"Light of My Life"

"Light of My Life"

Love, Time and Memory in Nabokov's *Lolita*

JAMES D. HARDY, JR.,
and ANN MARTIN

McFarland & Company, Inc., Publishers
Jefferson, North Carolina, and London

LIBRARY OF CONGRESS CATALOGUING-IN-PUBLICATION DATA

Hardy, James D. (James Daniel), 1934–
   "Light of my life" : love, time and memory in Nabokov's Lolita / James D. Hardy, Jr., and Ann Martin.
      p.   cm.
   Includes bibliographical references and index.

   ISBN 978-0-7864-6357-2
   softcover : 50# alkaline paper

   1. Nabokov, Vladimir Vladimirovich, 1899–1977. Lolita.
   I. Martin, Ann, 1970–   II. Title.
   PS3527.A15L6326   2011
   813'.54 — dc22   2011002278

BRITISH LIBRARY CATALOGUING DATA ARE AVAILABLE

© 2011 James D. Hardy, Jr., and Ann Martin. All rights reserved

No part of this book may be reproduced or transmitted in any form or by any means, electronic or mechanical, including photocopying or recording, or by any information storage and retrieval system, without permission in writing from the publisher.

Cover photograph © 2011 Ruslan Gilmanshin

Manufactured in the United States of America

McFarland & Company, Inc., Publishers
  Box 611, Jefferson, North Carolina 28640
  www.mcfarlandpub.com

To our spouses and our children,
whom we love in ways
never described in *Lolita*

The object matters, but the fire consumes

Table of Contents

Acknowledgments — viii
Preface — 1

ONE: The Word Known to All Men — 11
TWO: Marriage — 62
THREE: Irregular Adventurers — 100
FOUR: *Exeunt Omnes* — 154

Bibliographical Reflections — 185
Index — 195

Acknowledgments

Our primary obligation in writing this book is to Mrs. Dorothy McCaughey, of the English Department at LSU, who is also the director of the Herget Residential College, and our colleague in teaching literature, history, philosophy, and art in the basic interdisciplinary courses for that college. She was more delighted than surprised that we planned a book, and has given constant and generous support to this enterprise. We have also benefited from the wisdom and advice of another colleague, Mrs. Christine N. Cowan, once also of the English Department. She has provided bibliographical suggestions, along with apposite comments on the nature of love. We deeply appreciate the support from colleagues, and we also wish to thank our chairs, Dr. Gaines Foster, Dr. Anna Nardo, and Dr. Irvin Peckham, who approved our project and left us alone to do it.

The book had its origins in casual conversation about a traditional topic, the relative merits of the ancients and the moderns. While the superiority of the ancients is acknowledged by all, at least by almost all, several modern novels were put forth as classics. One of these was James Joyce's *Ulysses*, structurally revolutionary, psychologically acute, and certainly a profound examination of truth both personal and social. Nabokov's *Lolita* was also suggested as a novel of depth and subtlety. This appreciation produced a certain amount of discussion. Out of the discussion, we somehow agreed to write a book on *Lolita*. Having announced our intention to write about *Lolita*, we found it impossible not to do so. A decision like that, to write a book, cannot be disavowed without displeasing God, astounding the Muses, disappointing ourselves, and abusing the faith of friends. So, in the fullness of time, this book has appeared.

Whether books are the result of long deliberation or snap decisions reeking of bravado, the result is still the same: this book, like all others, has errors. We would like to blame these errors on somebody else, and deep in our hearts we probably do, but publicly we accept responsibility for them. Whatever that means. We hope only that the errors are minor, that the "palpable hits" are important, and that the text confirms the wisdom of Horace, to delight and instruct.

PREFACE

This work about Vladimir Nabokov's sensational and signature novel *Lolita* explores its enduring themes, and attempts to place them in their cultural contexts. It is designed for the general educated reader, so we have not constructed an esoteric conversation with other critics, nor a commentary on the various schools of *Lolita* criticism.* Because are writing for people, not professors, we have omitted the technical jargon. Nor have we concentrated on minor textual detail, offering an addendum to the annotated *Lolita*. We have tried to see *Lolita* as a whole, because its major themes are universal. It's also important to consider biographical, social, cultural, and historical contexts which every novel must inevitably reflect.†

---

*See Mark Edmundson's article in the *Chronicle of Higher Education*, "Against Readings" (April 24, 2009): "If I could make one wish for the members of my profession, college and university professors of literature, I would wish that for one year, two, three, or five, we would give up readings. By a reading, I mean the application of an analytical vocabulary — Marx's, Freud's, Foucault's, Derrida's, or whoever's — to describe and (usually) to judge a work of literary art." Edmundson argues that "the critic's objective is to read the author with humane sensitivity, then synthesize a view of life that's based on that reading. Schopenhauer tells us that all major artists ask and in their fashion answer a single commanding question: 'What is life?' The critic works to show how the author frames that query and how he answers it. Critics are necessary for this work because the answers that most artists give to major questions are indirect. Artists move forward through intuition and inference: They feel their way to their sense of things. The critic, at his best, makes explicit what is implicit in the work."

†We are aware, as is everyone, that Humbert was not Nabokov, nor was Nabokov Humbert. Still, parts of the author seep into the novel. This is inevitable, and desirable. What of Nabokov that seeped into Humbert was the author's long time habit of engaging in romantic encounters/conspiracies with women. Affairs began at an early age, as Nabokov revealed in *Speak, Memory* (New York: Vintage, 1989). They continued, as his and Vera's biographers have noted. Loath though we are to engage in biographical speculation, and fearful as we are of falling into the tar-pit of the intentional fallacy, we still have a suggestion. Affairs, which for Nabokov meant secrecy, flirting, flattery, closeness, and being "in the

Preface

The main theme of *Lolita*, and of this work, is love, in all its forms, turns, manifestations, twists, aberrations, expressions, and failures.* Beyond love there is time, equally central within *Lolita*. The third general theme we consider is memory, encapsulated in the form of memoir, which here presents Humbert's "confession," or at least his explanation. Therefore, we examine *Lolita* in terms of the narrative of Humbert's life, and the development of his character, within the persistence of memory, within the change of circumstance.

Of these three themes, like Humbert, we give love pride of place. Love often drives, and simplifies, the plotline of one's life. That is true in *Lolita* where the power of passion drives its straightforward plot. Humbert finds girl, loses girl, finds girl, loses girl, and loses life. Incidentally, everybody else dies also. But the power of that driving force rumbles under Nabokov's stylistic lacquer. Readers recognize the intensity of Humbert's erotic passions, which consume him both in the absence of the beloved and in her reappearance, and are of such intensity that all the rest of his life appears as nothing compared to them. Humbert, we dare say, represents everyman in his experience of love's power. Everyone has loved something deeply, and perhaps everyone has experienced love as a gravity well, sucking the rest of life in toward it.

Humbert never breaks free of the orbit around *eros*. The story of his life is the story of his bondage to *eros*, and such bondage does not promise a happy ending. Nabokov tells an anti–fairy tale, where love debases and destroys its practitioners. And *Lolita*'s plot trajectory is not unrecognizable or surprising. We have known the unfortunate among us to have been made worse, not better, by love, to have become more selfish, less compassionate, more self-absorbed and destructive. Fortunately, most of our fellow human beings do not appear to have been changed in this way. The

---

[*continued*] know" as well as a bit of sex, were a long-term habit. It probably came to an end in America about the time the Second World War ended, about the time he gave up smoking, about the time he put on weight, and about the time he shifted his base of operations from Harvard and Wellesley to Harvard and Cornell. In many ways, *Lolita* is in the nature of an elegiac novel.

*For an interesting modern analysis of love, see C. S. Lewis, *The Four Loves* (New York: Houghton Mifflin Harcourt, 1991), which deals with love in an Aristotelian way, commenting with particular emphasis on the excess of each of the forms of love.

interesting question for readers of *Lolita* is why Humbert was. For him, the gravity of love leads not towards bliss but towards the berserk. Everyone has seen it. The divorce courts are filled with this stuff. So are the police blotters of stalking and murder. *Lolita* presents a disturbing fable of love turned towards sin and crime, towards disaster and death. It resembles most an ancient myth, in which everything is true but the story itself.*

Frames and Directions

Nabokov wished *Lolita* to be understood within a framework of closed-system formalist analysis. *Lolita* was not supposed to be drawn from "real life," most emphatically not his own. Rather, he made it all up. The world of *Lolita* began with the foreword, ran through Humbert's memoir, ended with the afterword, and that was all of it. The characters, the scenery, the décor, the plot, even the imagined readers: just a product of his imagination. Nabokov did not see *Lolita* as a myth, nor as a psychological cautionary tale, nor as something emblematic of the then-fashionable school of moral lostness in the Western world. A New Critic produced a New Critical book. Whether or not one can do that is not the issue. Nabokov imagined that one could, and that he had.

---

*We concur with Denis de Rougement with respect to the contradiction between love as *eros* and love as social responsibility. See Denis de Rougement, *Love in the Western World*, trans. Montgomery Belgion (Princeton, NJ: Princeton University Press, 1983). Our point of agreement with De Rougement is greatest in the specific area of love as a destructive force, which is so powerful that it cannot coexist with the other aspects of the lover's life. We find its origin with Helen of Troy, with the pattern repeated often enough that it becomes a commonplace without ever becoming a cliché. We do not, however, contrast *eros* with *agape*. Our contrast is primarily of *eros* with *philia*, a loving concern for family and community.

Love has continued to enchant modern scholars, as well as those who write popular songs, Hollywood scenarios, and all-too-explicit blogs and television shows filled with sexual tension and the desire for "luuve." See Cristina Nehring, *A Vindication of Love* (New York: Harper, 2009) and Meghan Cox Gurdon's excellent review of Nehring in the *Wall Street Journal*, June 16, 2009. In her call to arms, Nehring defends "imprudent ardor and romantic excess." She favors the erotic immersion of a heedless grand passion. But these things rarely work out, whether they are tried or avoided. If tried, they end in disaster; if avoided, they end in deep and perennial regret.

He also sought New Critical criticism. He expected readers to take his characters and their words and sensibilities seriously, but only within the context of the novel. We give due respect to Nabokov's intentions. Style and character are matters interior to the novel itself, and hence proper New Critical fodder. Of course, they are also figments, and dance and dangle according to the whim of the omnipotent author.* The critic, like every other reader, should fall to some extent under the novelist's spell. Not every critic does. There are those who say that Humbert is utterly untrustworthy, and nothing he says can be believed. Fine. However, if one places no credence in the only words that the novel contains, what can one say about it? All that's left is to say: "Gee, I liked this; gee, Nabokov is good; Nabokov is tricky; I can't figure out what can be believed." This kind of criticism does not advance readers' understanding, so we have attempted to avoid it.

Nabokov built *Lolita* like the proverbial Russian nesting doll, using the literary technique of a frame, which adds narrative and psychological complexity to the story. A New Critic looks for frames, and in this case, supplied one. Actually, more than one. Nabokov scaffolded *Lolita* with at least three frames. The most obvious is the frame of Humbert writing his memoir. Added to that is the frame of the critic, "John Ray, Jr.," in the Foreword. Added to that is the frame of authorial commentary in the Afterword.

Given Nabokov's delight in indirection, the reader can only understand these frames as a group when he/she has finished the book. The Foreword, by "John Ray, Jr.," purportedly a scholar entrusted with the editing of Humbert's memoir by Humbert's attorney, pre-pends a statement about the fate of *Lolita*'s main characters. Ray also adds a critical

---

*See Artur Schnitzler, *Der Reigen* (1900), presented in French as *La Ronde*, both on stage and in the movie, starring Gerard Phillippe. In this overtly sexual play, which at the time was regarded as pornographic, every character is treated as a marionette, dangled by *eros*, each in love with someone who loves another, in an endless circle of desire and disaster. We do not suggest that *Lolita* plays upon the theme, or that Nabokov knew the play, though he certainly did, but rather that the playwright in Nabokovian sensibility creates his own world out of the realities of imagination. In Nabokov's case, however, he was never able to stay completely behind the curtain, and the reader is forced to pay attention to "the man behind the curtain."

Preface

commentary on what it all meant, theories of social responsibility to which Nabokov himself did not wholly subscribe. Ray's, and Nabokov's, intentions (sometimes at cross-purposes) aim to shape the reader's response to Humbert's autobiography, which itself gave a consistent Humbertian interpretation to the events of the plot.

That innermost frame of Humbert's memoir adds shifting perspectives to the narrative by presenting events first-hand, even if some were seen second hand, or sometimes third hand, or sometimes just imagined. All know how the law treats hearsay testimony, though it might be argued that Humbert's narrative was a dying declaration, and we regard it as such. Nabokov in the second edition added an afterword to the "novel proper," which seems to serve as an anterior self-justification as well as a further frame. In front, Mr. Morality; at the end, Mr. Aesthetics. It all fits. The double-headed frame, reminiscent of the Habsburg double eagle (or perhaps Søren Kierkegaard's *Either/Or*), produces a complexly structured novel, which in the best Nabokovian tradition repays rereading.

We have added to the formalist close reading technique a more expansive analysis of the overriding themes of *Lolita*: love, time, and memory. We consider love with relation to its classical form as a trope, as, literally, *polytropos*, with many turns. Love as narcissism, turned completely inward, love as *eros*, turned to a single beloved, love as *philia*, embracing community, love as *agape*, reaching for God: these are the main currents, both as presence and absence in *Lolita*. An essay about *Lolita* and love must include, as classical and modern authors understood, the idea that failure and doom are common, while success and happiness are rare. As much as love is the core of life, it is also the anteroom of death. Dido and Francesca and Paris are not casual nor accidental artistic inventions. Neither is Emma Bovary nor Anna Karenin, to say nothing of Leopold Bloom, whose creator Nabokov knew from their days in Paris.*

Concerning the theme of love, we note that Nabokov, like Dante and Euripedes and Flaubert and Tolstoy before him, understood erotic love as

---

*We suspect that the picture that Lolita had ripped from a magazine and pasted to her wall, of a man bringing a breakfast tray to his wife in bed, was meant to evoke Leopold Bloom in the imagination of *Lolita*'s close readers. One of Nabokov's little jokes. See *Ulysses*, part II, chapter 4.

more danger than delight. The lover, engulfed by erotic passion for the beloved, is isolated from the wider human community by the intensity and single focus of his/her consuming, almost idolatrous, desire.* Only the beloved and her surroundings are real, and the rest of the world becomes indistinct through unimportance. Isolated within love, the erotic lover loses connection to those obligations and professions and persons unconnected to the lover. The lover becomes a singularity, within society but not a part of it; even if some know of this love none can appreciate its depth. Isolation is only increased by secrecy, as the lover must appear to be normal, interested in normal things, to be *simul, semper, ubique et ad omnibus,* exactly what he is not.

If isolation from the world were the whole consequence of intense erotic love, the secret lover might still manage well enough, through ceaseless vigilance and constant imitation of ordinary behavior. The lover might seem preoccupied, perhaps a bit sad, but this could be explained away as a result of writing a book, or some other not very useful but still legitimate activity. But the lover faces an internal compulsion that can neither be surmounted nor avoided. He inexorably seeks to swallow the beloved whole, so to say, to adapt her person to his love, to enhance her perfections, to make her totally his and his only and his always. Erotic love alone, untouched by anything wider and more general, compels the lover to engulf the beloved. "I could just eat you up" is the colloquial form of this widely recognized feeling. Failure, though anticipated beforehand, is irrelevant. The lover pursues the absorption of the beloved to the extinction of exultation though not the pain of passion. At this level of intensity and secrecy, the lover's satisfaction remains always beyond reach, though constantly in sight, a living experience of the mythic torments of Tantalus,

---

*C. S. Lewis expresses directly what Nabokov presents as parable: *Eros* "seems to sanction all sorts of actions they [the lovers] would not have dared. I do not mean solely, or chiefly, acts that violate chastity. They are just as likely to be acts of injustice or uncharity against the outer world. They will seem like proofs of piety and zeal towards Eros. The pair can say to one another in an almost sacrificial spirit, 'It's for love's sake that I have neglected my parents — left my children — cheated my partner — failed my friend at his greatest need.' These reasons in lovers' law have passed for good. The votaries may even come to feel a particular merit in such sacrifices; what costlier offering can be laid on love's altar than one's conscience?" (*The Four Loves* [New York: Houghton Mifflin Harcourt, 1991]).

Narcissus, and Echo. Passion that attempts to absorb the other always absorbs the self, to the great damage or destruction of both.

Erotic love can be kept from destroying life when it is transformed into something larger. Such transformation can be found in the ordinary, conventional, and widespread public ceremony of marriage, which is contract and rite, both social and personal. That public affirmation, in joining personal passion to social recognition, limits the damage that *eros* can do, and increases the benefits that *eros* can bring to person and community. Humbert Humbert, however, marries for convenience, though this is not necessarily a bad thing. And his marriages do not work out. It's *eros* that does him in, whether the beloved is a dream or a living girl. Eventually, Humbert just gives up on marriage, asking Lolita to leave Dick, to come away with him, but not to marry him. She is willing to grow up and marry, and to accept the responsibility of a child and a home. He is not. Humbert remains always the same, always the importunate lover. *Lolita* does not pretend to be an Humbertian *Bildungsroman*.

Eros and Marriage

Lolita appeared at the same time as Nabokov was examining love, time, and memory in his literature courses at Cornell University. Most of the books he chose for those European and Russian Fiction courses dealt with complementary themes of erotic love run to destruction, or transformed into loving and successful marriages. Nabokov himself had engaged in an extended affair which ended in a return to marriage, and he was sensitive to the tides and pulls of *eros* and obligation.* Nabokov emphasized these forces in his teaching, particularly in working with *Anna Karenin*, *Madame Bovary*, *Bleak House*, and *Mansfield Park*. He explained in his lectures that marriage, enriched by love and mutual regard, was the goal to be reached. The way might run through *eros*, but came out the other side. Marriage justified itself, primarily by improving the partners involved, but also by improving the society at large.

---

*Stacy Schiff, *Vera* (New York: Modern Library, 2000).

Preface

Besides presenting the contrast between *eros* and married love, *Lolita* explores time and memory. Within Humbert's narrative, years pass, but he remains always in the summer of 1923. He is untouched by time in a fundamental way. Humbert persists in the condition of his first, stunned grief and passion. He remains always thirteen: for him the Riviera idyll alone is real, the first love alone contains the fullness of his life. Eden may be lost, but Humbert just won't leave. For Humbert, things are what they have always been. Although adolescent love is a common experience, it becomes a fixation for Humbert. As the years pass, the pain never abates. Neither does the longing. Like Tennyson in "In Memoriam A. H. H." Humbert refuses to forget, refuses to allow the hurt to diminish. Unlike Tennyson, he achieves his goal. It is this retention of loss complementing the experience of young love that sets Humbert apart from the common run of those whom he always regarded as having a lesser capacity to love.

But if time stands still, memory does not. Our power of memory often softens pain, improves outlines, makes facts bearable for us endure. It works as a force for good, contributing to our psychological stability. Who of us could bear to remember the whole truth about our past? Humbert's memory, though, does not serve its owner in this way, does not function as psychic stabilizer. Humbert abuses the power of memory, calling forth out of it an Annabel who does not fade. Her existence is so vivid to him that he expects to find her again in the everyday world, in a subway perhaps, on a park bench, in a schoolyard. Humbert's vigil requires him to be prepared: he dare not grow up and away from Annabel. Unfortunately, though memory allows him to call spirits from the vasty deep, it cannot prevent him from growing old. The past cherished in memory beyond reason stands as a parable for exile, particularly for those interested in the author's life and/or subconscious. We do not go so far, but merely observe that memory can produce effects nearly as destructive as *eros* can.

Humbert, the "author" of this "memoir," remembers more of his past than just scenes involving Annabel, a great deal more; in the full text of his memoir/confession statement, he deliberately, and slyly, embeds her in a fleeting episode of youth. Those early pages of narrative sparkle with passion and detail; then Humbert's account loses verve. Form follows function, as the critics say: Humbert's post–Annabel life was boring too. A succession of drab details serves either to set the idyll off, or to obscure the idyll's importance. The reader chooses, dependent on how slippery he thinks Nabokov is. Humbert, as disguise, from himself or others, glumly evokes the world he saw as a young adult. He includes a sketch of Paris. Paris was not for Humbert a "moveable feast" or a place to get a drink, to become an artist or scholar, or to engage in a festival of sex.* Humbert's Paris was "dull and dingy," and he appears to have been glad to leave.

Well, how about America? It didn't impress him more; actually, less; but Humbert spills a lot of ink describing it anyway. He is particularly verbose about the American road, from gas stations to motels to scenery, museums, and sweet shops, presenting it with great vividness as a series of snapshots filled with detail. He condemns at length the plastic, philistine American culture; his prolonged sermon is dotted with examples from movies, song, and magazines, all dripping with disdain. America may not have been dingy but it was the soul of dull. And after the ecstatic moments of passion, Humbert found dull the worst condition of all.

In Humbert's descriptions, it's clear that scenery also follows function: as with the special moments experienced through *eros* and memory, in the landscape Humbert inhabits, nothing moves. He preserves static *tableaux* in the amber of memoir. For all Humbert tells the reader, the auto courts and popular songs might have been there forever. American popular culture was in Humbert's memoir a fixed thing, not the fecund process of change and diversity it has always been. The *tableau vivant* of Annabel froze every vista that followed it, at least in Humbert's apprehension of them. Humbert's memoir is that most paradoxical of literary creations: memory in the absence of time.

Within *Lolita*, Humbert's presentation of America also serves as a way to understand the characters. Tawdry American culture defines

---

*The fictional Humbert appears to have missed a great deal of what went on in Paris. He never recorded meeting anybody like Ernest Hemingway, F. Scott Fitzgerald, Henry Miller, James Joyce, Samuel Beckett, or any of the Russian émigré intellectuals. They were all there. Humbert missed the artistic ferment of Paris, at least in his memoir. We can think of two reasons for that. In the first place, although art may be the emblem of love, and the survivor of love, this did not apply to the artists themselves. Secondly, Humbert evidently lacked the capacity to admire another adult. And another thing: can anyone who has been to Paris and spent time in cafes regard the city as dull? Perhaps some dinge, but never any dullness.

through examples the cultural gap between Humbert and Lolita, which expands through their years together. Lolita grows ever more a part of her modern world, while Humbert strains to assimilate her ever more tightly into his lost Eden. The widening distance between the two is represented as a juxtaposition of opposites, Lolita's cultural/personal identity and Humbert's obsession with *eros*. And those opposites do not merely represent the personal expressed as cultural; it is also moral. The abuser is in constant contrast with his captive, but the two are never on the same page. Juxtaposition takes the place of explanation and of the forward movement of the plot. It is the show without the tell.

It is also a bit like a parable, in which the story itself is not told by the story. So, we have paid a great deal of attention to Humbert's view of America, both as a manifestation of its time and Humbert's memory within the novel, and as a point of entry into his memoir.

Chapter One

THE WORD KNOWN TO ALL MEN

One may be pardoned for being pleased, or at least not disappointed, that a line was dropped from an 800-page novel. But in James Joyce's *Ulysses*, an ironic imp caused the deletion of the single indispensable line in all those pages: "Love is the word known to all men." Love is the word without which nothing converges in *Ulysses*, a novel as immense, disordered, and undisciplined as life, and love plays a similar part in *Lolita*, Nabokov's elegant, circumspect, and polished novel. Joycean love involves marriage, ideas, fellowship, family, and society, however imperfectly these were embodied, while in *Lolita* love burns as an eternal erotic flame, consuming Humbert, scorching everyone he knows, and leading all to a sad whimper of time and hope lost.

Humbert insists on the centrality of erotic love, which devours the lover's life. Humbert himself loved pre-pubescent female children, making him a creepy person whose erotic passion was a social disgrace. But the passion would have twisted him no less had the woman been of marriageable age and station. The object matters, but the fire consumes. Humbert grasped that, all right, and began his memoir by describing his passion, not its object. "Lolita" is the first word of the memoir, but only the name is given, with varying pronunciations, and there is no description, and no mention of age. "Lolita," whoever she was, was for Humbert, the "light of my life, fire of my loins. My sin, my soul."* Me, me, me: The first sen-

---

*Vladimir Nabokov, *Lolita* (1955), Pt. I, ch. 1, in Alfred Appel, Jr., *The Annotated Lolita* (New York: Random House, 1991), p. 9, and see also the notes on p. 328. All quotes from *Lolita* will be taken from *The Annotated Lolita*, and its pagination will be used. Part and chapter are given for those using other texts.

tence of the novel is about nothing else. The lover's passion informs the book, Lolita or other incidental nymphets notwithstanding.

The rest of *Lolita*, that is, the entirety of Humbert's memoir, is given over to anecdotal illustration of that first line. It is an exclamation, an ejaculation. Humbert does not spin theories of love. Love for Humbert, and for his creator, is not a syndrome, or a complex or condition that could be treated symptomatically. *Eros* can't be treated at all. Nabokov's presentation of love in *Lolita* avoids explanations provided by modern psychology and sociology, which tend toward fragmentation of people into symptoms, clinical conditions, and natural selection.* Although Humbert's complaints and attitudes beg for a Freudian interpretation, it is likely that this is a wry device of authorial distance, separating the creator from the creation.

Nabokov's understanding of man arose from his sense that we are *what* and *how* we love.† People can love well or badly, of course.‡ The acts of love, from monstrous selfishness to astounding altruism, from tepid affection to consuming intensity, matter as much as the object. Actually, they matter more. The emphasis in *Lolita*, and in most novels about love, is on the lover's acts rather than the beloved's experience of them.** In

---

*Within the modern social sciences, from psychology and sociology to economics and education, theorists operate with various definitions, or at least examples, of love. Psychologists consider love the offspring of the raging unconscious; sociologists think of it as a social construct; economists think of love as one of the reasons people lose money in the market; educators think of love in terms of self-esteem. As a result, these modern theorists tend to illustrate particular circumstances in which love appears or, is sadly absent. Self-esteem in education, an attachment to conventional economic decisions, an emotional force of nature, the personal love of one for another, or for things, or for memories, or for commodities, or for ideals: all fit the modern taste for love within circumstance. For further example, scientists are exploring the relationship of neurotropin levels (NGF, BDNF, NT-3, and NT-4) to romantic relationships.

†Nabokov announced that *The Gift,* his last novel in Russian, expressed his love for Russian literature and language, not inappropriate for this permanent refugee. In *Bend Sinister,* one finds the love of a son, in *Pale Fire,* written in English, Nabokov celebrated his love of mystery and its antidote, literary explication. In *The Real Life of Sebastian Knight,* Nabokov used the theme of brotherly love, while in *Ada,* erotic love took the place of sibling love, with predictably bad results. Instance could be expanded, but the point has been made.

‡We have taken our direction from Plato's *Symposium.* In matters of ethics and love, words cannot be univocal, but we have attempted to apply at least a modest amount of discipline on meaning.

**See, for example, a book Nabokov did not like, though most other critics think is stupendous: Fyodor Dostoeysky's *Crime and Punishment* (1866). The novel follows Raskolnikov, the lover, rather than Sophia, the beloved.

Chapter One: The Word Known to All Men

Lolita, Humbert justifies his dangerous erotic behavior, which while informing his life destroys the lives of those he meets. It's entirely appropriate that he should begin with "me," with "fire," with "loins." *Eros* will do that to you.*

Eros, in its positive definition, expresses the emotional, romantic love of another person, with marriage its mature form and appropriate conclusion. Within marriage, *eros* evolves (usually, if things go well) into the multiple connections of a familial community.† If things do not go well, *eros* becomes monstrous. Selfish needs blot out any thought of the other's well-being. And then things never go well.

Ovid's *Metamorphoses* is a direct ancestor of *Lolita*: both tales represent love as tending to run amok, to become deformed, to destroy lover or beloved. In *Lolita*, Humbert exhibits a limited but deadly range of emotion. He doesn't get past narcissism and *eros,* and thus his story reveals what Greek tragedy, philosophy and poetry reiterate: love can be wound, fire, and unreason, leading inevitably to disaster. That view fits Humbert's memoir and illuminates Humbert's adventures. Nabokov did not shrink from this dire Greek view. Actually, as a Russian Formalist and moralist, he reveled in it.

Nabokov understood love in a Christian as well as an Ovidian context, even though he was not a conventional Christian.‡ Nor did his character Humbert ignore Christian attitudes towards love, at one point going so far as to seek sacramental absolution for damage done by *eros*. Dante's *Commedia* and Milton's *Paradise Lost* are instructive here. So are some nineteenth-century novels, which Nabokov taught in his university courses. We examine Nabokov's own novel with the approaches he used

---

*In this connection, see Aristotle, *Nicomachean Ethics*, Books One and Two. Here, Aristotle explains that happiness comes from practiced virtue, which benefits the community and *eudaimonia*, a great spirit which benefits you. In Aristotle, unlike Humbert, the individual is always connected to the community.

†A single example, relegated to a note, must suffice for an essay, which is always short of space. See Rebecca West, *The Meaning of Treason* (New York: Viking, 1947). Ms. West viewed love as a circle radiating outward from the self. In the Epilogue, on page 301, she wrote: "We live outwards from the centre of a circle and that what is nearest to the centre is most real to us." This applies, of course, to the secular working out of any definition of love we wish to accept, from self to other to things to community to God.

‡See Vladimir Nabokov, *Lectures on Russian History*, ed. Fredson Bowers (New York and London: Harcourt Brace Jovanovich, 1981), pp. 137–244.

"Light of My Life"

on the novels he selected for undergraduates: Flaubert's *Madame Bovary*, Tolstoy's *Anna Karenin,* and Joyce's *Ulysses.** In these texts, love in its full forms appears in central theme and illustrative detail, whether as love's labors lost or won, love given or compelled, love misdirected, excessive, or defective, *eros* ripened into marriage, or not, love as wound and love as healing, and love as word and also Word.

In his university course, the novels Nabokov taught were mainly love stories. They were not all happy love stories. These novels depicted love as extraordinarily complex, embracing a fearful intensity, shifting from joy to despair, being lost in indifference or enshrined in memory. Emma Bovary was coarsened by her affairs, made ever more forward and vulgar, whether her love grew or declined. In *Swann's Way*, M. Swann, as he felt his love for Odette waning, strove to recall how he had felt when he still loved her, but found that the very act of trying to remember altered the memory of love. Humbert might have done better had he remembered that. Readers of *Lolita* cannot avoid this insight.

Initial erotic attraction may fade, as it did for Emma and Leon in *Madame Bovary*, or it may deepen over time into a "relationship" or marriage. *Eros* usually requires two people, and Humbert, after Annabel's death, was down to one. Never mind. In the realm of memory, narcissism functions in the service of *eros*, because narcissism denies the erosion of time. Humbert imaginatively improved and then fixed the moment of Annabel into a permanent memory, which was proof against moth and rust but not against abuse or obsession. First love became perfect love. That doesn't happen often. Most people grow and change. They daydream, construct an Edenic love, enjoy it a while, and then move on. There is never any confusion of imagination with reality. But Humbert carried that entire process to excess, to wild excess. And he tells the story with pride. In constructing his memoir, Humbert tells a story remarkably similar in theme to Wordsworth's *The Prelude: The Growth of the Poet's Mind*.† Both

---

*Vladimir Nabokov, *Lectures on European Literature*, ed. Fredson Bowers, intro. John Updike (New York: Harcourt Brace Jovanovich, 1980). Nabokov's lectures, which were given at the same time he was writing *Lolita*, are his main published critical comments, and, in light of that, have considerable weight as evidence for Nabokov's views on love.

†1798–1799.

Chapter One: The Word Known to All Men

describe the development of an artist, which Wordsworth was, and which Humbert believed he was.

Through the life described in his memoir, Humbert recounts, and demonstrates, how he worked with his memories, refining them, nurturing and cherishing the intense erotic passion of first love, reliving that time and refining that experience. The continuity of remembered and reconstructed passion is as central to loving the nymphet Lolita as is the fire of his loins. Humbert's remarkable steadfast devotion to an increasingly abstract erotic passion stands as the thematic counterpoint to the "light of my life." Humbert balanced past and present, real and enhanced, memory and lust; actually, he saw it all, lust and memory, as the same thing. Humbert did not, as so many in *Lolita* did, live a fragmented life. In spite of movement and marriages, Humbert's memoir unifies his life as devotion to *eros* in general and to nymphets in particular. For Humbert, past is prologue, the prologue to past revisited.* Humbert artistically merges memory into anticipation, Annabel into Lolita. His memoir cannot avoid the elegiac theme of time lost and memory grasped.

In *Lolita*, love and time seem to stand still, with the passage of years having no effect on Humbert's memory or his affections. This is not the usual case, of course, but Humbert is more constant than anyone ever known or imagined. He astonishingly maintains the same insistent driving passion and search for passion that emerged from his first and only love. The interplay of love and time forms a core dynamic within *Lolita*: while Humbert insists upon love that repeats and replays, time brings him a love that grows in loss. In dealing with remembrance and meaning, T. S. Eliot sighed:

> People change, and smile, but the agony abides.†

In *Lolita*, Humbert abides, people too rarely smile, and the agony for all deepens.

---

*This Proustian quality of Humbert's memoir has been often observed. But it is sufficiently important to be noted again. Humbert bears more than a passing resemblance to Proust's narrator, Marcel, particularly in their joint efforts to recall past time through the medium of reliving it. We suggest, and there is no proof of this, that *Lolita* includes shards of the novels Nabokov taught, which is not unusual, as literature, like all arts, is self-referential. We maintain, however, that Proust has pride of place in this process.

†T. S. Eliot, "The Dry Salvages," II, l. 66.

"Light of My Life"

Humbert and Annabel

The persistence of love and time in Humbert's memory begins with his brief love affair with the young Annabel Leigh.* That love erupts during a summer vacation, an hiatus within the ordinary business of life, which for adolescents is school. During a summer vacation, or spring break for that matter, anything can happen, including love. Because it is summer vacation, the process of falling in love accelerates, and a young man who would love first the woman and then her body comes to love both almost simultaneously.

Humbert's love took him by surprise. One day he and Annabel were just kids playing on the beach; the next, or the day after that, they realized they were in love. It was the first time for each. Their love became the center of everything. But only for them, and its intensity served to separate them further from the adults around them, and to emphasize further the fragility of their circumstances.

Neither Humbert nor Annabel had experienced anything like this before, of course. Consequently, unfamiliarity added a piquancy to the velocity and intensity of their descent into *eros*. Unfamiliarity leant apprehension to love's delights, novelty added something close to terror to the intensity of their feelings. Utterly caught up in the experience of love, they were also utterly caught up in wanting each other. This kind of passion happens to all, but seldom with the violence described by Humbert. His experience of erotic love was so overwhelming that it came to define life itself. One could not live without passion; at least one could not live as Humbert knew as he ought to live. We are all the stars of our own personal narrative, but Humbert added to this the sense that he, and he almost alone, had and could live life fully and appropriately. Teenagers tend to think that their passion is greater than all other passions; now, then, or

---

*The evocation of Edgar Allan Poe we take for granted; *ca va sans dire*. Though the evocation is clear, starting of course with the name, we do not think it adds much to the understanding of the Annabel episode beyond the obvious of love, youth, loss, and memory. The fact that she was an American may also matter. Nevertheless, we find her not so much a type but a literary convenience. And, perhaps, an evocation to confuse the critics. Nabokov does those things, providing surface similarity (kingdom by the sea) to conceal essential difference (a post-romance lifetime of pedophilia). The book, after all, is entitled *Lolita* and not *Annabel*.

ever. But they grow out of it. Humbert never grew out of it. His relationship to Annabel, and the power that relationship inspired, simply proved to Humbert what he doubtless already knew: that he was superior to those around him. Having experienced the power of erotic love, Humbert resolved to see love in no other way, and kept this promise to himself As is often the case with women, Humbert identified himself with love, with the power of the emotion lending power to the person. He believed that he understood life and love more deeply than others, and would say so, when looking back on his time with Lolita. Loving Annabel and reliving that love with Lolita made Humbert an exemplar of love, even an epitome of love. What could any man know about love that Humbert did not know? This overweening attitude explains why Humbert turned a simple legal confession into a fable on the nature of *eros*.* Who else could do this? It is no exaggeration to say that Nabokov, though always suspicious of symbols and emblems, made the love affair with Annabel the emblem of the memoir.†

The fearful immediacy of young Humbert's love for Annabel, which was fully requited, cast the two of them into a world beyond ordinary time. The grown Humbert would suggest that their time together had the sacred quality of things deeply felt that could only be clumsily expressed. But *eros'* sacred happiness never exists alone. Behind the joy of togetherness lies the nagging certainty of a constant anxiety that routine will catch up, that the moment will be lost, that the enchantment will be shattered. Humbert remembers his teenage consciousness as being as aware of time as of love. He vaguely grasped, even at that young age, that the process of mutual discovery must be stuffed into a few days or weeks. How long

---

*Fable in this context suggests the French *fabliaux*, a medieval genre of popular poetry that emphasized clever wordplay, tricksters, and sexual contretemps. Fabliaux stand in contrast with the more elevated poems of courtly love, in which the Muse does not enter the bedroom. In *Lolita*, Humbert presents himself as the last courtly lover, as Lionel Trilling pointed out ("The Last Lover: Vladimir Nabokov's Lolita," Encounter, 11 Oct. 1958). It's an odd form of courtly love that involves kidnapping, pedophilia, and murder. Of course, those can be the wages of *eros*, which is never courtly.

†Emblematic recapitulation is not a new technique, of course. We merely observe that Nabokov did it extraordinarily well, largely by letting Humbert speak in his own voice, combining childhood and adult memories into a single paradigm of erotic obsession.

"Light of My Life"

would the Leighs remain on the Riviera? There was no time for anything to ripen. Only if passion dominated time could Humbert's love for Annabel prevail. But the ecstatic moment always ends. No one wishes this, but the moment passes, and ordinary time reasserts its sovereignty. Vacation is over. It's back to school. The magic lingers, the moment recedes, but the fragrance of love and idyll dominate memory as they once dominated life.*

Like so many Romantics (Emma Bovary comes instantly to mind), Humbert never moves beyond the notion that the idyll should, could, must, continue indefinitely. Romantics don't grasp that mature love is able to begin only when the ecstatic moment ends. They resist the fact that love carried into ordinary time is the love that ripens. With Annabel, of course, it was over so quickly that there was nothing but idyll. That simple fact escapes the Humbert who is writing the memoir. Neither time nor experience had provided perspective. Humbert remained thirteen, though a more experienced thirteen than most. Of course no thirteen-year-old understands time and change. Not even the always-superior young Humbert. But the grown Humbert should have. All of the rest of us do. Still, judging by his memoir, and that's all we have to judge, Humbert never learned that time can add depth to love, that intensity can be transformed to devotion and mutual support. These things remained permanently absent from the *Humbertiad*. In this crucial way, Humbert remained always a child. His example suggests that Nabokov regarded Romantics as children who never develop the moral distance that separates feeling from thought.†

The intense idyll with Annabel occurred within a reasonable facsimile

---

*David Rampton observes that the lost idyll was a signature Nabokovian trope. He points out "a coherent pattern [in Nabokov's novels] whose significance is clear. Once upon a time there was a garden, and a cool house, and a warm summer. Children played there and grew up slowly. Then there was a fall and they were ejected. They succeeded well enough in their new world, although they always felt out of place in it and dreamed of getting back to the one they had lost.... Nabokov did not think much of 'mythic criticism' but this myth, with its suggestion both of triumphant recovery and the difficult acceptance of inevitable loss, informs everything he wrote" (*Vladimir Nabokov* [New York: Cambridge University Press, 1984]).

†We further suggest that Nabokov viewed life, and marriage, as a test of strength of character. Life knocks people about, and intensity of feeling is inadequate to deal with bumps and bruises. In short, we do not doubt, not for a moment, that Nabokov viewed adults as very different from children. Humbert, however, agreed with Dickens and Rousseau in regarding a child, in Humbert's case a newly pubescent girl, as the high point of all creation.

Chapter One: The Word Known to All Men

of the *hortus inclusus*, the enclosed garden that defined paradise and was depicted in monastic and academic cloisters.* Ecstatic moments tend to happen to those who have regular meals and lots of leisure. Humbert, with his private income and simulacrum of work, would find plenty of time to remember Annabel, dream of love, leer at nymphets, and make those summer weeks in 1923 the center of all his life. At the time, Humbert and Annabel were sheltered by age, thirteen in both cases, from the adult necessity of getting a living and maintaining a station.† Both were sheltered by space as well, which Humbert remembered as a shining world, "a kind of private universe."‡

Humbert remembered that he and Annabel were precocious as well as leisured. They connected to the wide world almost as if it were the abstraction, with the garden alone being real. Humbert recalled proudly their conversations, idly discussing the world beyond themselves. He maintained that they typically discussed "the plurality of inhabited worlds, competitive tennis, infinity, solipsism, and so on."**

---

*For example, the Cloisters, a branch of the Metropolitan Museum of Art. Its guidebooks are clear and informative on the meaning and the function of the cloister. See the *Guide*, re-edited each year. For the academy, see New College (1379), Oxford University, for a cloistered interior.

†This necessity pressed long and hard on Nabokov himself during the 30s, when he was struggling to support himself, a wife, and then a child in a postwar mess. It got really bad by 1937, the time when Nabokov's reputation as writer was skyrocketing but his economic situation was as bad as ever. Talent and culture didn't fill the belly; empty belly hurt the soul; Nabokov embarked on an intense erotic affair with another refugee, Irina G., which lasted for several months.

‡Nabokov, *Lolita*, Pt. I, ch. 2, p. 10. As a general note for social and historical context, we add the story of Gerald and Sara Murphy, rich American "expats" who settled in France in 1921, and began the habit of summer vacations on the Riviera in 1923. They persuaded a hotel, not too similar from the Mirana, we suppose, to remain open so that the Murphys could entertain their friends. Most of these were artists, including Fitzgerald, Hemingway, Benchley, Jean Cocteau, Picasso, Dorothy Parker, Cole Porter — in short, the reigning arbiters of artistic style. As a result of the Murphy's efforts, 1923 stands as a transition year in Riviera life. It is entirely appropriate that the Leighs to have been on the Riviera that summer. Fitzgerald tells their story in *Tender Is the Night*. In spite of Nabokov's formalist sensibility, the patterns of reality nuzzle *Lolita*.

**Nabokov, *Lolita*, Pt. I, ch. 3, p. 12. It might be added that solipsism was the modern version of Greek Sophists, notably Protagoras and Gorgias. After the time described by Nabokov, sophism was given its characteristic modern form, existentialism, by French philosophers and writers, notably Jean-Paul Sartre, Eugene Ionesco, and Samuel Beckett. Whether or not these topics were, in fact, the general interests of European children of brains and privilege in 1923, must remain an unanswered question.

"Light of My Life"

Every teenage couple in love has pet topics of talk. The distinction here is the snobbish patina that Humbert valued. He and his beloved thought of things both distant and elegant. Their list of interests reveals the older Humbert's desire for readers to admire a "smart set" of European preadolescents, whose communal preoccupations omitted all consideration of school, dress, acquaintances, music, or entertainment, including movies. Those interests belonged to modern American teenagers, almost a different species entirely. Lolita, though incomparably provocative, was vastly inferior to Annabel. Back then and over there, they made kids better.

The esoteric topics of talk suggested that Annabel and Humbert's brains were turned entirely away from themselves, even while they were "madly, clumsily, shamelessly, agonizingly in love." But it's also true that one can only talk of love, per se, for a short period of time. In such murmurings, there is so much repetition, so little variety. Symbol, therefore, takes the place of declaration, and brings the lovers themselves even closer, since they alone know the full meaning of what they say. It serves as protective coloration. Tennis and infinity were the impersonal topics reserved for public discussion with the outside world of doting yet censorious adults, who can, after all, communicate only over vast distance with the sexually budding young. These topics comprised an interesting and probably impenetrable code for love, which excluded adults through surface plausibility, which hid the subtext of *eros*.

The progress of this love was determined by those same adults to whom Humbert and Annabel were able to speak only of tennis and philosophy. Humbert had no parental supervision, as his father was touring Italy with a current *inamorata*. Humbert's aunt and her suitor, Dr. Cooper (whose name Humbert the memorialist unaccountably remembers) joined the Leighs in the task of overseeing the secretive but not bumptious teenagers. They interested themselves, as adults always do, in limits, imposed on the semi-conscious but powerfully felt basis of common sense, social convention, and on what was good and desirable for the young. They set these limits intentionally, without having to speak of them, and enforced them with constant vigilance. What seemed reasonable to adults appeared intolerable to youth, not an uncommon situation, even in the absence of a "generation gap." The gap here comprised intensity and style,

Chapter One: The Word Known to All Men

and stretched as wide as the difference between the clumsy passion of Annabel and Humbert and the decorous courtship of Humbert's aunt by Dr. Cooper.

Humbert described their passion as a "frenzy of mutual possession," that might only be satiated by "actually imbibing and assimilating every particle of each other's soul and flesh; but there we were, unable even to mate." They would touch, gaze, speak, and made two attempts at something more, one thwarted by watchful and disapproving family adults, the other by a chance encounter with watching and approving "bearded bathers." Mating, of course, has little connection to the frenzy of mutual possession. It is merely the outward and visible sign of it.

The attempt to mate, repeated a second time, seems daring, and a leap of erotic imagination not usual in thirteen-year-old boys, and perhaps not in girls either. Girls might have been more mature and subtle in these experimental matters, but at that time (either 1923 or 1947) thirteen was below the ordinary age of sexual initiation for either sex. It was largely a matter of class and property. Persons of property had a fiscal value, which in young women was called "the little capital." That capital would be invested in the marriage market, but not until the age of eighteen or twenty, and only after a debutante season or two. For males also, love was more a matter of decorum than of excitement. Among the well-to-do, particularly on the Continent, young men did sleep with women at an early age, but these were rarely the sort of women one would be able to marry.* In the then European society of class distinctions and a European economy of some scarcity of opportunity, sex was neither casual nor early. Was that a bad thing?

Parents did not think that restraint in matters of desire, and postponement in matters of gratification, were bad things at all. And they kept watch. After the Great War, the institution of the *duenna* had become a

---

*An example can be found in Nabokov's own personal history. In his own memoir, *Speak, Memory*, Nabokov related an intense and extended affair with "Tamara," whom he loved and asserted (and perhaps believed) that he would marry. She was wiser than he. She laughed at him. Tamara knew. She was a middle-class girl, a learning experience for a young nobleman, as had been the case for generations. When Nabokov saw her summer-house (rented, of course) he still professed the possibility of marriage, more, his hope that they would marry. But he was young.

"Light of My Life"

bit quaint and old-fashioned, at least in France. But the watchful battalions of maiden aunts, family friends, and female cousins remained on guard. Property, which bred propriety, and propriety, which guards property, both demand constant vigilance.* Chaperonage, though not actually a profession, was common nonetheless, a constant and almost reflexive family habit.

It was, perhaps, a good thing for young boys especially that chaperonage was tight, and relationships inevitably more public and more formal. Chaperones, though often unwittingly, protected the hesitations and doubts of thirteen-year-old boys, who were then (and still are) sexually confused and ignorant, hopeful but fearful, unsure of how to proceed, especially when constrained by love to seek the good graces of the beloved. But Humbert reports that he was different at thirteen. He lacked doubts and hesitations, he tells us now. He knew what to do. He knew how to do it. The reported fumbles were merely matters of technical detail, rather than existential ignorance. Precocious Humbert. He persevered, progressed, and was thwarted, rather than failed. An exceptional episode altogether, beyond the normal expectations and actions of a very young swain. Humbert was so sexually skilled as to be a miracle, or a freak, or a fictional personage. The "brooding good looks" and "foot of engorged brawn" were present from the very start. Humbert does not conceal from readers of his memoir the one thing he was good at, then and always. For Humbert, and for Humbert alone, curiosity instantly became mastery.

In these short passages on Annabel, Humbert the narrator spends a substantial amount of time describing efforts to mate. Not that these efforts are uninteresting, or unimportant, but they are yet only brief moments, a few minutes there, a half hour there, taken out of an entire summer. It is the intensity of erotic desire that Humbert reports, rather than the personality of the other. The reader knows almost nothing about Annabel. Humbert does remember that she wished to be a nurse, an example of giving, of love extended beyond the beloved. In contrast, he himself had wished to be a spy, an intensely private profession, with its stock in trade of misrepresentation. Humbert admits he can no longer describe Annabel's

---

*In matters of marriage, and its unruly companion, sex, it's always *DEFCON 3*, at least.

Chapter One: The Word Known to All Men

appearance; he reproduces nothing of her conversation. What he remembers is the power of his own passion, as Annabel fades into merely the opportunity for *eros*. And, of course, Annabel dies. Quickly. There can be no second acts in first passions.

The reader might legitimately wonder if Nabokov is playing tricks with Humbert's passion for Annabel. Is Humbert revising history, just a bit, to influence the jury? Anybody able to believe that these thirteen-year-olds were actually sexually mature is also able to fall for Humbert's claim that Lolita too was ready and eager for sex at twelve. Humbert is a wily teller of his own tale, and may well "misremember" his age. His behavior with Annabel suggests that of a young man in his later teens, sixteen or seventeen.* The older Humbert, reconstructing the tale for confessional purposes, will strive for a sympathetic hearing. If he asserts that he and Annabel were fully ready for sex at thirteen, he has primed the jury to accept his claim that Lolita, too, was fully ready for sex. The jury will certainly be convinced that Humbert, young and old, was always ready for sex. And his problem, which he ascribes to the intensity of this encounter, consisted only of the regrettable inability to find a proper object for his affections.

No matter what their age, the apprentice partners Humbert and Annabel found the failed attempts at intercourse irritating and frustrating. Their failure would have been a relief to watchful adults had they known. Humbert presents their love, though, not as a casual grope, but supreme desire, previously unknown to mortals, on the Aristophanic model of joining two into one:

> The spiritual and the physical had been blended in us with a perfection that must remain incomprehensible to the matter-of-fact, crude, standard-brained youngsters of today.

Such perfection in love must always remain a singularity, in the nature of things never to be repeated. It can only occur to a narcissist. His experience was unique; it defined the best. No love affair afterwards, even his own, certainly no others', could equal the merger of Humbert and Annabel into

---

*Think of Romeo.

each other. Humbert alone was the perfect lover, just as Annabel became through time and longing the perfect beloved. Poor Lolita Haze. She could only, always, fall slightly short. This inevitability was Humbert's fault. He grasped that his grasp of the essence of love, honed on memories of Annabel, was so profound, that Lolita, provocative though she might be, could never fulfill every nook in his imagination. She merely personified the "standard-brained" fallen world, the incarnation of the ordinary, with her absorption into the banal and disposable contents of American popular culture. Where was the concern with other inhabited worlds, infinity, and competitive tennis? Even Lolita's tennis game was hopeless.

Humbert casts an analytic eye on his love affair with Annabel only to wonder if that was when the "rift" in his life began. Rift is the appropriate word, all right, since it indicates a separation of Humbert's life into two stages: the Annabel episode, and the rest of his life. For most of us, of course, thirteen is the nadir of life and love, when everything, from school to family to love to identity, goes wrong, when even things that go right seem to have gone wrong. Who remembers junior high (then, now "middle school") with affection? Imagine being stuck permanently at age thirteen; the thought evokes an endless nightmare. But not for Humbert. He alone, found thirteen an age of fulfillment, amatory mastery, and supreme social success. Humbert, as they say in sports reporting, peaked too soon.

Well, what about the "inherent singularity"? To deal with that, we might resort to psychologists, the ungainly descendents of the "Viennese medicine man," who combine the talking cure with purple imaginations. Psychology is not *always* a poor path, though Humbert preferred metaphysical interpretation:

> Long after her death I felt her thoughts floating through mine. Long before we met we had had the same dreams. We compared notes. We found strange affinities.

Here was connection; "strange affinities" always carry more emotional weight than ordinary occurrences. They are certainly more impressive, if for no other reason than that every reader wishes they had happened to him/her. The ideal of love is general, and by writing as he does, Humbert

Chapter One: The Word Known to All Men

constructs himself as having tasted it, and implies that others may as well. The conjunction of Humbert and Annabel appear not as a prologue to Humbert's life, but as both the apex of his life and as a template for others' experience.*

Readers will also sympathize with Humbert's grief. The "strange affinities" were heightened by the teens' failure to mate, which made the affair both poignant and perfect by leaving one thing undone and making anticipation permanent. Of course, that is a cliché, but that does not mean it is untrue. Perhaps the love of Annabel and Humbert had existed before they met and lasted after they parted. It marked the permanent participation of each with the other.

The strange affinities marked a love more intense and prolonged than is usual for young adolescents, but the phenomenon of *eros* amongst the young, from Romeo and Juliet to the popular music of modern America, insistently plays this theme. As these things generally go, the onset of adolescent passion is rapid and intense, often overwhelming what little sense and emotional stability those between childhood and maturity possess. The young lovers are quite literally, madly in love, gripped by that "frenzy of mutual possession," longing to merge their two persons into one. Aristophanes did not exaggerate. And then it ends. Obstacles or fulfillment, and each can trigger the dawn of falling-out of love, begin the painful process of separation. As John Donne wryly lamented in "A Lecture Upon the Shadow,"

> Love is a growing, or full constant light
> And her first minute, after noone, is night.

Joyfully come, painfully gone. Also, not an uncommon experience.

Beyond physical readiness for *eros* and emotional un-readiness for obligation, Humbert and Annabel exemplified another typical aspect of teen romance. The intense attraction can flower because adolescents have little else to do. Mostly too young for work, at least among the propertied classes, and mostly marginally interested in school, and mostly interested overwhelmingly only in themselves, those in their teens have time but lack

---

*See John Donne, "The Canonization." The opposite, of course, is always more interesting. See Jason and Medea.

occupation.* Puberty demands some response, and passion is not an unreasonable path for a couple in search of meaningful activity. Additionally, love brings the adolescent's most needed and desired feeling, that of external validation. The pursuit of that, whether as love, or popularity, or expertise, certainly makes itself into something to do.

Still, as John Donne knew, lovers experience intense emotional attachment as growth or subsidence, as fulfillment or frustration. Humbert and Annabel were cut off at "noone," a case of idyll *interruptus*, as it were. For them there was no disappointment, only perfection. The couple remained suspended in time, outside the passage of the ordinary; their love had no definite beginning, nor would it have any decisive end until Humbert encountered Lolita.

No surprise that Humbert eventually discovered Lolita in a garden. For Humbert, the idyll could resume, not as if nothing had happened, but as if nothing important had happened. Still, it must be said that, in the aftermath of Annabel's death, Humbert did not succumb to the wistful romance of heartbreak. Nor did love frighten him, or make him shy. He remembered how he had loved more than what he had lost. Humbert found life worth living only when it was illuminated by the uncontrolled ferocity of erotic desire Humbert had felt vibrant, excited, transformed: nothing would do but to regain the intensity of that erotic passion. His Annabel idyll also apparently fixed the object of Humbert's love, which would be directed only to girls of twelve or thirteen, just arriving at puberty, who alone possessed the fey charms of knowledge and innocence mixed, of sureness and confusion combined.

Most interestingly, Humbert's psychic inheritance from the Annabel idyll included a sharp separation of erotic passion from mere sex, a practical convenience, and from mere marriage, a social convenience. Further, erotic passion after Annabel also became, for Humbert, divorced from simple

---

*Today in America, young adolescents are in school, not in the enclosed garden. The problems of location are readily apparent. In the garden, young adolescents madly in love can pay attention only to each other, thus enhancing the sense of connection and discovery. But school involves "activities," some curricular, some extracurricular; but all required. It is, therefore, a common lament among young lovers that "he doesn't pay enough attention to me." This complaint, and those of a similar nature, is true. It is also inevitable. It is no accident that Humbert and Annabel were on vacation.

Chapter One: The Word Known to All Men

affection, for caring about the welfare of the other. *Eros* ruled supreme and alone. Ultimately, which in Humbert's memoir is 1947, erotic desire became entirely one-sided. Unwelcome sex (for the nymphetic recipient) supplanted the mad mutual passion of Humbert's early youth. The solipsism or narcissism implied by one-sided erotic passion is what the reader has to piece together for himself, as he hears *Lolita*'s narrator insisting on his exceptional "love," and at the same time recounting endless instances of grubby passion and sexual abuse. Humbert consistently fails to explain the distinction in his own attitudes towards love and sex in his memoir.

Many explanations can be constructed for Humbert's emergence from puberty into a male maenad, but on this point Humbert's memoir is reticent. Perhaps it was Humbert's insuperable resolve of character* reflecting on the heady Annabel idyll. Humbert consciously decided to reproduce the whole erotic scene. Or, perhaps, Humbert was driven by an obscure Freudian quirk of unspeakable depravity. Perhaps Humbert's memoir set in amber a changeless version of the past as contrast to an always-changing present.† It might have been youthful misunderstanding of the varieties of love and the meanings of commitment. Memory and love seem to us the most likely, given Humbert's scrupulosity with regard to chronology.

---

*One ought to remember that Vladimir Nabokov felt Nikolai Gogol inferior only to Tolstoy in the pantheon of Russian novelists. He thought *Dead Souls* (1842) was one of the supreme achievements of nineteenth-century Russian prose, and he taught Gogol to his students with loving care. One recalls that in volume one of *Dead Souls*, Gogol described Chichikov's strength of character, which overcame all obstacles in a relentless search for wealth, comfort, status, and ease. Disgrace, arrest, threat of prison, did not deter him. Chichikov would start again, from the lowest depths of the Russian bureaucracy, where "everything reeked of indecorum and rotgut" and work his way back up. Whether Nabokov modeled Humbert's obsession on Chichikov's determination can never be known. Nor do we speculate. We merely suggest the similarity in character.

†In this connection, see George Poulet, *Studies in Human Time* (Westport, CT: Greenwood, 1979), p. 306. "For the adult being, there is something incurably imperfect in the present, something impure in exterior perception, which leaves the perceiver indifferent and incapable of believing in it; but let this present become past, let this perception become memory, and immediately, with the same energy as the child in its act of faith, the adult adheres to this memory." In general, Nabokov would not have agreed with Poulet on much of anything, because of Poulet's insistence on interconnections rather than formalist isolation. However, this quote certainly expresses an Humbertian view, in which the past (Annabel) is enshrined as a permanent icon, to which all lesser things are compared, and from which all lesser things are detached, keeping the memory pure.

"Light of My Life"

But in any event, the long-term effects of the Riviera romance, the ideas about love that Humbert took from the megawatt emotions of those few summer weeks in 1923, set the arc of his life. The "strange affinities" Humbert felt with Annabel, and the obsession they renewed, were permanent.

Dolly would not come to supplant Annabel, but she did update her, and bring the nymphetic desire from memory to pursuit. Dolly possessed Annabel's fey grace in sufficient wattage and amperage to recreate the fullness of Humbertian desire, though girl and garden had changed. The details of Annabel's person began to fade in the intense light of Dolly. Memories of Annabel became more intellectual and less specific. Humbert here illustrates the nature of recall: modern memory overlays the earlier impressions, complementing it. It is the palimpsest principle. Humbert and Annabel could not merge, but the memory of Annabel could merge with the appearance of Lolita.*

As this coda to *Lolita* indicates, the metaphysical, with Humbert, as with all, sought corporeal representation; the word, as so often happens, became flesh. Humbert remained trapped in this ongoing relationship with Annabel. Perhaps mating could have freed him, but that cannot be known. Instead, a succession of nymphets appeared before Humbert's libidinal gaze, a sufficient number to allow Humbert, who had a substantial streak of reflection, to create an Aristotelian category of enchanting pubescent girls, of nymphets. They needed to be between nine and fourteen, at the oldest. A nymphet had a "faery" nature. She was a *daimon*, a romantic and almost unearthly essence, with a "shifty, soul-shattering, insidious charm." Most young girls, whether plain, plump or pretty, remained just young girls, the same to Humbert as to all the others, and he passed them by as part of the scenery of life. Only a few staggered and stopped him, bringing Annabel back, not as a person but as a type, to remind him of forbidden delight. Humbert's description was imprecise and vague, accessible only in terms of moods and fancies felt.

Beyond always-elusive adjectives, Humbert used two indices that would identify a nymphet. The first of these was age, which applied both

---

*Nabokov himself, like his creation Humbert, lived a life informed by Proustian memory, as one can see in both their memoirs.

Chapter One: The Word Known to All Men

to the nymphet itself, between nine and fourteen, and to the man she enchanted. Humbert asserted that a significant age difference must exist between lover and nymphetic beloved. He suggested twenty years, or perhaps even forty, as appropriate, but it must be at least ten years, and could go as high, perhaps, as sixty. Always, there was the gap.

He admitted that the gap had not applied to his relationship with Annabel. Both had been children together; if she were a nymphet, he was a "faunlet." They were a special case. The beginning of love in an expected and appropriate setting distinguished origins from coming attractions and consequences. For the rest, distance lent enchantment.

The second, and darker, index was death. In the case of Annabel, physical death in 1923 or 1924 did not end love but preserved it in the eternal spring of future desire. The succeeding nymphets were (we must take Humbert at his word on this) the genuine article but of lesser quality than Annabel. But they too were damned to death, not by the typhus that killed Annabel* but by something equally inexorable, and that was time. A girl of nine does, by and by, become fourteen, and the fey grace seems to vanish into the more easily recognized charms of womanhood. The death of charm turns the exceptional into the ordinary, and pubescence, while a process not an event, does proceed at a pace that inclines the coupling of a Humbert and a nymphet toward an encounter rather than a relationship.

Humbert himself thought in these terms; he knew how important age was and how fleeting the nymphet years must be. Spying upon girls passing through that phase, Humbert could unleash a secret pulsating lust in his imagined and brief romances. The nymphets' transit through adolescence allowed him to live for a while on the surfaces of desire. Although the individual girl's transit would necessarily be brief, Humbert could enjoy her youth forever by simply replacing the accidents of flesh. His atti-

---

*Before a vaccine was developed in World War II, typhus was a devastating disease for humans and has been responsible for a number of epidemics throughout history. These epidemics tend to follow wars, famine, and other conditions that result in mass casualties. Consider the influenza epidemic of 1918 and 1919, through which Humbert and Annabel lived. See John M. Barry, *The Great Influenza: The Epic Story of the Deadliest Plague in History* (New York: Penguin, 2004).

"Light of My Life"

tude was the opposite of Platonic, where the physical world is a poor imitation of the fleshless ideal one. It resembled, though, Wallace Stevens' insight about beauty's persistence in the endlessly regenerating physical world:

> Beauty is momentary in the mind —
> The fitful tracing of a portal,
> But in the flesh it is immortal.
>
> The body dies; the body's beauty lives,
> So evenings die, in their green going,
> A wave, interminably flowing.*

And if indeed Annabel's "body dies": Humbert would find again her "body's beauty" alive in another incarnation. Humbert's need for that beauty, in fact, proved stronger even than his own adolescent search for validation. Given the choice between seeking a loving mutual relationship, or seeking a type of young girl whose appearance replicated the original's, Humbert elected for appearance. That option would, of course, demand less personal engagement. It would allow him to keep a safer distance, close enough to delight the aesthetic faculty, far enough away to preserve his emotional stability. At least, that should be the appeal of the aesthete's life.† Humbert's soul would be refined, his heart would be comforted. The reality did not work out. Humbert quickly and implacably sank from his transcendent thirteen-year-old transports to the common lust of a common adult, for no good reason that the text describes.

The only thing that made Humbert's ignoble experience different from that of every other sex-crazed adult was the object of his passion. He was forced underground. Adventure came in daydream and voyeurism and propinquity. Humbert sat upon benches in parks, while nymphets played with their friends around him, and "caught glimpses of an incomparably more poignant bliss." But it was bliss at a distance, and time was never far from his thoughts. But time ignored is not time denied. Humbert wondered what happened to nymphets grown to young womanhood. Did some

---

*"Peter Quince at the Clavier."

†Kierkegaard's own super-aesthete, the "author" of *Diary of a Seducer*, had revealed the despair attendant on a life devoted to aesthetic passion, but the widely-read Humbert either did not happen upon *Either/Or*, or did not apply the lesson to his own situation.

Chapter One: The Word Known to All Men

hint of his longing drift through their lives, much as Annabel's thoughts lingered after her and were felt by Humbert? What did they become?

The deceased Annabel herself grew into more than a love and an echo, more than a memory. She, and the love she shared with Humbert, became the *point de depart* for all the hierarchy of loves in *Lolita*. Humbert consciously (and literarily) compared Annabel both to subsequent nymphets and to the women he married/endured/consorted with after her. The nymphets themselves fell short of the apotheosized Annabel, although they exuded provocation just as Humbert oozed desire. Only one, and only for a moment, a post-nymphet but barely post, the prostitute named Monique, tantalized Humbert for a single encounter. The encounter ended, Monique was less enticing the next time, and she soon became a woman among the other women.

Then came Lolita Haze, whom Humbert avowed as being sexually exciting to a degree that she could only be compared with Annabel. But the mad mutual passion was not repeated. Lolita, unlike Annabel, revealed herself quickly to his discerning taste and memory as banal; and there were no "strange affinities" as had existed with Annabel. Humbert's *cri de coeur*, "Oh, Lolita, had you loved me thus!" was, in its essence, about the absence of affinities. Monique had, for an instant, and Lolita had, for the remainder of Humbert's life, aroused only the first rung on the hierarchy of love, that of physical attraction to another. *Eros*, of course, is an invitation to ascend, not an excuse to remain.*

We suggest further that the *belle moment d'amour* on the Riviera may have exhausted, by its alchemical "strange affinities," the love that Humbert had to give to things and persons beyond himself. That was it. The idyll, so well remembered even after Lolita Haze, did not transform Humbert or the objective reality he disdained. Interior reality stayed the same. No latent hint appeared that love was liberating, or that *eros* led upwards towards convergence. What Humbert and Annabel's young love seemed to do, only too briefly, was stimulate the expression of juvenile dreams and

---

*The idea, though not the exact expression, can be found by Oliver Wendell Holmes, Jr., *United Zinc and Chemical Company v. Britt*, 258 U.S. 268 (1922): "A road is not an invitation to leave it elsewhere than at its end."

"Light of My Life"

transform possibility: perhaps she could relieve suffering in some famished Asian place, perhaps he could become famous. This typical teenage boasting normally functions as an ego boost. In this case it served as an aphrodisiac.

But the idyll with Annabel was not without its uses, both to Humbert himself and in Nabokov's explanation of what love was. It exposed for the young lovers (and for Nabokov's readers: let's not forget them) the incredibly powerful nature of desire. Annabel's death underlined the central truth about *eros*—it is never satisfied. And Humbert having to live out the rest of his life hyper-conscious of their unconsummated passion underlines another truth about *eros:* no matter how powerful the emotions, the lover remains essentially alone.*

Humbert grasped the meaning of erotic passion and did not hide it in his memoir: his emphasis on the "singularity" of his experience highlights its double meaning. Besides the overt one of "uniqueness," it conveys the essential single-ness of even the most powerful and reciprocated erotic passion. There is no common enterprise, no wider scope than what's reflected in the lover's pupils.† There is only eternal desire, ever unfilled, ever deflected and delayed, even in the most edenic Riviera romance. Humbert wrote, and clearly meant, that the "frenzy of mutual possession might have been assuaged only by our actually imbibing and assimilating every particle of each other's soul and flesh."

There's Nabokov's genius apparent in the outlines of Humbert's foundational romance: the erotic passion is always expressed with the verb *want*, never about *give*‡ or *do*. The impression that remains with *Lolita*'s reader the longest is the "aching veins," the longing, not the joy.

Humbert, unlike Nabokov, could not understand that desire is always unslakable, and persisted in believing that, had Annabel lived, sexual consummation would have put an end to the "petrified paroxym of desire" in

---

*Humbert can't tell us anything specific about Annabel, only the innumerable subtle details of his own internal weather during the summer she was nearby. He experienced passion, but passion by definition is experienced by a person who is *passive* before its power.

†See Annabel kissing Humbert in "her solitary ecstasy" (p. 14).

‡"[W]ith a generosity that was ready to offer her everything, my heart, my throat, my entrails, I gave her to hold in her awkward fist the scepter of my passion" (*Lolita*, Pt. I, ch. 4, p.15). Hmph.

which the young lovers had existed. Ah, false faith in mere glands! Humbert, in the grips of an erotic power admittedly more powerful than he, believed that it could be tamed by mating, even "as slum children." Poor Humbert, who lived all his life believing that for a single moment he had actually been "on the point of possessing" his darling. But of course, possession, however intense, can never amount to absorbing the other. There is always a distance, and there is always the nagging sense that love has not been completely fulfilled. In this universe, physically or emotionally, there is no perfection.

Unwilling to acknowledge the frustrating nature of *eros* itself, Humbert blamed his frustration on bad luck. He rolled the dice again and again, betting that in a limited liability situation he would not risk, or lose, so much again. Unfortunately, even with his exclusively sexual goals, luck continued to elude him. During the time between Annabel Leigh and Lolita Haze, Humbert became desire thwarted by law and decency, and unfulfilled by mating or mate. His unhappiness at this condition did not move him to adjust his goals. Instead, he re-contextualized them. Justifying his addiction to nymphets, cited Dante's love for Beatrice, a pre-pubescent girl herself when Dante first sighted her. Humbert meant the age of social and customary consent, not, as had Dante, love leading from personal good (*eros*) to the greater good (*philia* and *agape*). *Nel mezzo del cammin*, in the middle of our life, is the beginning of the *Inferno*; in the middle of Humbert's life, in 1947, love led to the three beasts who blocked the way to the light.*

Love in the Western Tradition

Nabokov loved to play games with his readers, including "find the meaning." In *Lolita*, he presented several paradigms to "help" the reader

---

*For Humbert, the three beasts are essentially as they were for Dante. The lion of violence culminating in the murder of Quilty; the leopard of concupiscence symbolizing Humbert's constant erotic hunger, and the she-wolf of fraud and betrayal resulting in Lolita's captivity and exploitation. No wonder Humbert had no more success than Dante in climbing the hill toward virtue. For Dante this mattered; hence the pilgrimage. For Humbert, it was a matter of indifference. His was the life dominated by *eros*, not by journey.

succeed at this game. One was Freudian; if you were a Freudian, the text would work for you on that level. Nabokov himself was not a Freudian; he despised the fertile imagination of the "Viennese medicine man." But Freud can be imagined to pop up in *Lolita*'s very first sentence, where the "fire of loins" is juxtaposed to the "light of life." Further, Freud's concern with childhood would explain Humbert's adolescent, and permanent, passion. Perhaps Nabokov added a Freudian pattern to *Lolita* as a public blemish on Humbert's character. Perhaps Humbert is playing a little game with the reader.

Nabokov's more plausible paradigm concerning the nature of love comes from the Western tradition. Nabokov had an elite Victorian education at *gymnasium* and Cambridge, with its belle-lettristic emphasis on the liberal arts, supplementing his formal education with extensive readings in the western classics, from the ancients to the moderns. Much of it appeared by implication in *Lolita*.* Impossible for it not to; a novel often tells more about the author than it does about the characters.

In Nabokov's "Masters of European Fiction" course, Plato, Ovid, Dante, and Milton lay discreetly but clearly behind the novels we read. Jane Austen knew as well as Plato that part of love was to esteem as well as to do the right thing, and Nabokov knew it too. Nabokov *liked* to think of each great work as a separate icon, alone and undefiled by time and opinion, but the tradition was as much a part of him as he was of it; he could not omit Plato *et al.* from a book on love and time. Classical notions of love underlie the varieties of love enacted by Humbert and the other characters in *Lolita*.

The Greeks told tales of passion simultaneously immanent and transcendent, often involving Zeus' endless seductions of human maidens. This is the stuff of myth, a narrative exposition of truth in which everything is true but the story itself. William Butler Yeats, looking back, suggested

---

*Nabokov published the first edition of his memoirs, *Conclusive Evidence* (later *Speak, Memory*) in 1952. In it, he described his education and mentioned some of the things he read: primarily, it turned out, to be literature, butterflies and chess, which he fitted into a serious and time-consuming love affair. Immediately publishing his memoir, he was working on *Pnin*, and beginning to shape *Lolita*. He was also teaching literature at Cornell, where Hardy attended his course.

Chapter One: The Word Known to All Men

that western culture began in myth, with the erotic encounter between Leda and the swan, producing Helen and Clytemnestra, who, in different fashions, lived lives defined and defeated by love.* Leda, like Lolita, was an unwilling victim of a male possessed by the power of passion. Leda understood that love was filled with mystery and terror, with the sublime and the grotesque. Over time, the western concept of erotic love has expanded from Zeusian erotic passion, but has retained the power of transformation. Love will turn your life around, for better or worse, and the Greeks both celebrated and feared it.

The awe and power of love did not escape Plato, though, like most philosophers, he preferred to organize things into categories, rather than dwell on mystery.† His *Symposium*, the dialogue of a drinking party, presented several persons discussing what love meant, from reason to passion, from morals to madness. Because it came first, the *Symposium* has established a coherent vocabulary to describe love and its absence, coming down as standard to Nabokov, and beyond Nabokov to us. The *Symposium* presents the idea that love is as love does, that "nothing imports guidance as well as love."‡ Plato remained vague on where that guidance ought to lead, indeed, could lead, although he thought of the world in terms of a moral imperative admired in speech and ignored in practice. In his *Symposium*, the initial exploration of love "as the word known to all men" describes the public face of ethics. Phaedrus exclaimed,

> What guidance do I mean? I mean a sense of shame at acting shamefully, and a sense of pride in acting well.**

Love as an ethical guide goes beyond the ecstasy and fog of *eros*. Love also involves how we treat others and how we make moral decisions in the everyday world. In the *Symposium*, Phaedrus touched on the morality of

---

*"A shudder in the loins engenders there/The broken wall, the burning roof and tower/And Agamemnon dead" (William Butler Yeats, "Leda and the Swan"). We do not ignore the competing obligations of love found in Book 6 of the *Iliad*, where Hector is pulled in two mutually exclusive ways.

†Plato, *Symposium* (ca. 385–378 B.C.E.), trans., ed., notes Alexander Nehamas and Paul Woodruff (Indianapolis: Hackett, 1989).

‡Plato, *Symposium*, 178 D1 (Phaedrus), p. 10.

**Plato, *Symposium*, 178 D 2–3, p. 10.

everyday life, now called situational ethics. There was, Plato suggested, "Common as well as Heavenly Love," the ordinary love experienced every day compared to the occasional passion for divine good. In reality, everyone judges the effects of love in daily life, which meant that

> considered in itself, no action is either good or bad, honorable or shameful.*

Context being all, love acquires its public face. Such social obligation is about as far from Humbert's experience as one can get. While for Pausanius, passion was only the lesser part of love, for Humbert, it was all the world and more. Humbert had no "good to be preferred" beyond an erotic hunger, and like Antony, "appetite grew by what it fed on." That attitude would not have shocked Plato, but it certainly would have displeased him. For the Greek philosopher, it was the social that mattered. So, Pausanius explained that love

> depends entirely on how it is performed. If it is done honorably and properly, it turns out to be honorable; if it is done improperly, it is disgraceful.†

Never mind *hamartia*, the egregious missing the mark by Oedipus, the result of the inevitable imperfection of people and things. Forget the disasters produced by good intentions, or the road that they pave. All know from Thomas Aquinas, as well as from Humbert Humbert, that intention is only part of an action, and perhaps the smaller part at that. What we intend to do is often only a pious hope. There is also execution, which is what we *do* do. Execution is the public and consequential part of the action. We are all familiar with this: "I just wanted to do the right thing." Of course. For almost all, that is almost always the case. But how does it turn out? Plato was acutely conscious of how it turns out: he was, after all, an iron moralist. Humbert, on the other hand, didn't give two whoops and a holler about that "honorable" face of love.

And further, given the complexity of the situations in *Lolita*, and in life, and from life to fiction, for life imitates art, it is far from clear what the honorable intentions might be. What does one say about Humbert's

---

*Plato, *Symposium*, 180 E 7–181A1 (Pausanias), p. 13.
†Plato, *Symposium*, 180 E 7–181A1 (Pausanias), p. 14.

Chapter One: The Word Known to All Men

decision to marry Charlotte, or to marry Valeria? Or Humbert's identification of "love" with very unwelcome sex. Depending on where one stands, "honorable" can have very different meanings. Alas, the morass of moral designation of intention, always partly unknowable, leads only downward to picking nits or plucking lint, and worse yet, substituting the self for the character being dissected. So, Plato has Pausanias conclude with an expansion on his principle concerning intention.

> Love is not in himself noble and worthy of praise; that depends on whether the sentiments he produces in us are themselves noble.*

This statement is pretty dry, but it does have meaning. It pushes intention back from a specific situation to a generalized noble sentiment. One may hope and even suppose that love is a necessary precondition for honorable action. Sometimes, probably. Love can make you act badly, or lift you up to acting well, alas, regardless of good intentions.† Love as action and intention dominates Plato's *Symposium*; it is sometimes explained with thinly disguised moralism but sometimes appearing in the lush charm of myth.

Myth depicts existential reality, even though the story itself may seem fanciful. Plato unfolds, through the medium of the comic playwright Aristophanes, a delightfully fanciful myth which depicts *eros* with a charm

---

*Plato, *Symposium*, 180 E 7–181A1 (Pausanias), p. 14. Dry, theoretical, and dehumanized, the moral comments of Pausanius and Phaedrus in the Symposium are implicitly undercut, indeed set close to nought, by the parables of Aristophanes and the Diotima. Both of these deal with *eros*, which in spite of Plato's eternal moralizing, becomes the message that one takes away from the dialogue. Burning passion, that's the stuff everybody understands, that's the stuff everybody experiences, and moral definitions of love and good are pallid beside it.

We believe that, deep in his heart, Vladimir Nabokov was a romantic deeply attracted to *eros*, and the power of *eros* is the central force of *Lolita*. The train wreck which is the nature of everyone's life in the novel is pretty thin compared to bright purple passion and "light of life" stuff.

†Although Nabokov avoided Christianity in essay, in fiction, and in life, he was nonetheless brought up in a Christian world. One ought not to forget then Paul, *Corinthians* I, 13, 4–7 in which love is described as inspiring virtuous behavior:

> Love is patient, love is kind *and* is not jealous; love does not brag *and* is not arrogant, does not act unbecomingly; it does not seek its own, is not provoked, does not take into account a wrong *suffered*, does not rejoice in unrighteousness, but rejoices with the truth; bears all things, believes all things, hopes all things, endures all things.

None of this applied to Humbert, of course. Nabokov made certain of that. For that reason, we have put it in a footnote.

"Light of My Life"

not extended to love as good will or great soul. Aristophanes will find, two millennia later, an unexpected echo in *Lolita,* whose main character searches for the love of his life. Aristophanes says that we are all searching for the love of our lives:

> Each of us, then, is a "matching half" of a human whole, because each was sliced like a flatfish, two out of one, and each of us is always seeking the half that matches him....
>
> And so, when a person meets the half which is his very own ... then something wonderful happens: the two are struck from their senses by love, by a sense of belonging to one another...
>
> "Love" is the name for our pursuit of wholeness, for our desire to be complete.*

This myth depicts erotic love at its best: personal, intimate, bonding, the love that unites two persons and separates both from all others. Excluded in the severing and reunion described by Aristophanes are all forms and sorts of casual lust, of group eroticism, of modern pornography. While these things are real and often powerful and always around, they do not fall into Plato's definition of love, nor did they strike Nabokov as love or lovely. In the austere *Lolita,* as in the cheerful Aristophanes, the center of gravity lies not in lust but in connection. The longing felt by Aristophanes' un-named victims of divine wrath, and by Humbert as an example of them, is for connection, for completeness, for wholeness, for contentment, for the end of frantic and squalid searching, for rest.

People seek endlessly for rest and completion, which is the point of Aristophanes' myth. We fall madly in love, but only for a while; find comfort in a community, but the community changes; find solace in a doctrine,

---

*Plato, *Symposium,* 191D5–7; 192B8–10–192C1; 192E13–15 (Aristophanes), pp. 27–19.
Rest, the result of completeness and connection, was, for Plato, the end of love found in the ideal or form; for Aristotle, the perfection of love would be in the form within the thing; for a more recent poet of myth, John Milton, rest was found in God. God as the source of real and abiding rest, as the proper direction for *agape* (Platonic ideas certainly) can be seen in the two episodes of human sexuality, both within Paradise but one before and the other after the Fall. Before the Fall, Adam and Eve made love, with concern for the other and leading to contentment; after, they had sex, with wantonness and lust leading to dissatisfaction, each with the other. The Latin tag that man alone is sad after copulation captured the reality that the "fire of my loins," while an expression of *eros,* did not encompass all that might be thought and said about love, from *eros* through *phile* to *agape;* but instead, said only "a little little."

but doubt creeps in; if the person does not change, and of course they always do, then the world changes around them, as it always does. Rest is a journey, or at least a movable delight, for nothing in a single human life remains the same always. Ovid, the epic Roman poet, knew that as well as Aristophanes did. However, Ovid was much less sanguine about love's power to bring rest to lovers, or anybody else, for that matter.

Ovid in the *Metamorphoses* described the emotional impact of love upon those unfortunate enough to experience it. Narcissus gave his name to the emotional sterility of the seriously self-absorbed. Medea endured the agony of passion which she repaid with rage and betrayal. The love of power and violence, or the boasting of pride, leads humans to destruction; though gods were spared the hideous consequences of love defective, excessive, or misdirected, they still shared the emotions. The light ironic tone of the *Metamorphoses* contrasts so sharply with the earnest instruction of the *Symposium* that it sometimes seems as if they were not speaking of the same thing.

The central theme of the *Metamorphoses* is that change affects individuals, often adversely, by bringing outside appearances and actions into harmony with internal attitudes and intentions. Who wants to be known as we really are? Sins, warts, insecurities, lewd and unjust thoughts brought to the view of all: does that sound like fun? And yet we do give ourselves away. Poker players call it the "tell." It happens all too often for human comfort, and love, particularly as erotic lust, is often the cause. Ovid knew this; he gloried in it. Ovid taught the prudential doctrine that love is to be feared.

Love, often excessive and misdirected, but always fierce and unyielding, demands the uttermost that desire can imagine and the body can create. While the *Symposium* contains only the single myth told by Aristophanes, the *Metamorphoses* contain nothing but myth. Ovid illustrates the attitude of erotic love, matured and enlarged by the social harmonies and duties inherent in *philia*, in the tale of Baucis and Philemon, where hospitality and domestic love were rewarded by the favor of the gods.* Philadelphic love expanded into *agape*: Deucalion and Pyrrha were devoted

---

*Ovid, *Metamorphoses*, tr. and intro. Horace Gregory (New York: Viking, 1958), Book VIII, pp. 234–238.

to each other and solicitous of the community at large, revering the gods and giving hospitality to the stranger. When destruction came upon the wicked (Noah is not the only such tale) the good Deucalion and Pyrrha were spared. Right repaid right, which is as it ought to be, but not always is.

> Their first
> Thought was to pray, to praise the Delphic nymphs,
> To give their thanks to Pan and most to Themis
> Who from her grottoes was the voice of Fate*;

For Ovid, *agape* is the primary expression of love and the essential personal virtue. Not surprisingly, Ovidian *agape* resembled Roman *pietàs*, a social duty meticulously performed in ritual as a protection for the community as well as an expression of individual character.

The opposite of Roman duty was Greek *hybris*. Arachne, a poor girl of Maeonia, worked in wool with a skill that enchanted the nymphs and a pride that filled Athena with envy and rage. Arachne was

> So artful with her needle that one knew
> No less than Pallas was her inspiration.
> Yet she denied the goddess was her teacher,
> And took offense when art was called divine.†

Presumption always leads to test, and the contest with Athena, too familiar to repeat, brought to Arachne the same reward earned by Lycaon for consuming rage, violence, avarice and a lust for destruction.‡

In the Ovidian world, people often experienced punishment, whether deserved or not. Suffering was often the outward and visible manifestation of change, not the reason for the change. The cause and origin of change lay in love, and Medea was a classic (even for Ovid) example of *eros* unattended.** Medea, the Persian princess of Calchas, fell immediately in love

---

*Ovid, *Metamorphoses*, Book I, pp. 36–37.
 †Ovid, *Metamorphoses*, Book VI, p. 163.
  ‡Ovid, *Metamorphoses*, Book I, pp. 39–40.
   **Two major pre–Ovidian redactions of the Medea tale have come down to the modern world: *The Argonautica* by Apollonius of Rhodes and *Medea* by Euripedes. These sources were already standard by Ovid's time. Ovid's view of love has been called one-dimensional, even cynical. One must remember that "cynical" describes an idea or an attitude that romantics disapprove of, even when they know it is true.

Chapter One: The Word Known to All Men

with strikingly handsome Jason. That was before she knew he was an idiot; but first impressions are powerful. It would be a shame for such a splendid man to die (as he surely would without her help). But to help Jason was to betray her father and her people, and to use her magic in wicked, even fatal ways. Duty or love? This is not an uncommon dilemma. Ovid knew the answer. People prefer desire to duty. And the dire consequences to come? The hell with them. But....

>Ovid depicted love coming to Medea as a curse.
>Sharp-eyed Medea, burned with quickening heat.
>She fought against her fever: it was madness.
>Nor could she cool her brains with hope of reason.
>....
>I see the wise,
>Yet I take the wrong.*

Eros did not triumph without resistance. Reason and good sense are not nothing: Medea had rallied:

>Daughterly
>Affection, Modesty, Right Thinking shone†;

They shone only briefly. Medea abandoned duty amidst increasingly frantic thoughts of Jason, thoughts that were simultaneously composed of worry and wantonness. Oh, Jason, Jason.... *Eros*, as Humbert in his turn would also discover, is not an easy boarder to repel, nor an easy companion to entertain.

Eros, as Humbert would never discover, can broaden into a more inclusive affection, philadelphic love, the love of family, community, and society. Ovid, for all the fun he had with the wreckage wrought by *eros*, described philadelphic love in that sensitive myth of Deucalion and Pyrrha at the very beginning of the *Metamorphoses*. Tone was not the only distinction between the solemn moralist Plato and the usually flippant Ovid. But Ovid's touch, usually light, could not disguise the seriousness of his thought nor the darkness of the lessons he taught. Ovid presented the randomness of evil. In the *Metamorphoses,* punishment and disaster were not

---

*Ovid, *Metamorphoses,* Book I, p. 187.
†Ovid, *Metamorphoses,* Book VII, p. 189.

"Light of My Life"

essentially connected to moral turpitude. Sometimes bad things happened because they happened. Always, the rain fell on the just and the unjust alike. There were in Ovid, some just deserts, but mostly, there were just deserts. Actaeon, the hunter, stumbled unwittingly on the naked Diana. Not his fault, really, but he was turned into a deer and hunted to death nevertheless. Life happened, and fortune was as important as virtue.

Transformation of people in the *Metamorphoses*, for whatever cause or excuse, normally meant a permanent trip down the evolutionary ladder. Actaeon became a deer, Arachne a spider, and Lycaeon was transformed into a wolf. All down, down, and never mind Darwin. At the core of this devolution lay *eros*, as later with Jekyll and Hyde, (another book Nabokov taught) and the same thing occurred, although metaphorically, to Humbert. He was at his best, body and soul, during the brief idyll with Annabel. But as time went on, Humbert slipped down, as his erotic passion continued to dominate his psyche. He consorted with prostitutes and took captive Lolita. Humbert became a modern metaphor for Lycaeon.

Still, Humbert never "deserved" his obsession, though he might have earned it after the fact by vast and continuing moral lapses. He lived a life informed by attraction to nymphets, choosing to cherish and embellish that taste instead of suppressing on moral or prudential grounds his nymphetic absorption. This deterioration would have been a matter of Ovidian interest. All the participants in the *Symposium* would have condemned Humbert, not sexually but socially. Solemn Plato would have moralized. A cheerful Ovid would have told a good tale. Like Nabokov.

Love in the western tradition, as Nabokov knew and often ignored, also had a strong Christian component. Christians regarded *eros* with almost as much horror as did Ovid, and emphasized community (*philia*) and the love of God (*agape*). Nabokov (and Humbert) found this, for the most part, pretty sappy stuff. In *Lolita*, the red meat of *eros* dominates all consideration of love. Of course, the story is told by the carnivore. Nevertheless, triangulation is a useful instrument in criticism as well as surveying. So it won't hurt, and ought to be instructive, to mention the Christian attitudes towards love. These were, after all, the views of every character in *Lolita* except the ravenous Humbert.

The Christian sensibility concerning love did not exclude sexual

Chapter One: The Word Known to All Men

attraction or the communal good, but it did emphasize the importance of loving God, of *agape*. Consequently, Christian culture enthusiastically embraced the Roman ideal of married love, which, tied to God by sacrament, brought *agape* into the daily life of all to make the mundane holy. At least that was the hope. But there was also the continuing Ovidian tradition, which would reappear in courtly love's schizoid emphasis on adultery and fornication as well as chaste adoration* Humbert practiced just one kind of courtly love, the lusty variety, flaunting the essential selfishness of Ovidian courtly love. Only the selfishness. Humbert, for all of Nabokov's complexity, was a simple character, with a life devoted to a single goal.

Humbert's choice of love, with erotic desire rampant, was the classical form that Christian theology understood existed, but invariably condemned. In the courtly Christian tradition, which Humbert professed to practice, and did practice, in the outward forms of giving gifts and pining and sighing, erotic passion should function to make the lover a better man and bring him closer to God. Pretty to think so. But Humbert's goals were divorced entirely from his rhetoric. He was interested in the sex. Of course, people usually ascribe a nobler motive to baser actions; consequently, even the most casual coupling could be described by lovers as leading to God. Humbert, with his modern sensibility, left that part out, though he did not neglect to say that he loved Lolita and that this love justified all.†

Over the centuries, Christians organized love into doctrines of pastoral theology, a system of instruction and counseling that sought to bring Christ into daily life. It emphasized hope for the good and for salvation, which are rarely erotic goals. Nowhere is this clearer than in Dante Alighieri's *Commedia* and John Milton's *Paradise Lost*. Humbert strategically touched upon both in his memoir, making himself look better to his readers. Noth-

---

*Reflected here is the Humbertian and profoundly Platonic distinction between body and soul. Humbert's duty was only to himself.

†Again we refer to Lionel Trilling, not only to what he gets right (Humbert's rhetoric and his passion) but also to what he gets wrong (the value of that passion, and all the rest of the thing Humbert did). We suggest courtly love lyrics, a selection of which can be found in *Lyrics of the Middle Ages: An Anthology*, ed. James Wilhelm (New York and London: Garland Press, 1990). The lyrics have a much clearer exposition of the values of courtly love than do the longer, more complex tales, for example, Chrétien de Troyes.

ing like a touch of Christianity to elevate *eros*. Humbert was no fool; predatory, but not a fool. He wished the readers (who might well be fooled) to know that he was dwelling within "the first circle of paradise." A subtle misreading of Dante, it combined the *Inferno* and *Paradiso* into a single never-to-be-fulfilled moment of ecstasy. For different forms of love, *eros* for the body and *agape* for the soul, this is a Dantean description of love.

Humbert could not help but misread Dante, whether he was aiming to impress a reader or just make sense of his story for himself. Dante, after all, had found the right path, helped by the right young guide. Humbert, although of a reflective temperament, lacked all sense of savvy with respect to the Christian journey. The notion that *eros* leads you up to the "bright uplands" of communal and divine love was utterly lost on him. If Humbert's *eros* devoured his victims, it devoured him as well. It's the rare person who can engage in these erotic predations and not experience blowback. One has to be a lot more of a sociopath than Humbert was. In spite of the guilt he felt, Humbert did not attain an understanding of what his life meant. He failed the Eliot test: could he understand what he had experienced:

> We shall not cease from exploration
> And the end of all our exploring
> Will be to arrive where we started
> And know the place for the first time.*

Like memory, the *Commedia* is circular, implying an ever-present possibility of the new beginning for each and for all. It assumes a Providence which ameliorates (forgives) sin and error by divine love in a world that ultimately makes moral sense.

Humbert's secular *sensibilite* did not allow for the journey toward grace. But *Lolita,* like the *Commedia*, demands rereading. The reasons are different. In the *Commedia*, circularity lies in the moral meaning of the epic; in *Lolita*, circularity resides in the structure of the novel, with its cryptic Foreword and ambivalent Afterword. The reader finishes the novel by returning to the Foreword. Then, of course, it's time to reread the whole thing. Reading *Lolita* is not a casual undertaking.

---

*T. S. Eliot, "Little Gidding," Pt. V, ll. 27–30.

Chapter One: The Word Known to All Men

A secular understanding of people, which is now the standard, treats betrayal and lust as nothing beyond themselves. They happen because they happen. Moral judgment must be suspended. That was Humbert's world. In his memoir, he asks for "understanding," and is assisted in his plea by John Ray in the Foreword and "Vladimir Nabokov" in the Afterword.* *Lolita* taunts the reader with an aggressive tolerance of chaos, along with a bland acceptance of what once was called wickedness. Humbert measures every action by the single standard of "how does it help me?" The self is everything.† Love veers always to narcissism, with betrayal nothing more than a convenience. In *Lolita*, Nabokov shows us a chaotic life and does not judge; in the *Commedia*, Dante shows us the same thing, and both judges and preaches.‡

Dante's misdirected love gets an ironic twist in *Lolita*, where it characterizes not merely Humbert's passion for nymphets but also Humbert's cynical motives for marriage. Marriage, though Humbert never acknowledged it, has always been a social good, combining *eros* with community. Whether or not marriage is viewed as a sacrament, it is certainly a beneficence, a gift given and received by each to the other, and set within a framework of general community approval. These are not small things, not least as they direct love away from narcissism. Humbert, of course, saw it differently. Get close to the daughter by marrying the mother.**

---

*The real Vladimir Nabokov disapproved strongly and consistently of Humbert's behavior, while the literary Vladimir Nabokov in the Afterword pulled all his punches. One ought not to forget that Nabokov was a secretive man who hid in plain sight behind alleged openness, behind interviews and commentary which were ambiguous. Perhaps it is simply the exile's caution. Perhaps it is the remembered patterns of childhood. This last possibility depends upon the close reading of *Speak, Memory*. Note that what Nabokov tells of his childhood is that he did everything alone, except chess with his father. The rest, from butterflies to love affair, was conducted outside the intimate family circle.

†The godfather of this appalling selfishness in the modern West was, of course, Jean-Jacques Rousseau. Nabokov, to our understanding, was not in any way a disciple of Rousseau.

‡In Canto 5 of the *Inferno*, the circle of lust, Dante provides example from Francesca and instruction from Virgil. No instruction in *Lolita*. Each reader is his/her own Virgil. You cannot make a judgment that you have not brought with you.

**The opposite can be seen in the first volume of Sholom Asch's *Three Cities*. Although both were Russian, we see absolutely no sign in Nabokov of any influence at all from the Russian Yiddish authors who were his contemporaries. Not Sholom Asch, certainly not Sholem Aleichem, or, later, Isaac Bashevis Singer. They wrote, frequently, about the same

"Light of My Life"

Humbert viewed marriage as a profoundly self-centered arrangement. Not everyone did. Many, in literature and in life, have subscribed to a Miltonic view of marriage. In *Paradise Lost,* John Milton situated love in the direction it ought always to face: away from the self and towards others, both individuals and groups. Adam and Eve fell short, of course. People always do. Nevertheless, Milton pointed the way, the pilgrim journey of love within the joys and obligations of marriage. *Eros* becomes imbued with *agape.* Even in the fallen world, love in marriage fulfills *caritas*:

> Hail, wedded Love, mysterious law, true source
> Of human offspring, sole propriety
> In Paradise, of all things common else!
> By thee adult'rous love was driven from men
> Among the bestial herds to range; by thee,
> Founded in reason, loyal, just and pure,
> Relations dear, and all the charities
> Of father, son, and brother, first were known.
> Far be it that I should write thee sin or blame,
> Or think the unbefitting holiest place
> Perpetual fountain of domestic sweets*

Though not synonymous with salvation itself, wedded love presents a daily refuge for post-lapsarian humanity, and a very present help for *agape.* Humbert, it appears, missed all that, though doubtless felt self-recompensed by sating his lust. Not uncommon.

The *don gratuit* of life and love that each spouse offers the other in marriage may, in daily reality, be less intense, permanent, or satisfying than Milton depicted it, or the partners desire or society prefers. Nevertheless, married love is, often enough, an incredibly rich experience and, usually, a serious personal good. Wedded love, with its emphasis on erotic attachment to a single other, argues for the immediate to stand as emblem of love in general. It insists that the immediate is as communal in effect

---

[*continued*] things, and appeared to share the same values. See, for example, Singer's Nobel speech: "The genuine writer cannot ignore the fact that the family is losing its spiritual foundation.... There must be a way for man to attain all possible pleasures, all the powers and knowledge that nature can grant him, and still serve God." We can suggest no reason for the distance between Nabokov and the Russian Jewish writers.

Paradise Lost, Book IV, ll. 750–765.

Chapter One: The Word Known to All Men

as it is erotic and individual. Marriage becomes the outward and visible sign of inward and spiritual grace.* Milton celebrated this view of love, which Nabokov excluded from *Lolita*. However, Humbert did not speak for Nabokov.

Marriage persists even into our post-modern world, as husbands and wives can hardly doubt, and so does the poetry of love and marriage. Nevertheless, love's sweet song, in the most recent centuries, has appeared more in novels than in the traditional genres of poetry, philosophy, and drama. In the nineteenth century novel, a deluge of detail replaced a spare phrase, making for a measured pace through the journey of reading the story. Nabokov was raised with these novels, wished to write them himself, and taught novels for the twenty years he lived in America. The novel form of extended narration has become the standard and appropriate manner of story-telling; and, after all, our cultural heritage is not just what went before but also is what is all around us. Nabokov absorbed wisdom and attitudes and outlook and technique from that novelistic sensibility. The novelist's craft resembles other skills. One learns by teaching as well as by doing.

Of the novels Nabokov taught to undergraduates in the nineteen-forties and -fifties, two in particular, though all in general, fit the central themes that inform *Lolita*. These two are *Madame Bovary* and *Anna Karenin*.† Both illustrate the similar and disastrous path of erotic love run unchecked unto death for the women and destruction for all about them. For Emma Bovary, the path of adultery drifted along the common road of dreams. Emma fondly evoked exotic enchantments, emotional excitement, enhanced economic circumstances, all avidly pursued through two lovers

---

*This formula is the standard definition of a sacrament. Generations of scholars have insisted that Milton's systematic theology was Protestant. Not entirely true. Milton's ecclesiology was Protestant enough, but his systematic were profoundly Catholic. The sacramental view of marriage is a case in point. Omitting the Tridentine words occluded, did not obliterate, the Tridentine spirit. As we know from Paul, "The letter killeth, but the spirit giveth life."

†See Vladimir Nabokov, *Lectures on Literature*, ed. Fredson Bowers, intro. John Updike (New York: Harcourt, 1980), pp. 125–179; see also Vladimir Nabokov, *Lectures on Russian Literature*, ed. and intro. Fredson Bowers (New York: Harcourt, 1981), pp. 137–236. In the Anglosphere, Tolstoy's novel is known as *Anna Karenina*, the feminine form, to which Nabokov vigorously objected. To him it was properly *Anna Karenin*. That is how he taught it; in a book about *Lolita*, we have used Nabokov's formula.

whom she barely loved but deeply desired, without regard for family or society or God. Anna Karenin had the appalling misfortune to fall violently in love, and in the months she spent resisting the consequences of passion she found her love deepening to absorb her entire life. Her erotic passion, abundantly returned by her lover Vronsky, rapidly engulfed families and friends, to the disadvantage of all, and compromised her sense of an appropriate relationship with God.* The two erotic passions had different hopes of what the fulfilled life meant, with Emma looking for the romantic excitement found in novels while Anna sought marriage and motherhood. Each dream was as impossible as the other; good intentions meant no more than ordinary self-absorption and indulgence. The result was the same. In the novels that Nabokov taught and admired, *eros* alone could have no good end.†

For all to prosper, love must expand beyond the self and the beloved, and by its nature, erotic desire does not always move in that direction. Recall the lawyers in *Bleak House*, or the lying lovers in *The Wings of the Dove*, or the selfishness of Maria Bertram in *Mansfield Park*. The novel's narrative form seems expressly adapted to the tug between desire and decorum. Nabokov exploited this tension in *Lolita*, reinforcing the erotic destruction with abundant detail, allowing the story to emerge from within the lover's emotions. *Eros*, as Ovid knew, is a dangerous and painful gift, and, whether the passion was genuine, generous and reciprocated, as it was with Anna and Vronsky, or the restless and pedestrian narcissism of Emma Bovary, the results were equally unhappy. External conditions were no more a prophylactic against erotic wreckage than were good intentions or the endless delusions of hope. Things usually thought favorable, such as affluence or high social rank, serve only to increase the severity and extent of secular doom. Maria Bertram Rushworth, having run away from a wealthy marriage with the dashing and deceitful Henry Crawford, was immured in perpetual isolation

---

*Nabokov, in *Lolita*, had no role for *agape*, and Flaubert treated religion as a social pose, but Tolstoy wrote of Anna's distance from God as a genuine loss, for life could not be complete without it.

†Nabokov, as Trilling accurately observes, brings "passion-love" to life in Humbert Humbert. Nabokov pointedly makes an example of *eros*, showing what terrible destruction ensues from the practicer of it. It is a good thing that the entire world is not populated by great lovers of Humbert's caliber. We suspect that Trilling would not agree.

Chapter One: The Word Known to All Men

deep in the country.* For the lower orders, of course, intemperate outbursts of erotic fulfillment were expected, and life went on, while novelists from Balzac to Nabokov invariably excused it.† But, such events and attitudes were still meant to be morally instructive.‡ Always, *eros* flared and guttered dangerously on the unstable edges of personal and social control. It is a short step from Helen of Troy to Anna Karenin.**

The leisurely narrative pace of a novel gave Nabokov space enough and time to describe all the details of the push of erotic passion, and it was details in style and structure that he fancied. Nabokov's attention to a novel's formal structure was almost Flaubertian in its precision, and in its success. Like *Madame Bovary* and *Anna Karenin*, *Lolita* is a well-crafted novel. Detail in *Lolita*, and there's a lot of it, is always apposite. Besides well-chosen detail, well-placed incongruity also emphasizes the theme of unruly *eros*. Nabokov crafted, in a tale about off-beat (to say the least) erotic passion set in an orthodox scenery of American normalcy,†† but with an exotic male lead in Humbert Humbert In *Lolita*, the extended juxtaposition of discordant elements increase the reader's awareness of Humbert's fundamental isolation, and isolation is the consequence of erotic love, whether requited or not.

Narrative length also allowed Nabokov to isolate *eros* from *philia*, which scarcely exists in *Lolita*. Nabokov, the acute observer of Emma Bovary and Anna Karenin, understood *philia*, conventionally expressed as marriage. If it does not evolve into *philia*, erotic love often devolves into obsession, appearing in police reports as suicide, stalking, murder, addiction, or other sordid activities of dubious social value. The novel form enabled Nabokov to describe those realities about love without explaining

---

*Nabokov did not emphasize this aspect of Jane Austen's *Mansfield Park* when he taught it at Cornell, but it is an important part of the social lesson provided by that realistic novel. Still, we erotic minded undergraduates did not heed the warning.

†And that, even genealogists may attest, may be one reason the lower orders remained lower. A further example of social understanding may be found in Chapter 10 of James Joyce's *Ulysses*, where Father Conmee, S.J., gravely blesses the young couple who furtively emerge from the bushes after, well, we all know.

‡Although he professed to loathe moral instruction, Nabokov chose to teach authors who cherished it: Austen, Dickens, Tolstoy, and Gogol.

**And to Britney Spears, for that matter.

††We take "normalcy" from Warren Harding's speech to the Boston Home Market Club in May 1920, from which it made its way into American English.

them, to unite classical wisdom to modern taste, and to examine *philia* in its absence as well as *eros* in its excesses and failure.

The novel form embraces variety, of course. Nabokov straddled two of them in *Lolita*, the fictional memoir and the legal confession, and put both into Humbert's pen. The subtitle of *Lolita*, "Confessions of a White Widowed Male," suggests the standard form of memoir, and a formal legal confession of guilt.* *Lolita* includes a non-standard, lengthy memoir as legal statement, which conceals through verbosity a dying declaration. In memoir form, *Lolita* has a slight *frisson* of Augustine or Rousseau; it is, after all, a *confession*. In legal terms, a confession is the defendant's statement which may be cross-examined in court, though only in the defendant's presence. Its truth is not assumed. A dying declaration is different. The person making the dying declaration, being dead at time of trial, cannot be cross-examined. It is an exception to hearsay exclusion. A dying declaration is assumed to be true, a benefit of the doubt not given to confessions. The law gives these dying declarations enormous weight, regarding them as statements of truth, unless contradicted by substantial contrary evidence. The implicit assumption is that the expiring miscreant does not wish to go to his Maker burdened with sin, but in the profoundly secular world of *Lolita* "sin" is a comparative term, and "Maker" no more than a supposition. Ought one to give Humbert the benefit of deathbed veracity? Alternatively, should one assume that Humbert regarded approaching death with equanimity, seeing his life's work as completed, and not standing in fear of judgment? Humbert's memoir is an extended dying declaration, for it is the last thing he will do, and the last thing he contemplates doing. He has had, however, plenty of time to slant the story and gild the lily.

Les Fruits Verts

History and social reality, as well as literary text, lay behind the quasi-iconic figure of Lolita, who represented erotic love in the form of *les fruits*

---

*Of course, all this is American law. In Russia, and many other parts of the world, most confessions are dying declarations.

Chapter One: The Word Known to All Men

verts. These objects of desire were young girls, from age nine or ten, just before puberty, to age thirteen or fourteen, now leaving the coltishness of youth and beginning to enter the grace of womanhood. An erotic predilection for young girls during the Belle Epoque and postwar years was not a shameful secret, known only to the police, procurers, prostitutes, and aficionados. Quite otherwise. The taste for recently pubescent girls flourished in pictures and photographs, which were racy but certainly not illicit. This expression of appetite appeared in Colette's *Claudine* series of books, from 1900–1903, describing a schoolgirl, who though not yet sixteen was an accomplished coquette overflowing with erotic energy. The four *Claudine* books were bestsellers, so the name Claudine was attached to consumer products from lotions to perfumes to clothes. *Claudine* was adapted to the theatre in a three-act "comedy," starring an actress of eighteen, Polaire (Emilie-Marie Bouchard), who had come to Paris from Algeria at thirteen to conquer the stage. As Claudine, she exhibited a potent sexual force that was both innocent and knowing.* The nymphet was a part of public entertainment as well as private desire, and what began in Paris was translated and copied in all of the capitals of Europe. It was Paris, after all, which dictated fashion, not least in St. Petersburg, where the aristocracy spoke more French than Russian and visited Paris more often than their estates.

In France (and everywhere else), sexual taste and style was informed not only by social class but also by popular literature and, after 1900, by film as well.† This socio/sexual phenomenon reveals *les fruits verts* within

---

*Patrick Waldberg, *Eros in la Belle Epoque*, trans. Helen R. Lane (New York: Grove Press, 1969). See particularly Chapter 4, but the entire book is a witty and surprisingly inclusive examination of sexual desire centered on the major motif of undressing a woman. Of course, before the War, undressing a woman was a far more demanding and enticing task than it would be afterwards. Women then wore more and more variety of undergarments than is common today. And even the outerwear presented challenges. Why, merely undoing the endless pearl buttons of a woman's shirtfront added both anticipation and detail to the whole business of a gradual rather than an immediate reveal. The striptease, we suggest, probably began in the home.

†Mary Pickford, the actress who became "America's sweetheart," retained the then-girlish style of long, flowing hair well into maturity, indeed, into her marriage with Douglas Fairbanks. Even more apposite, Rosemary Hoyt, the seventeen-year-old star of *Daddy's Girl* in Fitzgerald's *Tender Is the Night* (1934), met her lover Dick Diver on the Riviera beach. The doings of celebrities are always well-known, and may, perhaps, and we cannot say more, find an echo in *Lolita*.

"Light of My Life"

the bourgeois familial religion of interiority and within the geographical segregation of prostitution. The bourgeois family protected the schoolgirl and her *petite capitale* from the erotic attentions of those uninterested in marriage. The schoolgirl was a family treasure, to be married advantageously, moved from the cosseted protection of her natal family to the equally close protection of her marital home. The bourgeois schoolgirl was never alone. Surrounded by family, money, status, and an appropriate social circle, she moved through a predetermined life to the defined goal of marriage, and eroticism played little part in either the journey or the destination. In these tender and domestic matters, property trumped everything.

For the prostitute, of course, it was all different. Having no family at all, or a family who leased her out, she was not destined for marriage but for the fleeting enjoyment of others. The poor and largely unwashed prostitutes roamed the grimy working-class streets, enduring a life that was nasty, brutish, and all too often, short. The better class of the newly pubescent toured the center of Paris, where wealthier clients paid more in coin but not in concern. At the top were those who became the *petites amies*, and in this case, *really* little friends, of a more or less constant protector. Society is always a pyramid, where the grimy waifs vastly outnumbered the perfumed princesses of a pedophile's cultivated desire.

In the presentation of the newly pubescent in theatre or literature, the schoolgirl persona was absolutely *de rigueur*.* The first of the Claudine series was *Claudine a l'Ecole* (1900), and *ecole* was culturally imprinted as a major marketing motif upon the appearance and mystique of *les fruits*

---

*That sexual motif remains with Western society today, and is seen in the continuing popularity of young teen pornography featuring parochial school or cheerleader costumes. It has not been uncommon for disapproved sexual taste and practice to combine lasciviousness with property and propriety. Sexually explicit images are the most stable area of representation. See Aretino.

On Paris, and its role in European fashion in license and dress, which are imaginatively the same thing, as well as art and social style, see Walter Benjamin, *The Writer of Modern Life, Essays on Charles Baudelaire*, comp., ed., and intro. Michael W. Jennings (Cambridge, MA: Harvard University Press, 2006). The volume contains the essay "Paris, the Capital of the Nineteenth Century," pp. 30–45, and the much longer "The Paris of the Second Empire in Baudelaire," pp. 46–133. These essays date from the 1930s, precisely when Humbert Humbert was in Paris. They look back to the world before the War, precisely as Nabokov had Humbert do in *Lolita*.

verts. French schoolgirls then wore short dresses, often plaid, atop black stockings, and had their hair done in long, loose, beribboned braids. That costume betokened innocence and property, along with a hint of sexual opportunity and the rewards of stolen ecstasy.* It also meant a profit on both book and film.

Approved nymphetic characteristics, an essential part of the ambiance and attraction of teen-age sexual provocation, were not easy to create, and got harder over time as erotic standards changed. Cultural tolerance for sex with thirteen-year-old girls diminished steadily after the Roaring Twenties, so Humbert Humbert, a bit too late, found himself cherishing an intense passion for a new Annabel in a cultural climate of disapproval and in a time of declining market supply of faux-bourgeois schoolgirls. Still, Humbert tried to recapture the elusive past, and was sent by a helpful madam to a repulsive mustachioed procuress. Her gross physical presence alone destroyed the dream, but then things got rapidly worse, as they often do in the risky business of erotic enchantment. Enter the girl. Instead of Annabel, or even the counterfeit-but-not-altogether Monique, there was revealed a fat young woman. She was indecently decked out in ribbons and braids, a last pitiful shadow of the slim, fastidious, and suggestive Claudine, now thirty-odd years in the past. All else was foul and ugly, from presentation to person.

Well, what else could Humbert reasonably expect? Casual commercial sex is *au fond*, emotionally ersatz. Still, the Annabel idyll persisted through it all as Humbert's dominant memory and constant touchstone of erotic satisfaction. He declares that it was Annabel with her "ardent tongue" that haunted him henceforth; she certainly haunts his memoir. Alas, Humbert was separated from the Belle Epoque by time and war, and from Annabel by time and death, and while both could be recalled, neither could be recaptured.

Humbert the Memoirist

The focus of a memoir may be upon the self, a novel of growth (*David Copperfield*), a story of origins (*The Voyage of the Beagle*), a series of anec-

---

*See Waldburg, particularly illustrations on pp. 108, 114, 116, and 122.

"Light of My Life"

dotes (Casanova), a comment upon the interesting times in which we have lived (*Reading Lolita in Teheran*); or a memoir may focus upon a single thread of life deemed by the author to contain the core of personal meaning (Wordsworth's "The Prelude: The Growth of the Poet's Mind"). At its largest scale, such as Winston Churchill's six volume *The Second World War* (1948–1953), a memoir may situate the self in the entire world. On a smaller scale, the emphasis is on private life. This kind of memoir demands that the storyteller be disciplined: it is far too easy to wander off into meaningless anecdote.

Before the Great War, biographers and memoirists usually wrote in the "life and times" style, devoting space and thought to the context of a life as well as the details of a life. This technique had two corollaries, then so obvious as to require no mention. In the first place, time passed, and the world at death differed from the world at birth. These changes were often due to the labors of the hero being chronicled. When Albert Einstein was born, physics was firmly Newtonian, but when he died, there were quantum mechanics, special relativity, black holes, general relativity, and much else as well. Secondly, biographers and memoirists recognized that "the times" affected the hero as much as the other way around, and perhaps more. The subjects of biography appeared in a context of culture, place, and politics. The relationship of hero to society was reciprocal and indelible. No man was an island, and all were part of their times. As late as early nineteenth-century England, one could have heard an old lady remark, "As my husband once said to Louis XIV...." Time and context: they fashioned a life and helped define its goals.*

In *Lolita*, the life and times becomes the life and time. No "*s*." Until 1947, just one time had existed, the summer with Annabel. A few perfunctory words of introduction led up to Annabel, and a whole lot of words of self-absolution led away from Annabel. But they didn't lead far. Humbert, both character and storyteller, stops the clock.† Humbert's "times"

---

*Today, of course, Western culture is caught up in the sludge of psychology, and the journeys described in biography and memoir have become increasingly interior and less communal. The emphasis increasingly is on "how I felt," and less on "what I did" and "what it meant." For an historian, this is not a gain.

†Having Humbert stop the clock is a clever narrative technique.

Chapter One: The Word Known to All Men

utterly vanished, vast amounts of illustrative detail to the contrary notwithstanding. He makes it clear that nothing that affected everyone else living through the twenties, thirties, and forties, had any impact on the utterly insular Humbert Humbert. Wars, depressions, moving to America, all were incidental details. His own marriages and encounters were all essentially decorative. They merely happened. Beyond Annabel, there is no *bildung*. That is Humbert's story, and he stuck to it. This gives *Lolita* its curiously hermetic quality. It is a novel of silence. There is no echo of the times. Even love, which changes everything, oddly remains a static experience for Humbert.* *Lolita* is an interior narrative of erotic passion misdirected, then repeated, always the same.

Humbert uses his memoir, a narrative form structured by time, to illustrate how he has denied time. For Humbert, memory performs an anti-chronological service by running all of the events of his life into the single matrix of the first event of that life. A memoir, after all, is no more than an organized form of telling our tale.† Having our say is as basic a human need as belief or connection. Memory is the deep well in which we preserve ourselves, and from which we call up the needed bits and pieces to explain ourselves and the world around us. We tell our story, and our story tells us. Humbert tells how he failed to grow, failed to love with generosity. This failure to grow, not his pedophilia, is Humbert's besetting sin.

In telling his story, Humbert recounts every misadventure and manages to find no moral, no meaning beyond the "palliative of art," with no goal for life and love. Reflection upon the past, and there is plenty of that, leads Humbert to no understanding, no organized pattern and certainly no sense of evolution. It started and then it ended. Humbert remains

---

*In that regard, consider Medea. Whether seen in epic (*Voyage of the Argo*) in myth (*Metamorphoses*), or in drama (*Medea*), it is always love, affirmed or denied, that changes Medea's life.

†The critic James Atlas argues in the *New York Times Magazine* (May 12, 1996) that, in the contemporary world, memoir has replaced novels. We assume that this development is part of the evolution of modern taste, and is analogous to reality television. Nabokov's *Lolita*, a faux-memoir, both captures the novel as craft and anticipates the modern taste. Of course, one ought not to forget that Augustine did much the same thing sixteen centuries ago. And then, *plus ça change, plus c'est la même chose*.

"Light of My Life"

caught in the eddy of *eros*, observing the fact of change in Lolita and interpreting it as a form of permission to murder the loathsome Quilty. Humbert did not move beyond the single summer at the Hotel Mirana with Annabel. In metaphors for the narrow and the static, consider John Donne's poem "The Sunne Rising," where the speaker insists his love can

> Make of this little room an everywhere.*

And for Humbert, it did.

The Great War

Where there is love there is always loss, and loss can dominate lives. For Humbert, the loss came in the exit from the enclosed garden. The greater blue cosmos that "blazed outside" of the Hotel Mirana was not the adult world, that ancient enemy of youthful passion. Things were worse than that. The Great War had blazed uncontrollably for seven years, in the process incinerating Europe and its civilization from end to end, leaving a bloody ruin prophetic of blood to come and already reeking with the sludge of fascism. Now, in 1923, the blaze had been reduced to general smolder and local flares, but these meant only exhaustion, not peace. The stable world of 1910 had vanished, leaving a sense of loss and longing for its return, a general and cultural nostalgia, in this case the pain of non-return.

The fictive young persons, Annabel and Humbert, were hardly aware that a world had been lost, with only the formal husk surviving. They were too young to understand that Europe now lived in the condition of exile, not from place but from the world before the war. For them, postwar ruin was normal, and if the world was broken, they still were fresh. They imagined there was hope for them. At age thirteen, it is hard to grasp that you, too, are the debris of war. It is hard for the young to look back, particularly after falling in love. Optimism is always the companion of young love, which is always also stuck in the moment.

---

*John Donne, "The Sunne Rising." See also W. B. Yeats, "Solomon and Sheba," where the wise pair agree that "only love can make the world a narrow pound."

Chapter One: The Word Known to All Men

Of their elders, few besides the poets and novelists immediately recognized the end of the world. They knew that a century of progress in the Western world had ended, and a time of troubles had begun. Few paid much attention. Artists were, after all, simply the modern form of Old Testament prophets. We know where prophets are honored.

Loss had come first for the soldiers. Ezra Pound saw the meaning of the Great War in terms of casualties, both personal and cultural. In 1920, even before the fighting had ended, he wrote "Hugh Selwyn Mauberly," bringing war home to the home:

> These fought in any case,
> and some believing,
> > pro domo, in any case...
>
> Some quick to arm,
> some for adventure,
> some from fear of weakness,
> some from fear of censure,
> some for love of slaughter, in imagination,
> learning later...
> some in fear, learning love of slaughter;
> Died some, pro patria,
> > non "dulce" non "et decor" ...
> ....
> Daring as never before, wastage as never before.
> ....
> fortitude as never before
> frankness as never before
> disillusions as never told in the old days.*

None understood the old world more clearly than James Joyce in his immensely sad *Ulysses,* an elegiac work of love as loss. Joyce wrote about the War without mentioning the War, but by comparing what all felt now with what had existed then. The form of composition was new, but style supported the sentiment, which evoked the warmth and comfort of remembered ways and a cherished home. The home was now gone. It could be felt but not recaptured, mourned but not recovered, a category of nostalgia and utter loss not unlike Humbert's remembrance of Annabel. *Lolita* tells

---

*Ezra Pound, "Hugh Selwyn Mauberly" (1920), iv.

a similar tale, a smaller version of *Ulysses*, both exploring the undiminishing pain after the loss of a child. In postwar Europe, everyone knew how that felt. As Bloom remembers, Humbert remembers. Joyce himself remembered even more, the loss of the whole world.*

In the world as in the books, a pervasive sense of loss had risen so high that it swamped "all the cultural resources of meaning available to Europeans in the first decades of the twentieth century."† Robert Graves described the general psychic fatigue and disillusionment with the bitter precision of one who remembered better.

> War was foundering of sublimities,
>   Extinction of each happy art and faith
>   By which the world had still leapt head in air‡

In its place Europeans were offered the pathetic delusion of peace through the League of Nations.

This general attitude of loss did not characterize the young Humbert and Annabel. They were merely inheritors of, not participants in, the collapse. Even for "intelligent European preadolescents" the end of prewar hope and security was indistinct, a part of the alien adult world that they were frantic to escape. And a form of escape there would be. The young lovers snatched their escape through their mutual passion and their relentless disregard of anything beyond it. An enclosed garden of wealth on the Cote d'Azur certainly helped. So did summer warmth. But summer lasts forever only in dreams. As must be, the Leighs left the south of France taking Annabel to her death and leaving Humbert to his. The garden emptied and vanished.

In *Lolita*, Nabokov included no sense of general cultural loss or disillusion beyond Humbert himself. Humbert did not emerge from the idyll with Annabel into a confused and cratered Europe; he emerged into a prolonged sexual malaise. Humbert's pain within mirrored, as it were, some of the general grief. He entered a prolonged bereavement, which blotted

---

*Humbert's memories are technically overdetermined, weaving bits of Nabokov's biography silently and secretly around Humbert's memoir.
†Eric Leed, *No Man's Land* (Cambridge: Cambridge University Press, 1979), x.
‡Robert Graves, "Recalling War."

Chapter One: The Word Known to All Men

out any serious appreciation of the damaged world around him. A lot happened in the quarter-century between 1923 and 1947, but none of it appeared to have had any impact upon Humbert. The interior monologue of anomie filled his years completely. Humbert carried an ill-defined but enormous burden of free-floating pain, always near the surface, always reappearing in the midst of love and sex, to deny fulfillment, to abort contentment.* Indeed, there is only a single oblique reference in all of *Lolita* to the aftermath of the Great War. It is Humbert's removal to America, leaving "dull and dingy" Paris to come to an undignified new world. Humbert never mentioned the cause of the move.

He never had to. Only the threat of war come again could have turned Humbert into a refugee, marginalizing him still further. Of course he recognized the gathering storm, having had grown to maturity in postwar France. Humbert was no fool. One day he is in Paris, offloading his first wife Valeria into the sympathetic care of the ex–Czarist colonel, and the next he is in New York, dodging the wiles of "perfumed and deodorized career women." The poets said, as with Eliot in the *Waste Land*, that after the Great War there could be no love, at least in ruined Europe. Humbert suspected that might be true. A new erotic passion could only come in a new world. He was sure that he had not lost his capacity for love, despite his overwhelming angst.

That passion would arrive, channeling his angst into the desires of pedophilia. Humbert would still call it love, as if his passion for Lolita bore no differences to his passion for Annabel. The intervening years would see no difference in his essential erotic passion, which was always for green fruit. Humbert would, however, age, growing further, chronologically and psychologically, from his chosen prey. Still, he told himself, as his memoir indicates, that things had not changed, that young love had not become full-blown dysfunction. He was deceiving himself, of course, and, as con men know, self-delusion is the most beguiling form of fraud.

Humbert wrote as if nothing that might be called an event had occurred to him in the quarter-century between Annabel Leigh and Lolita Haze. It

---

*See, for example, the role of pain and longing in Ernest Hemingway's *The Sun Also Rises* and F. Scott's Fitzgerald's *Tender Is the Night* and *The Great Gatsby*.

"Light of My Life"

was always 1923 out there, past the portal of Humbert. Humbert seems to have slept through the years. Of all the people in Europe after the war, he alone had lost nothing. Humbert's main claim in *Lolita* is that his vision of love had survived intact from the first days with Annabel to his last days in prison, dying with pen in hand. Though it covers the war years, *Lolita* is not a war novel about loss. There was just a lost garden to be regained.*

Part of the charm of the personal is that individual lives and fates can be, at least in part, disconnected from either general success or "boisterous ruin."† As Shakespeare knew, a low profile helps. In Humbert's case, that took the form of an intense devotion to privacy.‡ He attempted to slip through the years under the radar of history, avoiding a war he could not ignore and ignoring social contexts he could not avoid. Inward, turn always inward, cherish the secret love: that was actually Humbert' s motto. Never engage the world: that was Humbert's constant practice. He passed through the years, of war, ruin, twilight peace, and war again. In no sense, however, could he be called a "survivor."

And what did it mean to be a "survivor"? F. Scott Fitzgerald comprehended the psychic heritage of those who had survived the Great War. In *Tender Is the Night,* the horror of war and the guilt of survival had changed everything and everyone. The Western Front was part of us all.

> "See that little stream — we could walk to it in two minutes. It took the British a month to walk to it — a whole empire walking very slowly, dying in front and pushing forward behind. And another empire walked very

---

*We suggest that Annabel Leigh can be seen as a synechdoche for all of Western civilization, and further, that this was not an impossible idea for Nabokov.

†*Hamlet*, Act 3, scene 3:
> The cess of majesty
> Dies not alone; but, like a gulf, doth draw
> What's near it with it: it is a massy wheel,
> Fix'd on the summit of the highest mount,
> To whose huge spokes ten thousand lesser things
> Are mortised and adjoin'd; which, when it falls,
> Each small annexment, petty consequence,
> Attends the boisterous ruin.

‡Charlotte's openness and addiction to truth stands in contrast to Humbert's obsessive secrecy and mendacity. Humbert lied on their wedding license, and in the newspaper article about their nuptials, and pretty much everywhere to everyone. Though he complained when Valeria lied to him, his memoir shows no shame or discontent about his own habit of deception.

Chapter One: The Word Known to All Men

slowly backward a few inches a day, leaving the dead like a million bloody rugs. No Europeans will ever do that again in this generation."

....

"This western-front business couldn't be done again, not for a long time. The young men think they could do it but they couldn't. They could fight the first Marne again but not this. This took religion and years of plenty and tremendous sureties and the exact relation that existed between the classes. The Russians and Italians weren't any good on this front. You had to have a whole-souled sentimental equipment going back further than you could remember. You had to remember Christmas, and postcards of the Crown Prince and his fiancée, and little cafés in Valence and beer gardens in Unter den Linden and weddings at the *mairie*, and going to the Derby, and your grandfather's whiskers.

"...Why, this was a love battle — there was a century of middle-class love spent here. This was the last love battle."*

Fitzgerald recognized the nostalgia familiar to everyone who remembered life before the Great War. In *The World Crisis*, Winston Churchill wrote that the "old world in its sunset was fair to see," and none who had seen it could disagree, now that it was gone. In *Ulysses*, Joyce recalled a world that worked and made sense; its apparent chaos and the Brownian motion of the characters collectively led to the encouragement of love for the community. This was how those who had lived it remembered it, perhaps in Joyce's kaleidoscopic prose and certainly in the love that informed the pre-war world and which Joyce reflected. Again, Fitzgerald: "It is sadder to find the past again and find it inadequate to the present than it is to have it elude you and remain forever a harmonious conception of memory."†

Nabokov finessed that problem. *Lolita* was written, so to say, above its time, with nothing of elegy beyond the memories of Humbert, and nothing of lament beyond Dolly. Clever Nabokov. He wrote a novel in which the ruin of the individual is utterly divorced from the general ruin around him, as if the world of Humbert bore no relationship to the world of western civilization. We again observe, that *Lolita* has a curiously airtight quality about it; it is, so to speak, a closed system, almost a fallout shelter, set in, but not part of, the larger world around. Only an exile could write this way. Authors who are at home write about home.

---

*F. Scott Fitzgerald, *Tender Is the Night*, 1934.
†F. Scott Fitzgerald, *The Crack-Up*, 1945.

Chapter Two

MARRIAGE

In the 1950s, the era of "togetherness" when Nabokov was writing *Lolita*, the *Ladies Home Journal* carried an on-going series entitled "Can This Marriage Be Saved?" The answer, explained at length over several pages, was invariably yes, and the sub-text steadily implied that marriage was valuable in itself, worth every effort given to it, and wrought personal enhancement for both partners. Appropriate for multi-faith America, the *Ladies Home Journal* omitted any doctrinal justification for marriage as a sacramental union, but the series retained the essence of marriage from *Paradise Lost* as the foundation of "all the charities." Memory of sins past would lead to personal moral growth, and coincide with general social betterment. Wife and husband told their tales, and their personal memoirs were woven by the therapist into a new narrative of enlightenment, commitment, and mutually remembered history. The *Journal*'s story became the couple's new story; an unfolding memoir of enhanced romantic love amidst conjugal obligation.

But the memoir in *Lolita*, unlike the *Journal*, did not lead beyond present distress into improvement to come, but rather to Humbert's death. In *Lolita*, erotic love stood as an end in itself, and marriage represented its opposing force. Death, child abuse, banal philistinism, and central themes critics have often found, served as illustrative decoration. In the *Journal* narrative, marriage enlarged life; in *Lolita* it remained insubstantial because of Humbert's inability to transform *eros* into *philia* or *agape*.

The *Journal* did no more than speak the American civic faith that marriages ought to be saved, adding some phrases and therapeutic techniques gleaned from modern (c. 1955) psychological counseling, then at the height of its popularity. That sufficed. The pedestrian narratives of healing couples carried, after all, not only civic approval and pseudo-scientific cachet, but also the soothing sense of higher purpose and general good.

The *Journal* presumed that marriage could move man and wife beyond mere existence and inertia into two parallel narratives, one rising from *eros* to *agape*, and the other encouraging, even demanding, the moral growth of self and partner. Within a marriage that contains love, the participants merge into unity, while simultaneously remaining themselves. It is not that marriage *necessarily* leads up any specific avenue of human satisfaction; rather, as Milton described, marriage is a moral, psychic, and social condition profoundly different from what has come to be called "the single life-style." Commitment differs from convenience. The married partners, looking back over a life lived forward, realize that the fact of marriage itself, independent of specific events, slowly and unrelentingly changes every element of life and illuminates every element of love.*

Although marriage is formally contracted between two persons, its penumbra, to use a legal term, embraces the families specifically and the community at large. It is a public change of status, making sexuality open and desirable when previously it might have been furtive and slightly shameful. Marriage renders children legitimate, fruits of licit attachment and receiving communal blessing, rather than the result of carelessness.† Marriage brings stability to the community, to the generations, and to property. Marriage fixes a secure place for people within a context of social duty, which Charlotte willingly embraced when she became Mrs. Humbert. Marriage is often derisively described as the domestication of *eros*, the cooling of the gypsy's bellows, but lust must lessen a bit in any case, and better for all that it occur within a world of children and mutual work

---

*On looking backward for understanding and perspective on a life lived forward, preferably into grace, see Augustine, *Confessions*, Bk. XI. Augustine is on the same page as Nabokov: they both suggest that our crucial interpretive act is to be "re-readers"—we cannot make sense of something the first time around, so we return to the narrative, and make sense of it by reversing its direction. To be a "re-reader" means you have to go beyond passive "following the story" and take charge of the story. You have to enter the story itself and become owner, author of it. That is what Nabokov allows us readers to do as he strews important clues in the Foreword that we won't understand until we finish the first reading.

†Carelessness, let it be noted, is moral as well as physical.

than in the realm of single persons drifting apart amidst lies and recriminations. "Togetherness" is (and was) not just an advertising slogan.

In describing marriage, Milton sang of love and "all the charities," and the *Ladies Home Journal* emphasized community, but both dealt with sacrifice only through indirection. Sacrifice is part of marriage, occasionally of life, frequently of purse, and always of opportunity, and costs are part of the value of the community. Marriage, like love itself, often describes loss. For Humbert, the costs came through obligation, the opportunity to love and to support his wives, which he resolutely declined to do. He remained aloof and apart, with marriage a convenience (Valeria) or a conspiracy (Charlotte). Having said the vows, he remained essentially unmarried. Sacrifice was for the woman; the better, not the worse should accrue to him. Humbert entered no community; he omitted the charities; he would accept no loss. The incurably and erotically romantic Humbert never learned that one really married not to live in bliss forever, but to get to heaven, if religious, or to maintain social stability, if secular. The formal vows of marriage marked the farthest extent of what he would give.

Other marriages, besides Humbert's two barren episodes, appear in *Lolita*, but the text as memoir, with surgical efficiency, excises all that is tangential to Humbert, the erotic lover who aims to love passionately and dissolve into ecstasy. Humbert cannot describe or perceive or perform marital love. The absence of marital love in the book is a function of a narrator who cannot perceive it in the landscape. The ardent Humbert never, ever, talks about marrying Lolita. In *Lolita*, marriages fail. The reasons differ. The conclusion remains.

Humbert and His Wives

Humbert in Paris was a study in distance.

In my sanitary relations with women I was practical, ironical, and brisk.*

---

*Nabokov, *Lolita*, Pt. I, ch. 5, p. 15. We suggest, though cannot prove, that the "brisk" and "sanitary" aspects of these "relations" indicated oral sex, performed on but not by Humbert. We suggest further that the "practical" and particularly "ironic" elements of these relations lend support to our previous comment. *Eros* was involved, of course. Hence the need for the brisk and the practical.

Chapter Two: Marriage

His paid women, rented by the hour, usually less one would suppose, were biologically female, but beyond that one can say nothing. They formed no connection, demanded no commitment. Between the brisk Humbert and the boughten women was just a brief impersonal bump in the afternoon. Well, it was good enough, satisfactory if not satisfying, taking care of the moment without reference to anything beyond.* The brokenhearted lover of Annabel indicates that he still was capable of becoming aroused; at those times, he might desire an orgasm, but nothing more. There was no complementary object of desire. His need was not for a specific woman that he loved, or even just admired. His need involved merely physiological relief. If this condition of desire can be still defined

---

*There is more to prostitution than sex, which, we assume, is the primary interest only of the individual customer. Beyond the specific transactions lay the general sociology and economics of public sex in Paris before the Germans came in 1940.

Monique belonged to that class of working girls who worked the streets, having a block or two where she habitually strolled, hoping to catch a passing male eye. She did not "own" her half-mile of Paris sidewalk, but the competition was limited, for the most part, to regulars like herself. Monique worked a beat in an upper-class area of Paris near the Madeleine, perhaps on the Rue Royal itself. Attractiveness and sex appeal, qualities that elude precise definition but are nonetheless instantly recognizable, were required to hold down a position in that elegant venue. Monique also had youth, the quality that attracted Humbert, and caused him to part with 100 francs for a brief moment of impersonal *amour*.

The price of Monique's attentions is also of interest. It was 100 francs, c. 1932, a tariff which seems, in retrospect, quite modest. In 1926, the prime minister Raymond Poincare had stabilized the post-war franc at about 5 cents American. The depreciation of the franc to less than four cents American in 1928 made Monique's compensation even more modest. One hundred francs was less than five dollars, not outrageous for an aging veteran near the Rue Monge or the Luxembourg gate, but a bargain for a *gamine* near the Madeleine. Humbert also added a tip of 50 francs, not quite two dollars and fifty cents American, and the pleased Monique announced she could buy some stockings. At that modest rate of compensation, Monique would have had to work at industrial efficiency in order to prosper. But the nature of her enterprise prevented that. Commercial sex may have been common in Paris, but, in Humbert's salad days, the vast majority of working girls seem to have been poor.

This is not altogether surprising. Purveyors of primary products, from wheat to cotton to sex, are usually paid poorly on a piece-rate basis. Prosperity comes in the value-added category, which included, in Paris, the *grandes horizontales*, elegant women kept by the nobility. Their social identification as *grandes horizontales* expressed their status, with a frank description of their rank and a delicate hint of their function. For these elegant ladies of the *demi-monde*, charm, wit, and social presentation were more important than mere agility, and provided their value-added element. Monique, youth and attractiveness notwithstanding, could never join the ranks of these elegant entrepreneurs. In the sex business, it is not so easy to add value, as Valeria and Charlotte would show. Even love is not always enough.

as *eros*, it is *eros* taking form as narcissism. How likely is that mode of passion to have a happy end? Even *eros* focused upon an object of desire often leads to doom. Ovid was right. In matters of love, desire alone cannot succeed. Love is, after all, an offer, a gift, not compulsion. Humbert would learn this, but only through the extended (and for him) exquisite pain of his time with Lolita.

Humbert's brief, practical encounters with prostitutes took place in Paris, always an entrancing city, especially in the waning days of the *entreguerre*, when everyone knew that time was short and life was elegiac. However, the brisk Humbert remembered nothing about the city, beyond that it was dull and dingy. He was a student, an increasingly *manque* student, occasionally involved in scholarly pretentiousness, but otherwise simply existing, going nowhere, and becoming nothing. For the moment, Humbert just was.

Part of the reason for just making do with boughten women appears to have been Humbert's taste for nymphets of good family, like Annabel, rather than work-worn shop girls. The intensity of Humbert's memory demanded repetition. Do it again! the child cries when the game pleases him, and Humbert wanted nothing less than total repetition. Searching for Annabel, he watched and dreamed of school girls. Sometimes, he found one. Once a nymphet tightened her roller skate next to Humbert seated on his bench. Often he watched the moderately active sports of pre-pubescent girls. Another time a red-haired schoolgirl hung over Humbert in the *metro*, leaving him with a fiery memory. Humbert's fantasies often frightened him, and occasionally drove him so far as to consider the monstrous ministrations of psychologists. He was aware that his continuing attraction to schoolgirls was socially unacceptable, to which he added an internal judgment that it was also implausible. But Humbert knew in the core of his gut and soul, or something near it, that his fantasies of nymphetic love were of the most superior sort, better, more elegant, more refined, than the gross libidinous desires of ordinary men. Still, whether they were the approach to paradise that Humbert imagined, or something else, his idiosyncratic fantasies were all he had. He was stuck in his own grandiosity. And, confident that his fantasies were better than everybody else's fantasies, he pursued and embellished them.

Chapter Two: Marriage

Humbert's narcissistic imaginings could never shift from the barely pubescent to the charms of mature women. Nor did he wish to be different.* Eventually, then, he would find the opportunity and will to act upon his impulses. He would find that love, like stupidity, becomes what it does.† Humbert was not then (circa 1930–1935) as vile as he would be later, when he would imprison and abuse Lolita. As with Dante's *Inferno*, *Lolita* is the story of a trip down, from love to betrayal. Humbert did not understand his trajectory as descent, though he did know that that was the trip that he wished to take, that only nymphets could satisfy him. By the end of his life, does he see his journey more clearly? Telling his tale, Humbert describes it as if it were an involuntary fall. His perspective is not persuasive. Despite his explanation, readers clearly see Humbert deliberately stepping downward, sure in the guidance of his own narcissistic compass.‡

Not surprisingly, considering the impression Annabel had made on him, all of Humbert's adult fantasies involved girls of a certain social class: from propertied, established, respectable families, girls who went to school, who played decorously, who were washed and dressed and groomed as the settled bourgeoisie do. These girls looked like Annabel, dressed, walked, talked, played, smelled like Annabel. The chosen among them radiated an Annabelic aphrodisiac. The poor could not imitate the confidence of position; those young girls, even when not debauched, were too predatory and unpolished. Nor could the aristocracy simulate the momentary insouciance of girlish play or school; they were too conscious of social duty and distance, too languid, to participate fully in either games or laughter. Humbert

---

*Humbert's interest in his feelings is almost scholastic. Recall that Thomas Aquinas divided human action into intention and execution.

†See Aristotle, *Nicomachean Ethics*, Books 1 and 2. Aristotle asserts that if you do vile things, you become vile; if you do good things, you are good and on the way to becoming better.

‡We are reminded of Virgil, *Aeneid*, Book 6: 126; *facilis descensus Averno*. The usual translation, which is appropriate, is "it is easy to go down into Hell." One can also find a similar view of life in the broad way from the Sermon on the Mount in Matthew. In both cases, this reflects a certain opinion on the nature of humanity, that is, in the words of Ovid, "We reflect our stony heritage" (*Metamorphoses*, Book 1). As G. K. Chesterton pointed out, original sin is the only Christian doctrine that can be verified empirically. Indeed, it cannot be denied.

never mentioned social class, but he dreamt of propertied objects of desire.* *Eros*, as Humbert clearly knew, was not the nymphet naked but one clothed in context, and the context for him was always Annabel.

Even in Paris, where everything was possible, obtaining a nymphet of good family who was still in school was not possible. Bourgeois families had greater aspirations for their daughters. They were to marry men of property, not to be sacrificed as the erotic solace of a pedophile's fancy. Humbert did not have to exist only as the latter; he could easily have appeared as the former. He had sufficient social grace to advertise his position and conceal his disposition. Humbert could have qualified as eligible. He had position and property. But he combined an apparent eligibility for a bourgeois marriage with a profound emotional disqualification. Could he marry a mother to be near her daughter? Not yet.

Although women abounded, the bachelor Humbert was forced to look amongst women he could not love, but were available for marriage. Not unreasonably, he suspected that marriage would be safer than ongoing adventure. This was true even in Paris, the city of adventure. Marriage might even be beneficial, as the bourgeoisie so clearly thought. It would require little emotional commitment from Humbert, though that might develop. Humbert felt himself drawn to the idea of marriage as a social solution, even a moral solution, through uplifting his desires (with respect to age, not gender). He was aware enough, at this point, to know this as a good thing. He was optimistic enough, at this point, to hope that he might change. Maybe he would get better. Duty might redirect desire, although Humbert never recognized that improvement required effort.

Musing on his situation, Humbert made a bourgeois decision. He decided to get married. Marriage would bring regularity to his habits, and virtue to his life in general. This plan made perfectly good sense, far more sense than a maniacal attempt at a fling with a doubtless appalled and terrified schoolgirl. It remained only to find the willing (perhaps, though

---

*In his university lectures, Nabokov seldom mentioned social class. Personally, he was conscious of it constantly, belonging to the aristocracy but living amongst those who did not. This unmentioned but ever-present consciousness of class found its way into *Lolita*, and Humbert imitated his creator. Nabokov himself, in interview and commentary, emphasized that he was not Humbert. He was not entirely not–Humbert.

Chapter Two: Marriage

unlikely) virgin victim. Humbert could do this satisfactorily, could he not? He believed himself to possess what was then called "animal magnetism," a quality that F. Scott Fitzgerald thought, along with money, one of the best things a man could have in dealing with ladies. Animal magnetism worked its magic more often than not, at least in Humbert's case, at least in Humbert's account of it. He fancied that he could have any woman he wanted, that at a mere gesture or a cocked eyebrow, they would fall panting upon his extraordinarily virile person. There are never many who could believe that. But Humbert found it a necessary explanation (or excuse) for his sexual successes and marital choice. Some men must be just born for love.

Of course, the late thirties were difficult times in Paris, as war approached, with the Nazi net closing upon increasingly frantic human fish. But the fear and resignation of the times did not appear to have impinged upon Humbert's estimation of his person or his pursuits. Humbert's boast of animal magnetism is important for what it does not say. At points in the narrative where Humbert ought to have been describing his fiancée, we hear him describing himself ("one who could snap his fingers...."). Our self-absorbed narrator only steps outside the mirror's range far enough to observe that he has settled upon poor chubby and mature Valeria. It is, of course, supposed to be understood as a piteous compromise for Humbert, who felt no erotic attraction to Valeria. Not a word about Valeria herself. Was it a compromise, piteous or promising, for her? Humbert did not even consider it. At this point in the narrative, even casual readers will be struck with the seriousness of Humbert's problem. It is not that he has become a nymphetophile or a pedophile, serious as may be thought. Rather, his *philia* remains directed only towards himself, as he swings through the endless loop of his memory of Annabel. Humbert's offhanded and demeaning treatment of Valeria in the narrative makes his character clear.* It also makes clear the status of any other erotic

---

*Almost every critic has noticed that Humbert was a narcissist, and we do not present this commonplace as a new and startling idea. We do suggest that the reader of *Lolita* is more likely to read the novel than to read the critics. The idea that Humbert is a narcissist will come to the careful reader at this point in the novel, and from that careful reader's point of view, we describe Humbert's narcissism as a discovery.

prospect who might subsequently appear in that narrative. No matter who Humbert lusted after in the days beyond the idyllic garden with Annabel. He is unable to care for anyone besides the thirteen-year-old Humbert living and thriving in his memory.

The reality of Humbert's essential loneliness, a condition also known to all men, remained unchanged after marriage. What did Humbert want from Valeria? He mentioned regularity and safety; in internal dialogue, Humbert added to the list comfort, routine, and undemanding sex. All of these things might be regarded as useful, but they do not constitute criteria when searching for a person. They are only a list of needs. Valeria, somewhat to Humbert's surprise and greatly to Humbert's distress, turned out to be a person, even though she fit almost none of the criteria. She did have a gimmick which had caught Humbert's eye: she could imitate a little girl. Valeria exhibited that gimmick by dressing "*a la gamine.*" Further, she "pouted, and dimpled, and romped, and dirndled, and shook her short curly blond hair." This gimmick was sufficiently effective in the short-term: long enough for her to snag Humbert as a husband. But behind that girlish style lay a disillusioning and all-too-common reality. Her bleached-blonde hair showed black roots, she quickly came to resemble her dead mother, she waddled like a peasant woman, and she was already in her late twenties. Valeria was as far from a schoolgirl as it was possible to be. Beyond that, she could not cook, and had no domestic skills (which Humbert would treat with contempt when displayed by Charlotte). All she had to offer was "a muted nature which did help to produce an odd sense of comfort." Comfort was not, however, what a passionate gentleman like Humbert longed for.

Humbert responded at the time with what in modern America is called "buyer's remorse." Later, in his memoir, his reaction was harsher. He demeaned her as a comedy wife, which appears harsh and false, since Valeria was, as they say, not that kind of girl. Even in Humbert's carefully contemptuous description of the marriage, Valeria seems to have embraced the obligations of *eros* embellished with duties of marriage. Valeria did her best. She loved Humbert and tried to make him comfortable. But for Humbert, that only meant that she was at her best when she was at her least. She was, for him, essentially useless.

Chapter Two: Marriage

The benefits offered by married love could not enlarge the soul of a passive recipient. *Manqué* professionally, stunted emotionally, utilitarian philosophically, Humbert was not really there. He could not receive the genuine benefits of married love.* Attitudes "brisk, sanitary, and practical" hollowed out the marriage. Humbert would enter a marriage of convenience. A marriage of convenience is rarely convenient, particularly in a culture where love is deemed to be an adequate excuse for wedded bliss. Humbert indulged in a substantial amount of make-believe to suppose it could be otherwise.

This marriage of convenience did not enhance Humbert morally, nor did it bring him any real convenience, either sexually or socially. He had moved from Humbert the unmarried pedophile to Humbert the married pedophile. This was not a significant change. Humbert could not, as pop psycho-babble has it, "move on" from the lost garden to the found union; there *was* no real union.† He was united only to his image of Annabel.

Humbert was, so to speak, with child, or, more precisely, with the memory of a child. He did not change from adolescent passion, choosing, without hesitation, the memory of sex thwarted with Annabel over the love that Valeria felt and the duties each owed the other. Valeria could exhibit all the charities, while Humbert, because he could not give love, could not receive it.‡ For Valeria, marriage to Humbert was, beyond doubt, psychic frustration; for Humbert, marriage to Valeria was endurance. The absence of caring made the garden into a desert.

---

*Lionel Trilling argues that *Lolita* is about love, "on every page," and this is true. He insists that the book is about *eros*, and this also true. Not only is *eros* a form of love (see poor murderous Medea), it is the superior form of love, according to Trilling, and according to Humbert. Trilling, like Humbert, thought marriage a poor substitute for *eros*. Both are wrong, if for no other reason than that marriage is not tedium any more than life is, and *eros* is a recipe for a spectacular crack-up (again, see poor Medea, or Humbert for that matter). Marriage may lack the interior burning and longing of *eros*, but as we have previously stated, over more than a few minutes, hours or weeks, love is as love does.

†It is impossible to avoid the terminology of therapy. Its phrases, almost devoid of specific meaning but filled past the brim with popular significance, have saturated the language. So we have used them, though we admit that they are so equivocal that they now refer *only* to the reader's own experiences in a therapeutic culture. This leads to the general conclusion that Freudian literary analysis is, fundamentally, unhelpful.

‡Cardinal Humbert of Mourmoutiers (c. 1015 – 5 May 1061) held that, in the Mass, a priest who did not himself have grace could not give grace. Therefore, a Mass performed by a sinful priest was invalid. The discussion of love takes many forms.

"Light of My Life"

Life in this marital desert drifted in a routine fashion until something happened. In 1939, Humbert was making plans to take the couple to America when he sensed Valeria putting up passive but persistent recalcitrance. Humbert argued, cajoled, but nothing worked. Valeria, waddling ahead of him on a Paris street, shook her "poodle head" with the weight of the truth: she, not Humbert, had found love. Humbert had never noticed. A Czarist officer driving a taxicab, a social cliche, had come to life as the other man in Valeria's life, and she demanded an immediate divorce to stay with him in Paris rather than go to America with Humbert.

Humbert claimed to be enraged and outraged, not because he was losing the "stale flesh" or the muted comfort that Valeria provided, but because he regarded it as his place, and his alone, to make decisions. But the taxi-colonel appeared, and he took Humbert and Valeria to a small café. Valeria wept and primped and wept come more, and the colonel explained how he would take Valeria into loving custody. And he did. The brief *ménage à trois* went to the apartment and packed Valeria up. While the colonel moved Valeria from apartment to cab, Humbert sat and seethed. Humbert regretted never being alone with Valeria so he could pummel her for the offense of making a decision. The new couple drove off into the sunset. Like the movies.

Humbert got the last laugh, however, by including in his memoir a decorous but doubtless satisfying conclusion to the whole unfortunate Valeria experience. While he was forced to admit that she had managed to find care and love, and a marriage in which both partners contributed to the welfare of the other, he joyously included its depressing denouement. Humbert reported that the colonel and Valeria had been jointly reduced to quadrupeds in a typically vile and useless experiment in anthropology. To cap it all off, Valeria died in childbirth in 1945. Women dying are a constant leitmotif in *Lolita*, as is, also, with the exception of Annabel, Humbert's indifference or private pleasure at their demise.

After coming to America without Valeria, Humbert declined further, becoming more *manqué*, enduring (or enjoying) nervous breakdowns. He was given a good job in a luxury trade, perfumes, and collected a private income on top of it, added to some professional work on French literature,

Chapter Two: Marriage

with all of it crowned by his gloomy charm and handsome appearance. Humbert was as exotic as a movie star, and just as fragile. In the midst of things going well, he went badly. A tour in the Canadian arctic, lasting nearly two years, substituted the deliberate pace of nature for the frantic motion of New York, but Humbert was not "cured," whatever that might have meant in the now archaic psycho-jargon of the time. He went back inside, due to another attack of "melancholia and a sense of insufferable oppression." When Humbert emerged, it was not back into New York, but into post-war, small town New England.

To his other attributes of the fashionably European and exotic well-to-do scholar in exile, Humbert now could add the mystery of a non-specific "condition," due, doubtless, to the delicacy of his soul. Beyond all that, he displayed his Charles Boyer troubled elegance in a small town, where such things were rare in person, but culturally known from radio, magazine, and the silver screen. If he were not exactly the "glass of fashion, the mould of form," he was certainly the "observ'd of all observers." Enter Humbert, from stage left, presenting all possible aspects of desirability. Enter Charlotte Haze, stage right, who had a room to rent.

Humbert's first descriptions of Valeria merged her into the scenery, as she was painting unobtrusively in the corner of the room: he depersonalized her into interior decor. He performed the same disservice for Charlotte, whom he first identifies with her house.* Humbert noted with a snobbish horror that the house was white-frame (standard American philistine). Such a second-class dwelling would certainly have a rubber hose attached to the tub faucet in lieu of a shower. Such a dwelling was unworthy of him. He remembered better.

Even before viewing Charlotte's dis-spiriting suburban house, Humbert had already decided to abort his decision to spend a scholarly summer in the depths of small town New England. The house reconfirmed his flight response, but he could not flee. He had nowhere to go. Moreover, the chauffeur and a neighbor were watching. Trapped by desperation and decorum, Humbert rang the bell.

Things got worse at once. Humbert stepped into a front hall which

---

*This repeated James Thurber's cartoon of woman as house.

boasted a van Gogh reproduction. Pretentious, thought Humbert. There was "Mexican trash" in a corner cabinet. Junky, thought Humbert. In those days, Mexican represented a salient example of all that was "tacky," an adjective of moral and aesthetic opprobrium coming into general use along with the companion term "ghastly." Beyond the Mexican trash was "functional modern furniture," combining discomfort with ugliness, upstairs the "expected coils" of the tub shower. Downstairs again. A heavy mahogany dining table.* Then a kitchen. Would the tour ever end? Humbert had been planning his escape throughout.

Charlotte, his tour guide, concluded her presentation with the back garden, where her twelve-year-old daughter was sunbathing. Lolita. A stunned Humbert took in all of Lolita's features and conformation, comparing them to Annabel. They matched. Now, at long, long last, his "southbound mouth" could continue its journey. Nothing could have prepared Humbert for the reappearance of lost passion. There was only this tiny difference. Annabel had gazed moonstruck at Humbert, while Lolita seemed irritated at the interruption.† Charlotte heedlessly gestured: "'That was my Lo,' she said, 'and these are my lilies.'"‡ The lilies seemed to command more of Charlotte's affection.

Within the description of Charlotte as house had been a brief examination of Charlotte as person. She had appeared from upstairs, first as cigarette ash, then as gradually appearing, upscale casual wear. Humbert

---

*One is reminded of Nikolai Gogol's description of the furniture in Sobakevich's parlor and dining room in *Dead Souls* (1842). We cannot prove it, but since Nabokov loved and taught *Dead Souls*, we suspect that this bit of Gogoliana found its way to suburban America. Many and varied things cross the water.

†One should recall the fragment of Heraclitus, that no one can step in the same river twice. Humbert was to discover this, though at the time the startling resemblance to Annabel obliterated all sense of time and its changes.

‡Nabokov, who knew a lot of botany, had specific lilies in mind, as he did for most references to nature. He did not name the lilies. We suggest day lilies, probably of the then-popular tiger stripe variety, which bloomed early, as May is in New England, and grew in less than ideal soil, also a New England characteristic. The tiger day lily (*lilium splendens tigrinum*) bloom lasted only a day, but was spectacular, and the color of the bloom often deepened as evening approached. "Tiger lilies" combined reds, oranges, and yellows with shades of green, and when planted in curving clumps, as was the style a half century ago, made a striking appearance. Ever polite, Humbert would have been justified in calling the lilies beautiful, as Charlotte hoped he had.

Chapter Two: Marriage

sneered at her appearance in retrospect, remembering her artificial, movie-inspired visage. Charlotte combined these features with a "bronze-brown bun," obviously bottled, and a gaze that avoided eye contact.* In her initial conversations with Humbert, Charlotte appeared to reflect a suburban book-clubbish conventionality. Humbert pegged her as utterly humorless, an odd complaint, since he lacked humor himself. Humbert's more serious indictment involved Charlotte's intentions towards him. He had immediately surmised that she would doubtless expect him to supplement his rent payments with carnal service. Suave Humbert could imagine only one reason why a woman, not yet of a certain age, would take a handsome lodger under her roof. The reason must fall into the area of the brisk, practical, ironic, and sanitary. Other reasons, those beyond Humbert's imagination, might include a widow's need for income. Humbert supposed, since the price for room and board was suspiciously low, that he would pay the rest in trade.

Charlotte's presumed intentions presented comic plot possibilities. Humbert would have none of them. The deal-clincher, the high point of the tour, had been the eerie discovery of Annabel's twin, set like a gem in the superb American garden. Humbert's love story could pick up again.

As Humbert tells it, meeting Lolita was an interior climacteric. The past returned with overwhelming force. Once, Annabel, love, and the springtime of life and youth had enclosed him, and Humbert had convinced himself thereafter that the garden could be recaptured. Apparently it could. In an apostrophe uttering from a park bench in Paris years ago, Humbert had cried out to be left alone, for nymphets to surround him forever. His demand, almost a prayer: "Never grow up," was addressed to nymphets in general; yet Humbert had really been invoking himself.† Once Annabel's "faunlet," he had remained that. The world, nymphets included, had grown up around him, while Humbert had merely aged. Humbert still wished to love passionately, without obligation, living always

---

*Coloring hair from a bottle carried a social stigma amongst the propertied (and presumably philistine) bourgeoisie of those dear dead days.

†Nabokov, *Lolita*, Pt. I, ch. 5, p. 21. The Peter Pan motif here applied both to Humbert and the nymphet *du jour*, of course, is obvious to all. Still, critical prudence demands it be noted.

"Light of My Life"

between longing and ecstasy. Stephen Dedalus' command to master "silence, exile, and cunning" had become Humbert's motto in the intervening years.* Humbert had learned cunning, discretion, and dissimulation, and they served, so to say, as social make-up applied to the goat below. Here again was a nymphet in a garden, with lilies and all they implied, but what Humbert perceived now was a shimmering field for his limbic lust. For Humbert, the real garden was utterly detached from the vista before him.

But Lolita and the lost garden must wait. First came Charlotte. For Humbert to remain close to Lolita, he must earn Charlotte's approval. This proved to be a delicate task. Could he win Charlotte over sufficiently to remain in the house, yet not enchant her to the point of love? No. Charlotte fell in love with Humbert almost at once, if not at first glance, then in the first flush of acquaintance. Humbert did seem perfect, both exotic and dependable. And it must be said that Charlotte, like Valeria before her, anticipated a full life with Humbert. That expectation, which Humbert acknowledged, disparaged, found occasionally endearing and always tiresome, required from the memoirist further description of Charlotte. The brief picture of Charlotte gradually revealed, reminiscent of Duchamp's "Nude Descending a Staircase" (1912), was just the beginning of her part in Humbert's story.

Charlotte in love demanded careful consideration in Humbert's memoirs, as well as his short-term plans. He could not simply dismiss Charlotte with a few well-chosen sneers. He would have to explain her, and his relationship to her. Humbert made it clear that there had never been any diminution of his desire and determination to engulf, embrace, and enjoy Lolita. But with Charlotte thrusting herself at him in the sweet throes of epistolary passion, Humbert had to take her on as well, so to speak. Shocked and repulsed at first, Humbert had suddenly realized in a moment

---

*Stephen Dedalus, in Joyce's *A Portrait of the Artist as a Young Man*, hoped that these characteristics would make him a national bard, and would allow him to focus the essence of Irishness in a world where that quality seemed in danger of being lost. Stephen was, of course, entirely wrong. The essence of Irishness was to be expressed by openness, charm, communication, and amiability, precisely those characteristics William Butler Yeats displayed on visiting a thousand stately homes. And who was more Irish than Yeats? As it turned out, Irishness was something you did, not something you hid. In *Ulysses*, see Father Conmee.

Chapter Two: Marriage

of calmer reflection that to make love with one Haze he must marry the other. There was no other way. He remembered a "Dostoevskian grin" gradually growing in his soul and probably face as well.* When Charlotte came home after dumping Lo at camp, Humbert was ready and willing, and, as he remembered, able as well. Here as elsewhere Humbert remembered himself as extraordinary. Alcohol had no effect. Exercise did not exhaust him. When Charlotte presented herself, Humbert was ready to service her.

Suddenly and deeply and unexpectedly enveloped in erotic love, Charlotte had become a changed person, and Humbert, who noted every detail in Lolita, noticed a few in Charlotte as well. "The Haze woman," soon to become Mme Humbert, was not, it turned out, *entirely* an object of dislike and disdain.† Humbert, in order to be fair, admitted to a bit of sexual curiosity, and even some affection, though all was marked with a "pattern of remorse running along the steel of his conspiratorial dagger." Of course, Humbert's vanity was piqued. He was pleasantly surprised that Charlotte, who exhibited a total faith in the folk wisdom of her church and of the matrons in her suburban book club, could become "such a touching, helpless creature as soon as I laid my hand on her."

Eros improved Charlotte's appearance. Her affected smile became radiant adoration, her awkward caresses ardent, and she gazed across the plastic-topped (with tubular aluminum legs) kitchen table at Humbert "with intolerable tenderness." The beloved always suffers a sense of suffocation, and perhaps some guilt as well, since the erotic lover's passion encompasses everything, from making love to eating breakfast and everything. In that odd *ménage a trois*, Humbert was both impassioned erotic lover, and the victim of erotic passion. Both shoes were on his feet. It made for odd domestic arrangement. Again, Nabokov keeps a straight face as the comic possibilities of the situation remain unexplored. Humbert himself seemed to manage well enough for the time in a situation which

---

*We do not know, exactly, what a Dostoevskian grin might be. But it sounds unpleasant. At this moment, Humbert was perhaps at his worst, contemplating betrayal on every conceivable level of love. He was only contemplating, but he would descend, to abuse of all sorts based on what he then thought.
†Such a character would not reflect well upon the narcissist's own image.

must inevitably implode. And after all, *eros* does not, in any case, fit comfortably into domestic arrangements. But, in his memoir, Mr. Humbert wished to be generous, so he merely noted that by "marrying the mother of the child I loved I had enabled my wife to regain an abundance of youth by proxy." Not by proxy, but by love.

Love is always a journey of discovery, and *eros* demands that lovers acquire each other's past in order to possess each other entirely. The past must be known as the body is known. Humbert looked for snapshots revealing the physical origins of Lolita's "nymphetness."* Only twelve years old, she had, more or less, no story. But an idly curious Humbert sought out what story she had. Charlotte had a greater task. She wished to trace Humbert's undoubtedly exotic and romantic past. Charlotte craved tales about his life of loves gone by. He invented a harem. Protecting his privacy and sense of separateness from Charlotte's erotic appetites, Humbert concocted a past filled with romantic danger, not dissimilar to the fevered imaginings of Emma Bovary. The parade of lust and love past served several interlocking connubial purposes. It preserved Humbert while reinforcing Charlotte's view of Humbert as Charles Boyer, whose elegant continental charm could flourish only with true love from a faithful and domestic woman, while the shallow and glamorous social butterflies led only to doom.

For Charlotte, the movies had come to life. Humbert, as culturally acute as he was emotionally retarded, recognized that Charlotte sought narrative guidance and moral validation from movies, "soap operas, psychoanalysis and cheap novelettes,"† and valued the conventional attitudes of popular culture. So he gave her the stories she already knew. Humbert told these tales in Charlotte's language, careful always to imply Charlotte's movie-validated superiority of domesticity and virtue, which only made greater her desirability. Half a century ago in the movie myth, the homemaker triumphed over the harlot, the home-spun beauty from next door trumped the sleek sirens produced by the magic of cosmetics. It was the standard American middle-class fairy tale, secular, romantic, improbable and glamorous.

---

*Our use of "nymphetness" is purely arbitrary.
†Nabokov, *Lolita*, Pt. I, ch. 19, p. 80. *Lolita* came before the ubiquity of television.

Chapter Two: Marriage

Humbert's skills in art of concealment made him as entirely invulnerable to contemporary "arts" as he was to mature feminine wiles. He understood them all and deflected them easily. The life that the besotted Charlotte saw as a movie, with romance transformed into community, Humbert adapted as part of his own conspiracy, bringing him closer to his "downy darling." As Charlotte remade the house, Humbert courted his captive nymphet. Humbert exploited marriage to Charlotte as a protective cocoon, where he used all his wiles to practice the real art of his life. He lied constantly, hiding everything in locked drawers and slippery syntax. Humbert's essential life, as opposed to his social façade, remains at bottom even for the reader always hidden and hooded. Remember, as a child, he wished to be a spy.

Charlotte's suburban book club had not provided her with sufficient wisdom or insight to penetrate Humbert's disguise. Perhaps the books she had read were not good enough (Professor Nabokov would have recommended Tolstoy, Flaubert or Dickens). Humbert regarded Charlotte's books as he had Valeria's avante-garde French cubist coloring. He saw both forms of expression as chosen to separate, as far as possible, life from the mind.

Humbert did not fix his disdain only on the products of the arts themselves, but expanded his disdain to include the women who practiced them. He noted individual style, such as Valeria's girlish movements and Charlotte's plucked eyebrows, and considered the women's own efforts at artistic self-enhancement to be pathetically clumsy. They did not enhance, they did not deceive, they did not delight, and, for Humbert, they did not succeed. These efforts announced an ineffective pretentiousness, which Humbert held in utter contempt. He despised Charlotte and her ilk as failed artists, far inferior to his own presentation of a created persona. Better they not try at all. He compared them wordlessly to the naive naturalness of Annabel and Lolita. Cubist decoration and popular novels were made worse when respectable women took them seriously and pretended to acquire culture and remain in the wind.* Cultural glop was woman's

---

*The French phrase *dans le vent* means "hip" or "hep" or "with it." All were current in the 1950's.

imitation of art, and the fastidious Humbert dismissed them as another facet of the inferiority of women to nymphets. Always secretly unfaithful, Humbert looked down upon his wives as fools. His attitude was simple enough; he understood completely the shallow "them," while they had no idea at all about the deep "him." Humbert's world had room for only a single artist.

The tendency of adult women to practice bad art had always offended Humbert, even more than their unattractively mature bodies. He had been repelled by "the glitter of deodorized career girls" in New York. He had been soured by Valeria's efforts at painting "cubistic trash," which was no better than the "lilacs and lambs" which been the fatuous subject-matter of her mother's generation. Poor Valeria had ingenuously sported a mask of the artistic avant-garde that was inadequate and pathetic. The most infuriating aspect, though, of her artistic pretensions was that, on one level, it actually succeeded. And Humbert never forgave himself for falling for it. He had been fooled in marrying her. Artist though Humbert supposed himself to be, a cheap provincial masquerade had taken him in. Telling the story later, Humbert would turn his own disappointment with himself into contempt for Valeria.

A warier Humbert would not get so near a woman with a gimmick. Yet when married again, he again chose a woman of artistic pretensions, inadequately realized. This time, too, Humbert's attitude towards his wife was dominated by contempt for amateur artistic efforts that fell short of the mark. Unlike the last time, though, he was clear-eyed about his wife; with Charlotte, his contempt preceded marriage. This contempt allowed him to keep Charlotte and his own expectations at a psychological distance. He acidly sketched Charlotte's gimmick: sleek postwar American style. She crafted her persona through book clubs, cigarettes, sandals, plucked eyebrows. This persona sufficed for Humbert, whose expectations were low anyway. In place of intimacy with the woman herself, Humbert interacted with Charlotte's pathetic artistic avatar. From the very beginning, it worked for both of them. They could both participate in, for example, "a make-believe conversation about a false book by some popular fraud."*

---

*Nabokov, *Lolita,* Pt. I, ch. 11, p. 43. Humbert's contempt for bestsellers was not entirely misplaced; nevertheless, reading books is better than not reading.

Chapter Two: Marriage

In Humbert's memoir, grown women seemed to always seek contact with him through the "universal palliative" of art. All failed. Women, who used artifice reflexively, were bad at it, in Humbert's estimation. They were poor artists, unsubtle and unconvincing, and this was inexcusable. Women could not keep the illusion going. Bleached hair revealed its roots, improperly shaved legs turned to stubble, and plucked eyebrows appeared merely trendy. What sort of artist lets the audience see beyond the curtain? Failures. Ham actors. Women.

Humbert the artist admired, rather, the supposed naturalness of nymphets. They didn't try to enhance any illusion: and more importantly, they didn't compete with the greater artist, who was himself. Humbert lurked, cleverly concealed from prying feminine eyes. Humbert's art was concealment. As a child with Annabel, Humbert had wished to be a famous spy. In fact, that ambition was realized, but in love, not war.*

After marriage to Charlotte, Humbert turned his aesthete's contempt from false books of fiction to equally meretricious works of home decor. It is not that the novels and book clubs vanished, but they fell into the shade created by that enormous word "Home." Charlotte had moved her reading habits from popular fiction to how-to decorating books about the modern home. She went from absorbing advice to placing orders. Humbert darkly observed that she had delivered an elegant new mattress of the latest design, "although the old one seemed to me resilient and durable enough for whatever it had to support." A new mattress for a new love: could anything be clearer? The mattress was merely the climactic and most intimate of domestic improvements. It was not, of course, all of them. The public face of love also demanded polish and burnish. There was that piece in the society section of the paper, for which Humbert had supplied lies about name and profession, a mirror for the false love he had sworn to big Haze. And Charlotte, for her part, polished the venetian blinds, still in the forties something exotic and upscale on the east coast, re-arranged the furniture, cleaned tirelessly, all conducted "in a constant chiaroscuro of smiles and frowns, of doubts and pouts." This artist's genius was burning,

---

*As has oft been noted, from Homer, Ovid, and Apollonius of Rhodes onward, the boudoir is a battlefield.

and her new canvas clearly was her house. The ultimate goal of that art? Humbert could not imagine.

For Humbert, Charlotte embodied in house was mildly amusing: what else could be expected from a middle-class American girl? But it did not turn Charlotte from decor into person, from a means into an end. It all merely added to the sanitation of distance. Humbert, who grew up in a hotel and lacked all attachment to place, was homeless in every way beyond physical address. He uncomprehendingly viewed Charlotte's efforts to invest place with beauty and shared work, memory, and meaning as essentially silly. For the wandering Humbert, an endless exile, home was what women (not nymphets) did, and it was banal and philistine. Person merged into thing, and both were dismissed together.

As Humbert secretly disparaged her efforts, Charlotte openly rearranged the house. She set aside a study for Humbert's scholarly work on French literature. By establishing a study, Charlotte cared for Humbert as a person, not merely as a lover. Charlotte wisely ignored the details of his "scholarship." Woman know that men need a profession, or at least the pretense of a profession. The study was a larger version of the new mattress. Humbert, though, saw Charlotte's nesting in sinister terms. Her behavior increasingly revealed *philia* emerging from *eros*, community emerging from passion. Charlotte only did what wives do. She was creating a home. But a home with Charlotte was not what Humbert had in mind.

Charlotte retained an intense erotic curiosity about Humbert, convinced he retained important secrets. From early in their marriage, in fact, Charlotte had had vague suspicions and premonitions about Humbert. Her hunger to know more arose from *eros*; the intuition that there was *something* to know came from "huswifery." She had no idea what it was, but she intended to discover it.* Humbert was wary of Charlotte's possessive curiosity, perhaps recalling similar incidents from the days with Valeria, and tried on Charlotte a pose of distance that had worked before.

---

*We are aware that wives can get to know their husbands so intimately that it defies description, and can only be known by illustration or parable. It has been often noticed that spouses finish each other's sentences and thoughts. In myth, recall the stories of Pyrrha and Deucalion as well as Baucus and Philemon. Of course, it doesn't always work. See the example of Zeus and Hera.

Chapter Two: Marriage

He became silent, which used to terrify Valeria. It had no effect on Charlotte. She was not undone when Humbert escaped into himself, but she was sensitive to the phenomenon of a separation: the clichéd locked drawer and its hidden key disturbed her. Charlotte knew the lock barred her access to the real Humbert. She sensed that with Humbert, written documents really mattered. The distance of writing suited a man distant in all things. All but one. Charlotte found in Humbert's diary his passion for her twelve-year-old child. Not surprisingly, Charlotte was shocked, disgusted, horrified, and enraged. She had betrayed herself by loving him, and betrayed her child by trusting him. Her life crashed about her in an awful moment of truth. "'You're a monster,' she snarled, 'You're a detestable, abominable, criminal fraud.'" Those years in the book club had left their mark.

Humbert fell back on his artistic superiority again, which could no doubt get him out of this jam. This tawdry confrontation could be finessed. He readily admitted to Charlotte that the existence of the journals was an act of conspiracy. Confident in his verbal skills, Humbert would persuade his wife that she had "discovered" only notes for a book. He might quell her raging fury with an impersonal conversation about a literary thing, an object other than themselves. Fond and foolish fantasies! No sane man could think that a logical conversation, followed by physical reconciliation, would work. Humbert might pretend to have been a fool, proving again that his capacity for deviousness was unsurpassed. But in his cluelessness about how women operate, Humbert combined deviousness with naivete to an astonishing degree. Some spies are better than others.

Charlotte was not to be pacified by improbable explanations. Love had brought her not the sweetness of possession, but the bitter pomegranate of Truth. Truth may set you free, but it rarely lights up your life. Truth had ruined Charlotte's life. She was not prepared to pick up the pieces, bandage the wound, and soldier on. Once she discovered, not by accident but by unhappy intuition, that her Humbert was pretty close to a monster, her dreams and her marriage ended together.* She well knew that Humbert

---

*In Humbert's memoir, the chronology is occasionally shaky. Things fit together pretty well, but not perfectly. We have tried, in our comments, to straighten out the chronology a bit. But there are always outliers, bits of description that look back or look forward, and are technically speaking, misplaced. Many critics have noted this. One can be offended by

"Light of My Life"

himself would continue to desire Lolita. Charlotte was one of those "women of principle" whose attitudes were not merely fixed in content but also played a central role in the order of her life. Humbert thought of her as an "odious vulgarian," but he had always known that she was not a variable vulgarian. Humbert knew also that he could not persuade her to continue as his wife; he could not persuade her to ignore the words in front of her. Her rage was final. He was stuck.

For Humbert, the only solution was to kill her. But there were two problems with that. Most immediately, there was no time after her discovery, and after she had finished writing her letters. There was barely time to make her a drink. The other difficulty was the act itself. Humbert had already toyed with the idea of killing Charlotte for several weeks. As a solution, it was perfect; as an action, it had entailed vast and unavoidable risk. As Humbert had clearly seen, murder introduced technical, social, and psychic complications.

Nowadays you have to be a scientist to be a killer. No, no, I was neither.

And, nowadays, the police interested themselves in death, particularly when unexpected or irregular. They always began, in these matters, with the husband or the lover, and as Humbert was both, he wouldn't have a chance. There was also the matter of psychic cost. It is not so easy to kill people as it appeared in the movies then, and on television now. Violence on that level was not routine, an almost expected part of daily living. Humbert assured us that his special vice did not predispose him to violence. The odds were against a successful murder, and Humbert breezily admitted at one point, with unconvincing cheer,

But what d'ye know, folks — I just could not make myself do it.

[*continued*] a lack of chronological clarity, but we suggest it is better to accept the fallen world as it is. Things may fit neatly into time but they fit only appropriately into memory. So we have tolerated Humbert's memoir misfires and have coordinated what can be coordinated, and have gone with the flow where it illustrates the sensibilities of either author or subject. "One does what one can."

Would Nabokov approve? Yes, we think he would. The careful reader, as he proclaimed in his university lectures, is the rereader. The careful reader is not an accountant of minutes but a participant in the enchantment of good fiction. See also Vladimir Nabokov, *Lectures on European Fiction*, chapter 1, for Nabokov's introductory lecture to his assorted and mangy listeners (among them, one of us) on the nature of readership.

Chapter Two: Marriage

If Humbert could not do it, something else could. Novelists have in abundance that streak of ruthlessness that poets decry. Nabokov turned to an old friend, the *deus ex machina* from Greek tragedy.* Humbert recognized and renamed it:

No man can bring about the perfect murder; chance, however, can do it.

Humbert listed all the varieties of chance that came together in one perfect moment of slaughter. These included (but perhaps were not limited to) sun, shade, the wet, the dry, the dog, an idiot driving a car, Charlotte in blind rage, a moment of inattention on everyone's part, witnesses attesting to everything, a delightful thud with accompanying squish and squash. It took all of it. And it took all of it all at once. For something like that, of course, fault cannot be found. The culprit who lusted for violence in his heart escaped completely.

Deus ex machina normally comes at his own pace, and keeps his own tempo, as do the other unbribable ancient gods, Death and Time. But Nabokov made sure that Chance was prompt this once. Charlotte was more than merely prompt. She ran to meet her death.

Having discovered Humbert's secret love and secret distaste, Charlotte had responded with three letters, one to Lo, another to school, and the third to Humbert. These had been her exit lines. Crossing the street to mail them, she slipped on wet pavement and was struck by a car swerving to miss a dog. In an instant everything had come together, and Humbert was one of the reasons why, though for some reason or another he had left himself out of the list of visible causes. *Deus ex machina* had finished Charlotte. Exit. Kaput. Humbert even wept. A nice touch.

It had taken Humbert more than a brief paragraph, it turned out, to describe Charlotte and her forty-nine days of bliss and one of hot shame. Some of the memoir for those days was about Lolita, but most concerned Charlotte herself. The kinds of details omitted from his life with Valeria popped up with Charlotte. Did the time with Charlotte mean something

---

*Nabokov, in his university lectures, showed a certain distaste for *deus ex machina*, implying that it was a structural weakness. Hardly a surprise that Humbert's memoir turned so prominently upon the appearance of a *deus ex machina*. Humbert is a defective artist, and Nabokov is a sly, secretive creator.

more than momentary pleasure to Humbert, something more exciting than the first tryst with Monique? We tend to doubt it. Endurance rather than pleasure, conspiracy rather than loyalty, and burning proximity to a nymphet characterized Humbert's derisive view of marriage to Charlotte.

With regard to his second wife, Humbert, though, was genuinely garrulous. The literary discipline that abridged and focused even the idyll with Annabel, and certainly the dreary time with Valeria, deserted him with Charlotte. He went on and on. He included details of daily life, all of which showed the depth and variety of her love for him. In keeping with Humbert's usual practice, this section of the memoir was all about him. Charlotte appeared to have no life beyond interaction with the handsome and exotic Humbert. She was, after all, a postwar housewife and happy to be one. In that time, huswifery was a vocation, not an afterthought or a negotiation. And she does appear courtesy of her husband, a supremely self-centered memoirist.

We draw three conclusions from Humbert's detailed rendering of Charlotte. First of all, clever Nabokov. He sustained an extended contrast between the unselfish love of an adult (Charlotte) and the narcissistic passion of pedophilia (Humbert). The first giveth; the second taketh away. Beyond that, we note Humbert's habits in rhetoric. He always becomes wordy and diffuse when trying to cover up bad acts or bad conscience. The space he devotes to Charlotte, laying out their days spent at the lake, the friends they were beginning to make, the house she was beginning to embellish, looks suspiciously like sand thrown in the reader's eyes. The wordiness does not advance the memoir's putative purpose, confession of Humbert's relationship to Lolita, and the crimes appertaining thereunto. Humbert had committed no crime with Charlotte. Nevertheless, the episode with Charlotte is the only one in which Humbert felt that he might have wronged another, (omitting, of course, the faux-maudlin whines over Lolita). Charlotte he introduces as "the poor woman." Imagine that. Humbert admitting that someone could be "poor" for having been with him.

Finally, all of Humbert's memoir is implicitly a plea for understanding, an attempt to sway the jury. It is, after all, a closing statement. Humbert hopes his days with Charlotte will make himself look better. He treats

Chapter Two: Marriage

this marriage as complete in itself, not as a prelude to debauching Lolita. He might imagine his readers to be struck by his incredible generosity. Witty, sophisticated cosmopolitan Humbert marries the poor, mooning middle-class matron. What a decent thing to do. The episode with Charlotte suggests Nabokov at his most subtle, most indirect, and most efficient, making Humbert appear even more of a monster. Normalcy has the effect of heightening the horror of the unspeakable.

Lolita Married

In his lover's progress, Humbert bumped up against marriages constantly. He despised them all for smothering the erotic passion that alone, he thought, made one truly alive.* Yet his cynical observations of marriage arose not so much from malice as from utter failure to understand. Always turned inward, Humbert could understand nothing that he could not do. For Humbert, marriage was opaque. Nonetheless, his memoir recounts a string of efforts (beyond his own bad-faith attempts) to understand marriage from the outside in. From Annabel's parents to Lolita and her husband, Humbert peered uncomprehendingly into the closed system of wedded bliss or bust. The memoir ends (except for the Quilty coda), with Humbert dragging himself away from another marriage he could not comprehend. Ending Humbert's erotic journey by having him come face-to-face with a happily married couple was perhaps Nabokov's most brilliant stroke.

On September 22, 1952, wholly without warning, a letter, addressed to "Dear Dad," the one thing Humbert had never been, was dropped by impersonal fate in the person of the postman, into Humbert's glass-fronted mailbox. It came from Dolly, now Mrs. Richard F. Schiller, and six months preggers. The letter communicated clearly that Lolita had changed from the sullen nymphet that Humbert had lost and for whom he was still

---

*See again Trilling, with his intensely romantic preference for the erotic destruction of courtly love over the more placid but personally constructive habits of "wedded love." No one who is not crazy prefers Trilling to Milton.

"Light of My Life"

searching in a desultory way. Dolly's life had not been desultory. Having moved into the adult world, she was coming to grips with poverty, debt, and family. She needed a few bucks to tide things over in smoggy industrial Coalmont until she and her husband Dick could start again in Alaska. She concluded with a cryptic comment, filled with boundless meaning, some of which could have involved Humbert.

Write, please. I have gone through much sadness and hardship.

Humbert did not write. He appeared in person. He arrived in the sooty and desperate and depressed and featureless world that the trains traversed from New York to Ithaca. Here, in a *parodie de l'Enfer*, Humbert found Lolita, and found she was a wife.*

He saw that her marriage had stripped her of youth and bloom. The poor girl was now a woman, "frankly and hugely pregnant." Far from the vision described in women's magazines at the time as a lady-in-waiting or even a sacred vessel, Lolita had descended into the working class.† Pregnancy compounded by poverty will wear you down pretty fast and really hard. In her current world, far from movie magazines, malt-shop sodas, hotel dinners or department store shopping, Lolita's nymphetic past flickered only in Humbert's ever-green and ever-red memory.

That was only the first view, with Dolly in the doorway and Humbert standing outside, still caught between the pregnant now and the nymph then. The *then*, for a moment, still dominated, but the *now* has a sensual insistence that none but the pathological can resist. Upon further observation, punctuated by conversation with Lolita and her husband Richard, Humbert confirmed that during the time between 1949 and 1952 Lolita

---

*See "The Clod and the Pebble," by William Blake.

†The 1950's were a time of rapid population growth in the United States, and were also a period when the average family size rose to a bit over three children per couple. One must assume, and we do assume, that there was a corresponding increase in pregnancy, making that individually transient condition a culturally continuing phenomenon. This trend was noticed by the magazine press, as well as by those selling goods and services to mothers, infants, and prospective mothers. *Lolita* appeared in a heavily obstetrical moment in American popular culture.

We cannot say whether this circumstance had any bearing on Nabokov's hostility to children, except nymphets, in *Lolita*, or his tendency to bump off women so rash as to attempt reproduction (e.g., Valeria and Lolita herself).

Chapter Two: Marriage

had truly become a new person. And here she now was, "with her ruined looks and her adult, rope-veined narrow hands and her goose-flesh white arms," almost as if she had stepped out of *The Grapes of Wrath*, or one of Dorothea Lange's desperately dispiriting photographs of the Depression poor.*

For Humbert the aesthete, appearance always mattered. Humbert saw Lolita as ruined, bloated, sloppy, unshaven, manifesting an external decay that must reflect interior disorder. In reality, it was the other way around. The sleek, pampered nymphet had hidden internal disorder; the shabby wife was genuinely content. Appearance and reality is a constant cat-and-mouse game played by Humbert, and on Humbert, as he tells his story. On this occasion, the appearance is that of Lolita, and the reality is Humbert's reaction.

By his second look at Lolita, Humbert reverted to himself, interested in his own reactions more than he was in Lolita. He was devoted, as always, to love. Some readjustment was required. Seeing one's beloved poor and pregnant takes fortitude and ingenuity, after enjoying her prepubescent polish. Humbert decided that he was up to the challenge. He announced that, for the first time, his understanding of love expanded. His love was no longer tied to physical appearance and fey charm. True, Lolita was not at all the new Annabel. Yet Humbert wants his readers to know that

> ... I looked and looked at her, and knew as clearly as I know I am to die, that I loved her more than anything I had ever seen or imagined on earth, or hoped for anywhere else.†

This might be true. Humbert had always sworn undying love. Before the auto wanderings had begun, before he had ever agreed to rent Charlotte's house, Humbert "already knew" that he could not live without the child. That first time, five years earlier, might have been the moment of recognition; this time may, at last, allow for a moment of transformation. Per-

---

*John Steinbeck's *The Grapes of Wrath* (1939) was made into an Oscar-winning film, and won a Pulitzer Prize the following year. Dorothea Lange's iconic pictures were seen by everybody, appearing in *Life* magazine. Those are the obvious allusions. Time for a reach. Could this be the ghost of Annabel future? Normally we wouldn't ask, but Nabokov is tricky.

†Nabokov, *Lolita,* Pt. II, ch. 29, 277–278. Nabokov admitted that he wrote these lines in a teary haze, and could scarcely see the page. We take him at his word.

"Light of My Life"

haps it might have been; Humbert seems persuasive, even passionate, on seeing Lolita again. Still we recall (as do all re-readers) Humbert's musings on multi-generational child abuse, reaching into the third female generation. Hard to overlook that.

Humbert managed without stretching a psychic muscle. He claimed that he had changed even more than Lolita had. He had at last attained lasting amatory fidelity. The overt message is now that Humbert loved her "anyway" instead of "because," even if she had become a wife, great with child, and unkempt at that.* Did love, then, suddenly mean more than beauty, more than flush and fever and the idle dreams of gardens by the sea? Perhaps Humbert was momentarily jolted beyond erotic infatuation to a more serious appreciation of Lolita. At least that's what he said.†

If change were to come, it would come now. Might the first hint of love beyond the insatiable demands of pure *eros* lead to a new Humbert? To Humbert taking up the bourgeois American life of marriage, responsibility, and duty? To a Humbert no longer repelled by grown women? To a Humbert who would peacefully slink away from the Schillers without attempting to take Lolita off with him? Such questions address character, and "character is destiny."‡ Transfiguration, as Gregor Samsa and women after cosmetic surgery come to discover, may alter destiny, but leaves character untouched.**

Whatever its authenticity, Humbert's emotional turning point remained internal only. Humbert did not put into practice his new under-

---

*Friedrich Schiller, *Ode to Joy*, line 15: *Wer ein holdes Weib errungen*. The poet Schiller celebrated the joy of the devoted wife, amongst other forms of joy, which were, essentially, not Humbertian in nature. They were not erotic love. The wife comes closest, and it is here that Humbert begins to approach Schiller's sensibility. Lolita had ceased to be Humbert's *Tochter aus Elysium*, (line 2) but still remained his love.

†One mark of Nabokov's marvelous skill is his ability to fabricate a memoir that shows despicable behavior in a reasonable, though not favorable, light.

‡Heraclitus fragment, known to all.

**Franz Kafka's *Metamorphosis* (*Die Verwandlung*) (1915) was one of the novels Nabokov taught in his university course, "The Masters of European Fiction." *Metamorphosis* is divided into two parts, the first sentence "After a night of unsettling dreams, Gregor Samsa awoke to discover that he had been transformed in his bed into a monstrous vermin (*ungeheures Ungeziefer*)," being part one; and the rest of the novella being part two. Transformation or not, Samsa remained the same "person." As for women with face-lifts or implants of various sorts, the years may be denied and defied, but they do not disappear.

Chapter Two: Marriage

standing of life and love. Neither a sudden insight nor a true act of contrition, both barely understood at the time, guarantee that one will turn from his sin and live, leading a new life.* No time was left for the probably new Humbert, and no one existed to share that time with him. It happens all the time. The transfiguring moment comes, and though it is recognized, for one reason or another, nothing much happens.

Looking beyond himself, Humbert vaguely sensed that he was seeing a way of putting love into daily living. In front of him was Dolly the wife. She did not now represent an erotic moment, borne to ecstasy by passion imbibed by every sense and accompanied by "strange affinities." She had a marriage for "the working day," where partners cannot rely on *eros* for strength to meet the obligations of daily life. Another force must needs provide motivation. Lolita praised her Dick, who was, she informed Humbert, "a lamb"; his behavior represented work and loyalty, a form of togetherness that Humbert had never experienced, nor, apparently, had ever recognized. He could sense, though, that marriage, work, and a sense of a future had changed Lolita in character and personality as well as appearance. The trappings of popular culture were gone, replaced by a new (to Humbert) confidence of personal maturity.

In contrast to previous experience, Humbert had little trouble in getting Lolita to talk. She rattled on about life with Dick, which was quite happy, even though she admitted she had been crazy about the loathsome Quilty. Lolita, already more of an adult than Humbert would ever be, regarded *philia* and marriage as more important than mere *eros*. As for Humbert himself (he had to ask, naturally), he "had never counted, of course?"

Humbert's appearance provoked in Lolita genuine "remembrance of things past." What had those Humbertian years, so different in every respect from the pregnant spousal present, meant, as she considered her life as a whole? With a gesture, the Humbertian years were gone, weighed, measured, found dull, and then discarded. For Lolita, the past was the past, and, unlike Humbert, she did not live there. She had, as they now say, moved on, first to exploitive passion, then to marriage and mother-

---

*Augustine's insight that a person lives forward and understands backward seems appropriate here.

"Light of My Life"

hood. Those days with Humbert had become, so to say, almost another life, abstractly recalled as having happened but devoid of significance. She almost never thought of them now.

Humbert thought of little else, as he usually did, and he made a final effort to bring these thoughts from memory to living reality. He asked Dolly to leave Dick, abandon the "awful hole," and flee with him to golden vistas beyond. Humbert did not mention marriage, even now, at his last possible chance of being with the Lolita that he loved forever. Lolita had been that route before. The endless vistas, more than likely, were simply another series of motels, another tour of Dolly-world and Rita-land. Who could possibly turn that down?

Lolita would not go. She preferred the charities of marriage with the incidental Dick to *eros* with anyone. Having experienced *eros* as both beloved and as lover, she did not long to experience either version again. She had become an adult. As for Humbert, he supplied an epitaph for Lolita's former life, using words she did not say: "*He* broke my heart. *You* merely broke my life." Perhaps so, but Lolita had recovered from both. Did it matter to Humbert? What he had really meant was that Lolita had broken both *his* life and heart. Well, nothing of that would be fixed now. As he stood before the dry-eyed Lolita, piecing together fragments of insight, Humbert was speedily obtaining the "closure" that unhappy lovers all demand, and never really want to receive. His transfiguring moment was not going to entitle him to the happy ending.*

Weeping "the hottest tears I have ever shed," Humbert handed over to Lolita her "*trousseau*," four thousand dollars in cash and paper (which was hers anyway: no gift there!), along with the promise of more thousands when Charlotte's estate settled. It was a lot of money in 1952. Four thousand bucks was a year of modest middle-class living, more than enough to float Dolly and her lamb on out of Coalmont and onto the sea of settled married life. Humbert's last interaction with Lolita left her happy for the

---

*Nabokov was not alone in connecting death and transfiguration: see, for example, Arnold Schoenberg's *Tod und Verklärung*, opus 5. We do not imply that Nabokov was familiar with Schoenberg, or that he ought to have been. But we do suggest that Nabokov grew up in an environment in which death and transfiguration were connected phenomena. See Friedrich Nietzsche, *Also Sprach Zarathustra*, 1881–1883.

Chapter Two: Marriage

moment and hopeful for the future. He just drove off. Had that ever happened before?

As always, when faced with marriage, Humbert was in the mode of departure, for once accompanied by tears. Tears for what? Tears for whom? For an ending to his search for passionate intimacy, the divine Aristophanic coupling that made one whole? The tears did not announce the beginning of a search for a new person who might be shaped to fit inside the idyllic *hortus inclusus*. Humbert's tears were primarily nostalgic and elegiac, in the full meanings of aching pain of the lost past, now something that was utterly gone and done. Humbert's life was over, not yet literally but imaginatively. Time remains, meaning departs. It is not quite true that if nothing is going to happen, then nothing has happened, but it is certainly true that what has happened often becomes formal memory alone and loses the name of instructive experience.* Well, in Humbert's case, the past becomes organized in the only way possible: he put it into a memoir.

Nabokov's contemporary Samuel Beckett, whom he never mentioned in class lectures, but whom he would have at least recognized in pre-1940 Paris, examined fears similar to Humbert's in *Waiting for Godot* (*En Attendant Godot*, 1959), where a flat and featureless present was compressed into an absence of both past and future. Time had collapsed into merely physical presence. Humbert's tears upon leaving Lolita marked the real end of life because it marked the end of his life's work.

True enough, Humbert survived physically, and retained sufficient emotional command and control to plan and execute the entirely understandable, if not justifiable, shooting of the vile Quilty. That may be considered as the Nabokovian equivalent of the first and narrative epilogue in Dostoevsky's *Crime and Punishment*, just as his memoir, about love, resembles the second Dostoevskian epilogue, also about love. Humbert's purposive life ends when he hears Lolita "shout in a vibrant voice to her Dick." As with so much else, marriage is what it does.

---

*This attitude is entirely Augustinian, as any reader of the *Confessions* will recognize. However, the trope of journey, which Augustine exemplified, did not apply to Humbert, particularly after his last unsuccessful effort to take Lolita away with him on a third tour. For the full bitterness of nostalgia in matters of love, see the poetry of Sappho. Understanding backwards is often a tearful experience.

"Light of My Life"

Rita

We would not forget Rita, though that has been done. While Rita occupied two years of real time, Humbert skimped on her scandalously in the memoir. The Rita interlude between Lolitas lost and found was compressed into the seven paragraphs in Chapter 26 of Part Two. That is all. Still, Rita was the only woman who gained Humbert's affection, however tepid.

She appears in the memoir when Humbert's heart was most completely "a hysterical unreliable organ"; presumably, at the moment of Rita-rise, it was more unreliable and more given to hysterics than usual. Humbert had just lost Lolita, both as person and as dream. Rita filled the void as well as anyone could. She was not Humbert's wife, and for that reason, and perhaps because she was artless, was remembered with some grace and favor. Humbert recalls approvingly Rita's size (small) and coloration (pale), and even her asymmetry (eyes slightly askew). Her most charming characteristic was the childlike curve where her back joined her bottom. Humbert didn't react to her frailties with the hostility he brought to Valeria or Charlotte. Those women had both committed the unforgivable sin of pretending to artistic taste. Rita pretended to nothing. She was as honest about her desires as a child; in that way, she must have represented unimaginable freedom to Humbert, the consummate poseur.

Rita came into Humbert's life in a typical American way. He picked her up in a bar, where, "amiably drunk" and unquestionably lonely, she placed her little hand tentatively on his. He had difficulty describing how she appealed to him, not really sexually all that much, not really socially all that much, but as someone who appeared to radiate a gentle goodness.

> She was so kind, was Rita, such a good sport, that I daresay she would have given herself to any pathetic creature or fallacy....

Humbert was both.

Rita was, of course, born too soon to become a hippie; that brand of lostness did not surface for nearly a decade after *Lolita*. Rita was even a bit early to be "beat," a species of alienation that featured depression. Rita was disconnected from society in the traditional ways, through sex, alcohol,

Chapter Two: Marriage

and a kindly temperament adrift in a world of philistine sharks. One shark was her loathsome but culturally ordinary, even necessary, brother. This philistine mayor with his painted ties (a particular Nabokov horror) embraced the Rotarian et al. creed of "boost, don't knock."* Since Rita was a walking, talking, copulating "knock" on everything the voters of Grainball City held dear, her brother wisely paid "his great little sister several hundred dollars per month" on the sole but absolute condition that she stay out of town and sin elsewhere. Three husbands and countless lovers later, she was acquired by Humbert, and they traveled the country for two years, which appear in his memoir almost as an ellipsis. Nevertheless, if the years vanished, she did not, and she persisted in his memory as the "sweetest, simplest, gentlest, dumbest Rita imaginable. Sweet and dumb, sort of like Valeria, gentle and simple, quite unlike Charlotte, soothing and comprehending, the opposite of both wives, Rita was their superior in all things except formal intelligence. Humbert noted the deficit, did not find it serious, and thought it endearing enough to mention. The crowning mark of Rita's superiority was her willingness to travel, making with Humbert a cross-country jaunt through assorted auto courts reminiscent of the two wanderings with Lolita. The ostensible reason for a trip to California was to find Lolita, but the real purpose was to create movement within time, going round as she (Rita) phrased it, "like a God-damn mulberry moth."†

---

*On his cross-country butterfly trips in the late forties and early fifties, Nabokov had been through many midwestern towns with grain elevators, numerous churches and minor league baseball. Hutchinson, Kansas, comes to mind. The description of the mayor could have been written by H.L. Mencken, who similarly disdained middle America.

†*Lolita*, Pt. II, ch. 26, p. 259. The reference is ostensibly to Grainball, which the peripatetic couple visited, but we suggest more was meant. See Pt. II, ch. 26, pp. 261–262; and Pt. II, ch. 27, p. 264. The name "mulberry moth" refers, less symbolically, to the *Bombyx mori*, or silkworm, which eats only mulberry leaves, particularly from the white mulberry rather than the American mulberry. The mulberry moth does not long go "round and round." Quite otherwise, it settles down, weaves a cocoon, and becomes an entirely sedentary and valuable silkworm. The moth phase of life is considerably less important than the silkworm phase of life. Why did Rita choose as her symbol of aimless movement a mulberry moth? No answer comes readily to mind. What does pop up is the smoothness and value of silk, and the unbridgeable distance between a silk purse and a sow's ear, or the comforting connotations of cocoon. We can also suggest that the mulberry moth offers a glimpse, far too brief, at Rita's personality. Humbert did not include many of Rita's own words in his brief description of those two years.

"Light of My Life"

Connection survived wandering, and the castaways remained together when they returned to New York. Humbert became a poet/philosopher in residence in a pretentious college (Bennington, perhaps?) for a year, taking Rita and stashing her in a "roadside inn," where she continued her habits of drink and kindness to all she met. Then back to New York.

Humbert's relationship with Rita, the only satisfactory and therapeutic connection he ever had with an adult woman, lacked the torque to propel him beyond memory and anticipation, beyond the reality that "sex is but the ancilla of art."* But Humbert tried, with his typical ironic distance. He traveled with Rita, but looked for Lolita. He took Rita to the college town, but not to the college itself. Rita remained at one remove from what Humbert did and was. She could not lead Humbert even to *eros*, saying nothing about *philia*, imagining nothing about *agape*. Still, she offered the possibility, perhaps transiently even the hope, that Humbert could have a satisfying (on some serious level) relationship with an adult (in some ways) woman. Not a wife, of course; that demanded intimacy on a quotidian and (usually) non-ecstatic level, but Rita's function as traveling companion did not imply intensely erotic love tamed to the demands of life commonly lived. More, Rita offered Humbert a gift, with nothing in return asked, of a charm at once "cocky" and pathetic, and off-beat in every possible way. Rita was compassionate, and Humbert, like every man, badly needed female compassion. By the time he met Rita, Humbert had endured two years of his erotic passion combined with contemptuous Lolitan rejection; insolence, indifference, distance, hidden conspiracies, open attempts to escape, and philistine addiction to American popular culture. After a diet of feminine disdain, a dollop of compassion and giving is mighty welcome. Rita was a lover in the traditional ways, but she offered *philia* more than *eros*, which, over the long haul, is certainly relaxing.

Whether Rita gave more than she got can hardly be known, but she did soothe the fevered brow and heart, and Humbert did seem in better health with Rita than he had been before or would be after. These were great gifts, and though Rita was no nymphet and Lolita still burned in Humbert's soul, the years with Rita seem to have been the best of times

---

*Lolita, Pt. II, ch. 26, p. 259; see also pp. 260–261.

Chapter Two: Marriage

after the Annabel idyll.* Rita's offerings to Humbert were simple gifts, ordinary and humble, but not to be overlooked because they lacked the purple tint of passion. The Shaker hymn reminds the world of *eros* that simple gifts bring rightness, balance, and *agape*, which Humbert, addicted to passion alone could not accept. Life and things just went round and round, and Humbert fell back on nostalgia. What does memory always want and accomplish? It is the sense of self.

The interlude with Rita was, we suggest, a pause in Humbert's downward trajectory. He did less harm than usual. He even took care of Rita, after a fashion. When she got mixed up with a genuine criminal, of the more unpalatable (to Humbert) sort, he extracted her with some difficulty, taking her back, even more battered than usual. He also got Rita out of jail, where she was lodged after having been charged with a theft of Mrs. Roland MacCrum's furs, a gift, it appeared, from the incautious and inebriated (and perhaps slightly infatuated) Mr. MacCrum. All in all, though Rita's tale fell short of a saga, it did show Humbert demonstrating a pattern of concern and consideration, far removed from his usual attitude towards wives, especially his own. Humbert's best may have fallen short of the standard set by the *Ladies Home Journal*, but it was not so bad for Humbert. All things considered.†

So Rita, abruptly introduced, just as suddenly vanished. There is no Rita settling into memory. Humbert found Lolita again. Entirely appropriate. Had it not been Lolita, it would have been some other nymphet. That's the way things go for the addict of passion. *Eros* for Humbert was always the central need and value of life, and it forms the narrative core of his memoir. Still, if we may linger for a moment more, the intermezzo with Rita was the closest Humbert came to the idyll he had shared with Annabel. And it was not very close.

---

*Nabokov symmetrically balanced the two years with Lolita (*eros*) with the two years with Rita (*phile*). His telescoping of the Rita years into a few pages demonstrates how erotic passion distorts our perception of everything, even time.

†General decency often lacks a noteworthy narrative, which is one reason why Humbert's narrative about their two-year conjunction is so compressed. In a memoir about disaster, good news is more or less irrelevant. It is also boring. Things going well, and the self-satisfaction gained therefrom, do not induce either fear or pity, but instead a feeling that the author has nothing to say. And, of course, *hybris* ought always to be the beginning of the tale, particularly one about *eros* and heartbreak. Rita induced neither.

"Light of My Life"

Still and all, Humbert presented Rita mostly by omission and hint, so we have examined her episode with a tentative touch. Even those hints, however, offered several possible other Ritas. Perhaps Humbert understood Rita as a latter-day Monique, more enduring but not more important. Rita might be only a place-holder, required for narrative structure to fill two unimportant Humbertian years when *eros* was only a memory. Or Rita may have been even less, a clumsy effort to launch one more salvo at a philistine American popular culture that Humbert (and Nabokov) loathed. If so, enough already. We all get it.

The Limits of *Eros*

Movies have played a role in American culture analogous to the theater in Greece. They tell the great enduring tales, reflect American concerns, re-run standard American myth, and, because everyone sees them, movies nationalize American culture. This may be a commonplace, but it is not irrelevant or without value merely because people know it. So we make bold to conclude with a movie, *Shenandoah* (1965), a western of no particular distinction, but starring a major actor, Jimmy Stewart.* In *Shenandoah*, the character Sam asks Charlie Anderson (Jimmy Stewart) for his daughter's hand in marriage. Sam confesses love, but Charlie Anderson is not satisfied.

> *Charlie Anderson*: Do you like her?
> *Lt. Sam*: Well, I just said I...
> *Charlie Anderson*: No, no. You just said you loved her. There's some difference between lovin' and likin'. When I married Jennie's mother, I-I didn't love her — I liked her ... I liked her a lot. I liked Martha for at least three years after we were married and then one day it just dawned on me I loved her. I still do ... still do. You see, Sam, when you love a woman without likin' her, the night can be long and cold, and contempt comes up with the sun.

---

*A standard guide of the movies one needs to see omits *Shenandoah*, but an undistinguished movie is not, on that account, devoid of distinguished moments. See the glossy guide, Steven Jay Schneider, gen. ed., *1001 Movies You Must See Before You Die* (London: Quintet Publishing Limited, 2003). One thousand movies is a lot, and absence from the top 1000 may well indicate cultural or scholarly acclaim.

Chapter Two: Marriage

Just common sense, nothing more, born of long cultural experience that when the partners do not like each other the relationship faces problems.

Humbert clearly liked Rita enough, but that feeling never ripened into anything more. Many reasons can account for that; the main reason is that Humbert never stopped desiring what he had never really had. He remained still an enchanted hunter, pursuing an illusory dream of romantic union with Lolita. Caught by her fey beauty, Humbert accumulated only memories of orgasms in their two years together. He desired Lolita in the same way on the day he picked her up and on the day he finally escaped. That is certainly part of the meaning of *eros*: the lover never permits change in the beloved. Lolita was the permanent beloved, in this case, filled with contempt and distaste for her abuser/lover. Humbert's role was equally constant; he explained himself in the memoir as a great lover.*

Eros strikes a single note, giving *Lolita* its peculiarly hollow quality. The highs and lows of passion compare only to each other. Total absorption or casual contempt are the sounds of Humbert's voice on women, and on life itself. Readers are immersed, as it were, in nineteenth century Italian opera; it is always *soave fanciulla*, that instant of passion, that force of destiny, the trope of transfiguring moment, without which living could not make a life. *Che gelida manina*; after the little hand brings ecstasy, there can only be death. What Nabokov did not write was as important as what he did write, and the utter absence of married love within the shiver of passion leaves the reader in the hollow core of *Lolita*. If there is nothing to like, ultimately there can be nothing to love. The *Ladies Home Journal* knew that.

---

*Not surprisingly, love's opposite, contempt, has the same timeless and changeless quality. Perhaps this makes arrogance and disdain the really perverse form of love.

Chapter 3

IRREGULAR ADVENTURERS

Really, when you think about it, the only question concerning Humbert and Lolita is about the form that doom would take. In spite of Nabokov's distaste for Freud, Humbert suspiciously resembles an embodiment of the Freudian id, surging irrepressibly toward erotic passion and equally erotic death. As a character, Humbert is both powerful and simple. His emotional drives are obvious, their force overwhelming. Beyond the fixedness of character, however, there is also the constraint placed on plot by the irresistible force of time. In the midst of the red glow of lust, and even before marrying Charlotte to insure propinquity to his "downy darling," Humbert himself acknowledged the pitiless relationship of time and love.

> I knew I had fallen in love with Lolita forever; but I also knew she would not be Lolita forever. She would be thirteen on January 1. In two years or so she would cease being a nymphet....

Death is the only god unswayed by gifts, Aeschylus had observed,* but he was wrong. Time stands equally aloof. Nabokov knew that, and used time as the trigger of doom in *Lolita*.†

Passion Thwarted

Experience is adamantine only in facts, for everyone uses memory to resolve the past into pleasing patterns of either understanding or self-

---

*The only line left from the lost *Niobe,* quoted by Aristophanes in *The Frogs.*
 †In his later novels, time and doom are inextricably entwined. It is a Nabokovian signature.

Chapter Three: Irregular Adventurers

deception. Humbert's memory did both. Looking for the old idyll of Annabel and passion, Humbert created within himself an interior steady-state universe, a psychic bulwark against an outside where Lolita was growing up and away in a world informed by the kaleidoscope of American popular culture.

His memoir chronicled three meandering road trips through America, where aimless travel, random sightseeing, and popular culture remained constant, though the relationship between Humbert and Lolita changed. Internal change, however, came only to one traveler. Humbert stayed as he was when he first saw Lolita in the garden, and became fixed in the grip of erotic obsession. With Annabel, the gods had smiled indulgently on him, and Eros had been repaid with *eros*; now, Humbert's passion turned Lolita into a study in distance.

Beyond the once and present idyll, nothing seemed to form a pattern for Humbert. It was just wandering to him. But things did change. On the first and most substantially described meander, Lolita resisted Humbert only passively, through teenage moods coupled to movies and music. When the journey began, Lolita was at the edge of menarche, a beginning for her, and the beginning of the end for Humbert. It changed everything. Lolita, maturing into womanhood; Humbert, seeing his "downy darling" bloom before his eyes.*

How does the memoirist, years later, present the brewing disaster during the years when Lolita was becoming a woman, when Humbert simultaneously exploiting her vanishing childhood? At the end of his life, Humbert sketches his discomfort during this period only in the externals of cultural difference. The popular culture that Humbert snobbishly disdained, Lolita embraced. It was an unpleasant and enduring shock for him, after the cultural closeness he had experienced with Annabel. Traveling together, Humbert and Lolita existed apart. Humbert's description of the first trip, then, is something of an extended grumble.† Not exactly

---

*With culturally characteristic European reserve, Humbert left Lolita's emerging womanhood out of his memoir.
†See Robert Frost, "The Oven Bird" (1920):
  The bird would cease and be as other birds
  But that he knows in singing not to sing
  The question that he frames in all but words
  Is what to make of a diminished thing.

the romantic journey he must have hoped for. We hear Nabokov holding back his chuckle, imagining the comic possibilities inherent in the pairing of an American teenybopper and a middle-aged refugee. Solemn Humbert does not laugh. His intense erotic passion being thwarted daily by a thousand trivial offenses, he must have felt like a martyr to love.

Recording the second road trip, Humbert's grumble continued, but for different reasons. During that tour, Humbert was distracted from the pursuit of passion by his own paranoia. He imagined that he was under constant surveillance, being followed by a red car, and obsessively glimpsing detectives everywhere.* Worse, Lolita had taken control of the journey, including the daily agenda and destination. This was worse than movie magazines, popular songs, and bubble gum. Lolita was older now, more experienced in the ways of both Humbert and of teenage evasions, and she was leaving behind the fey charms of the nymphet, entering upon the more complex concerns of love as a woman. Neither practice nor passion could preserve for Humbert the stasis of his imagined idyll; things moved faster now that Lolita had awakened to love herself. Of course, she did not love Humbert. Of course, Humbert missed Lolita's transformation entirely. Passion sees everything but what is there in front of it.

Humbert hoped the second trip would enable him to hang on to Lolita, just a bit longer; perhaps Lolita could stay a nymphet, just a bit longer. But one fine summer morning in Colorado, Lo simply escaped, walking out to find her love, the pornographically inclined and unprepossessing Quilty. A casual estimate would have favored Humbert, with his animal magnetism and brooding good looks. But love makes its own judgment, and the tables were turned on Humbert. Live by *eros*, suffer by *eros*; perhaps not exactly what it says in Scripture, but it does convey what Ovid understood. Eros, who once had given, now took away.

---

*The trope of being observed is usually displaced guilt or fear. Humbert, however, did not feel guilty, and his fears centered on Lolita abandoning him, rather than his being arrested. He was careful, of course, but essentially on principle. After all, as Humbert himself acknowledged "[Lolita] had nowhere else to go."

Chapter Three: Irregular Adventurers

Time and the Nymphet

Though Humbert and Lolita equally shared the days and hours, they experienced them differently. Humbert had caught Lolita at the tag end of girlhood. Lolita was in that disorganized state of childhood outgrown and womanhood not yet attained. During the months before the menarche, girls often seem at a loss, without direction, unhappy but not knowing why, unpleasant and angry no matter what. To Humbert this capriciousness could be enchanting, echoing his own existential dissatisfactions. All others, and especially mothers, teachers and friends, endure this wretched time. The exasperated Charlotte had threatened to send Lolita to a boarding school, and get her out of the house. Fortunately, the distress does not last. Nature herself restores balance. The woman emerges, usually rather quickly, as yet without experience but no longer without direction.

Humbert's memoir barely acknowledges Lolita's growing maturity. A single, almost clinical description of physical change sufficed for those obvious alterations. Nothing about the emotional changes, or the increased maturity, or the beginnings of the sense of life's possible directions. Erotic passion blots out changes in the beloved; only the original perfection remains as the dream conquers reality. The object of Humbert's passion is unusual, but his obsessive attitude is entirely ordinary. In spite of the reality of a changing Lolita, Humbert retained the image of Lolita's fleeting nymphetness until the hideous epiphany at Coalmont when he discovered that his adored child was with child. Till the end of his life, he could never let that first image go. He would, as he said, "be always with child."

Was Humbert ever capable of making room for the mature woman Lolita in his erotic gallery? True, he proudly affirms, from the first to the last page of *Lolita*, lasting amatory fidelity. He is the epitome of the devoted lover. He is also a character who has a long history of rejecting adult women. The question carrying readers forward through the memoir (though not of particular interest to Humbert) is: will Humbert be able to love the older Lolita as well as the rapidly fading ghost of the nymphet he glimpsed in Charlotte's garden? Lolita was changing. Would Humbert change as well?

"Light of My Life"

In the grips of erotic passion, Humbert habitually lived in the present, seldom looking ahead more than a couple of days. His plans for Lolita included today's lunch, tonight's hotel, tomorrow's tourist trap. As for the years ahead, he visualized preposterous ways of circumventing Lolita's inevitably unfolding maturity. He thought of using her as a brood-mare for new generations of evanescent nymphets.* He imagined that "with patience and luck I might have her produce eventually a nymphet with her blood in her exquisite veins, a Lolita the Second."† Humbert thought further into the future, imagining a third generation of Lolitas, with him still potent and the child unutterably delicious. Can *eros* be more unsettling than this, in its irrepressible need to keep passion alive?

Humbert's function in this fantastic future would be to negotiate the grotesque complexities of being at once lover, father, and grandfather to Lolita. Such a refinement on incest might not have occurred to everyone, but it did to Humbert, answering questions about the possibility of faunlets evolving. It also suggests a narrative for Humbert's long trip with Lolita: they went everywhere, but he would go nowhere.

The actual outcome was still in the future as Humbert set off to pick up pre-pubescent Lolita up from camp. Always ironic in his sensibilities, Humbert knew that a road trip was uncertain for both parties. Yet in spite of his age, Humbert was new to relationships. Perhaps all it took was charm! Aided by the relative isolation of travel, the Humbertian charm might compensate for the uncertainties of a relationship, compounded, by Lolita's rapidly approaching maturity. If Lolita were to be loved "forever," and doom postponed until Nature's slow time arrived in later years, Humbert's love must grow in dimension and expand in goodness, concepts unfamiliar to him as the trip began. Love would need to evolve from intense erotic attachment into genuine concern for the other's well-being and patience with the other's faults. This was the personal incarna-

---

*Humbert's plan resembles the myth of the eternal return, the ever-young Kore reappearing in cyclical fashion. Humbert's plan, then, changes the nature of time: Instead of passing in a linear fashion, it would be cyclical

†Nabokov, *Lolita*, Pt. II, ch. 3, p. 174. This is the creepiest passage in the whole book; any reader who fails to experience a *frisson* of horror is either himself a predator or a blockheaded critic.

Chapter Three: Irregular Adventurers

tion of the general Platonic "guidance," expressed internally as a "sense of shame in acting shamefully, and a sense of pride in acting well."* For Humbert, and not only for Humbert, this was not as easy to do as it sounds.

Humbert had already spent a lot of time traveling, though mostly alone. The one extended trip with others, on the Arctic expedition, had ended with a nervous breakdown. Still, he knew that travel encouraged an ersatz intimacy between even the most mis-matched traveling companions. His future with Lolita would begin with that false intimacy. It did not matter to Humbert that their mutual history might be founded on this deception of convenience, to say nothing of deliberate lies. Deception came easy to Humbert, as it does to all with charm. So Humbert began the lies to Lolita before they even left camp, taking her away with the pretext that her mummy was ill. When Lo asked about Mother, Humbert airily replied that it was something, the doctors weren't quite sure, but it was serious, more than likely, and then he moved on to another topic. Lo had retorted brusquely, "Stop at that candy bar, will you." The child's seeming insouciance: did that justify the adult's lie? Not until the next day, after a night of love or at least sex, did Humbert finally come clean.

Lolita was not in good shape at the beginning of their road trip. It was the morning after her first encounter with Humbert at The Enchanted Hunters. Humbert tells his story, not hers, of course; but he does note alarmingly that she had been wincing in pain as she got in and out of the car, making "sizzling" sounds with her lips as they rode along, and complaining that Humbert had "torn something inside of her."† At a gas station, she asked to call her mother. Humbert figured it was time to assert

---

*Plato, *Symposium*, 1781 (Phaedrus), p.10.
 †Discreet Humbert gives no direct description of that first night's activities. But he takes pains to evoke them through a series of lurid images, such as a "choking snake sheathing whole the flayed trunk of a shoat" and "a sultan ... helping a callipygian slave child to climb a column of onyx." How the night went between the grown man and the twelve-year-old child, though, is exposed in the last few images of Humbert's lyrical evocation, "a last throb, a last dab of color, stinging red, smarting pink, a sigh, a wincing child." Intercourse may be intercourse, always alike in its technical components, but Humbert is at pains to remind readers that he (Humbert) was not Charlie.

control. Locking her safely in the car and speeding away, Humbert baldly announced that Charlotte was dead.*

Humbert's memoir cuts off at this point, and does not report Lolita's reaction. The narrative picks up again at some indefinite hour later that the morning. The child's mood was dangerously sullen and uncooperative. Humbert resorted to bribery. He lists off numerous items of junk he purchased in the attempt to lighten her mood: candy, gum, clothes, traveling alarm clock, chewing gum, sunglasses. One item well-buried in this list, suggests that Lolita's mind was not on toys: a box of sanitary pads.

He even got her a separate room that night. He does not explain how Lolita managed to acquire her own room, whether rage or pathos. But he does mention matter-of-factly that during the night a weeping Lolita came to his bed: "She had absolutely nowhere else to go." Captivity does not consist only of brick and bars.

Lies and abuse appear early as the leitmotif of what Humbert regarded as almost a honeymoon journey, in the European mode of the previous century.† For Lolita, captivity outweighed everything. For Humbert, it was love. Their trip, as always happens when two travel together, diverged into two journeys. Indifference and care, sex and parenting, exploitation and enjoyment, erotic play and burgeoning horror, existed simultaneously and might diverge dangerously. The trip began. Tally-ho!

On the Road

Wanderings across the face of America, with privacy Humbert's purpose and paranoia his inevitable accompanist, led to endless and incon-

---

*Nabokov, *Lolita*, Pt. I, ch. 32, p. 141. Again we see Nabokov's juxtaposition of love and death. Nabokov was certainly familiar with the Ishtar legend. Recall the "Babylonian" curve to Rita's back.

†It was not uncommon amongst the propertied to travel in a grand matrimonial tour for several months. This involved stops at fashionable watering holes and resorts, which Humbert and Lolita did. The happy couple would not be isolated, suffocating in each other's company, but would instead meet other peripatetic aristocrats moving slowly across the face of fashionable Europe. See Henry James. The War brought an end to all that, but the memories of better times and better days lingered on. Humbert's honeymoon across America is a tawdry and tattered reminder of what these things had been, and could be. In this case, was as far from the ideal as it is possible to get. In history, the pathetic often replaces the elegant.

Chapter Three: Irregular Adventurers

clusive episodes. Nothing Humbert said or did could make Lolita love him more or appreciate him better.

The tours of postwar America form a central static structure of the novel. It was less a trip of day after day, than of one day constantly repeated. This is an unusual narrative technique.* In Western literature, a road trip, even a picaresque tale, usually resolves into an ending allowing characters and readers alike to gain moral insight and social savvy.† In *Lolita*, though, the trips reflect the nature of *eros* itself: the scenery shifts around characters who do not. "Form always follows function"; here, like *eros* itself, the journey does not progress.‡ Nor does the protagonist. Humbert gains neither savvy nor insight.

Readers fare better than Humbert, or Lolita, for that matter. While Humbert remains possessed by desire, readers gain a bit of insight through observing Humbert's steady state of erotic itch. Readers also notice the contrast, as Humbert did not, between the misery inside the car and a friendly, prospering wider community of postwar America. Nothing wrong with the road; it was the travelers. Within the structure of *Lolita*, road functions as an emblem, not as a journey.

The road also reflects a postwar America, in 1947 beginning to adjust to the end of the Second World War. America was more prosperous than it had been just before Pearl Harbor. Men had come home from war and had gone to work, glad to do so. There was plenty to worry about — there always is — but things were better than they had been. This cautious but pervasive optimism, which would re-elect Harry Truman a year later, passed Humbert by completely, and the country he toured remained an alien land, observed, described, often deplored, but only dimly understood.

The late forties were a good time for a road trip through America. Now, people could buy tires again, gas rationing had ended, and the new

---

*At least it would be, until the *nouvelle vague* appeared in French literature, a style in which immense effort at detail was juxtaposed with an utter absence of action. Nabokov never went nowhere near as far as Robbe-Grillet, of course.

†Not here. No one gains any insight into anything except for Humbert's failure to launch. See, for example, most of the movie *Groundhog Day* (1993).

‡The quotation, from architect Louis Sullivan, refers to buildings, but narration is a form of building, is it not?

peace and prosperity made auto travel possible.* But the America that people saw still retained much that was traditional and local. Humbert and Lolita were immersed in the physical and social fabric of a country that still looked and sounded and tasted pretty much as it had a decade or so earlier. Air-conditioned cars did not yet shut motorists off from the sounds of people, birds, places and weather. Interstates did not yet send travelers through cities and around towns on roads designed to serve speed and movement. Motel and fast food chains had not yet brought the virtues of uniformity to travelers who, in serious ways, would never have to leave home. World War II had ended, the promises of a new and gleaming postwar America were still promises. An imagined future, with sleek art–Deco industrial design, elaborately exhibited by General Motors at the 1939 World's Fair, lay still beyond reach though not beyond expectation, for this was America where progress defined reality. This was not Europe where the general ruin seemed endless.

The Depression and the war had frozen America in physical and social place, halting for a time the constant rebuilding and expansion of cities, the constant consolidation of farms into larger units with fewer houses amidst the fields. The reason for this was money. Depressions preserve the past, both physical and social, while prosperity encourages new buildings and private purchases to keep up with the Joneses, or even get a bit ahead. It was still just too early for that. Only two summers ago Americans were fighting in Okinawa and the first nuclear explosion took place in New Mexico. Now, the veterans were finishing their first or second year in college on the G. I. Bill. The baby boom was just beginning. In the summer of 1947, before the oil shortage and the great blizzard of the coming winter, America was poised between depression and war past and Cold War to come. In that year, remembrance balanced anticipation, and the physical reality of the old was seen as soon to give way to the gleaming future promised by the World's Fair, the G. I. Bill, and the growing new families.

---

*The Joads of Steinbeck's *The Grapes of Wrath* (1939) reflected the desperation of a Depression decade. Jack Kerouac's *On the Road* (1957) still lay in the future. The Pennsylvania Turnpike (1940) was a harbinger of things to come, but it remained alone in 1947; the interstate system (Federal-Aid Highway Act) was not signed by President Eisenhower till 1956. The road trips Nabokov describes had an historical window of about a decade.

Chapter Three: Irregular Adventurers

Within the American town square, newspapers and the established electronic technologies of radio and movies still dominated the national culture. The old and familiar, for the moment, vastly outweighed the new. Local cultural and scenic variations greeted the tourist, while the rush of national homogenization, easily predictable and often predicted, was a decade away. In the South one still received an automatic helping of grits; in the west they used silver dollars in small transactions; in Texas the gas stations all had Dr. Pepper in the red soft drink cooler boxes. The American road reflected the places through which it ran. The American road that Humbert saw (through Nabokov's eyes, of course*) was reminiscent of the texture of Joyce's *Ulysses,* where a thousand fragments of reality connected in the character's mind; Humbert sees as Leopold sees, multiple discrete facets jumbled together.†

The infrastructure remained mostly pre-war. The roads Humbert and Lolita traveled were two lanes, usually concrete, often with meandering drizzles of asphalt repairing the cracks of Depression, neglect, and wartime wear. The roads were usually paved versions of the mud and dust ruts that preceded them, going, as roads then did, from town to town. They went right down the main street from residences to churches and business, just as in the Norman villages in *Madame Bovary,* though in modern (1947) America the roads were punctuated by red lights, perhaps, a grade crossing, then more residences and churches, then the countryside again. Forty-five miles an hour was a good clip on these roads that everyone used, both local traffic and those passing through. Passing a slow vehicle was an adventure, requiring careful calculation. Couldn't pass going uphill: few vehicles then had the horsepower for that. Couldn't pass on the numerous curves: impossible to see what was coming. The bridges of that era were narrower than the road and its shoulder: can't pass on a bridge as there was too little room. Most drivers sped up when threatened with passing: the American

---

*Nabokov traveled over America in search of butterflies, which he pursued with a scientist's focus and fervor. He knew America well.

†*Lolita*'s America functioned in an opposite way from the social and spatial geography of the St. Petersburg underclass in Fyodor Dostoevsky's *Crime and Punishment*.1 In *Lolita,* a distraught couple travels through a healthy America. In *Crime and Punishment,* a couple is saved within a society of social injustice.

"Light of My Life"

competitive juices flare up more often in automobiles than in love. You passed at your own risk and understood that around the next curve or over the next hill and certainly in the next town another slow driver would appear, and the drama of passing on a two-lane road would be replayed endlessly across the day's drive.

The travelers drove between the fence lines alive with birds in the countryside, and traffic through the center of towns great and small. Hawks sat on wires and poles that lined the highways, meadow larks perched on fence posts, cows spread across pastures and crops stretched from fence to tree line. These crops and cows might have seemed mundane, and Lolita Matrimonii aegre spinosus agnascor suis, utcunque chirographi suffragarit incre America fed the world. The farms were still mostly family businesses, and the road linked a line of farmhouses and barns that stretched from town to town. Rural America had the dual beauty of nature and fecundity, along with the satisfying rhythms of the seasons, and a primordial sense of peace and hope. Humbert was a bit out of place in that ordered world where the farms radiated a sense of place, permanence, and purpose, of the way things had been and would again. Travelers passed through, hurrying to a destination, but the farms and the woods were among those things which abide.

The pace of change and activity picked up as the road and the cars approached towns and their commercial busyness. For the voyager, this meant cafes and service stations. Humbert recalled gas stations, festooned with tire racks, and containing benches where old men sat, and large red coolers for Coca-Cola. The gas stations, whether under Pegasus, a star, or a lettered oval, all reflected the style and commercial acumen of individual owners, while still serving as the standard setting of social gathering.*

---

*In the years after the war, people used to gather at service stations to exchange news, gossip, and speculation about the ways things were going. Most were men, because the women stopped in to fill up, then moved on, the victims of errands and responsibility. In those days, men had more leisure than women. Perhaps they still do.

The social activity of gas stations reached its height on Sunday afternoons, after church and before sundown. The men all drank Cokes, and were dressed in clean clothes. Those at gas stations were respectable. The drunks, the bums, the marginalized, were elsewhere.

Today, gas stations have become multi-pump megastores, containing small grocery stores and often a fast-food restaurant, in addition to pumping gas. Located on the edges of town,

Chapter Three: Irregular Adventurers

Many had benches in front of the office, where local men gathered in good weather to chat about life surrounded by the masculine comfort of automotive sights and smells. Humbert and Lolita replayed this scene dozens of times in dozens of towns, until gas stations competed with cows and crops in terms of familiarity, and distaste.

But gas stations, and cafes, and towns in general, were for Humbert a time of danger, demanding increased vigilance. Humbert's nervousness reflected not just his peculiar position of traveling with a sex slave. No lover really likes to travel. Lovers aren't interested in wide-open spaces; just the space between the two of them, and how to contract that. However, the nature of travel — especially travel through the American countryside in the forties — forces the traveler's attention outward. The world was blowing in through the open windows. At any of the many stops, Lolita might communicate with the outside world, or even escape, exposing Humbert to police scrutiny and unthinkable emotional loss. By the second trip, he was sure that that had happened. In the Midwest, Lolita seemed to have made contact with someone, perhaps the bestial Quilty, resulting in their being followed across the Great Plains by a red car. Humbert must become ever more watchful, look more intently for the signs of fate and chance, which were once favorable in Ramsdale, but now malignant on the road.

Humbert's nervousness would grow as the travelers approached towns. There, the human scenery increased, from men at gas stations to people walking along the road or sitting on porches or standing in front yards chatting with friends and watching a world that still moved at a human pace. But for Humbert, friendliness merely heightened his anxiety and aloofness. After all, his irregularities were there to be seen because of the current method of travel. Humbert and Lo were not isolated from humanity and society, hermetically sealed inside air-conditioned cars cruising at

as close to the interstate as possible, their great signs stretch a hundred, two hundred feet in the air, visible for a couple of miles, giving the driver going eighty a chance to see them in time to stop. The social gathering function of the town station has been utterly lost, as has local ownership. Today all stations are alike, in sight, smell, and sound. Variety has given way to efficiency. That is the new American way. Gas stations are now as much a part of the assembly line as our automobile factories: quasi-automated activity in modern America applies to retail as much as manufacturing. Alas.

"Light of My Life"

high speed along interstates.* They were themselves part of the passing scene, with vehicles moving past homes, churches, store fronts, many from the last century, almost all from the times, then fondly remembered, before the Great War. That reality, of course, merely increased the danger that Lolita would talk, that their intimacy would be found out, that the authorities would intervene.

Nothing specific about nature or humanity interested Humbert particularly, so he and Lolita wandered aimlessly across the country, seeing with lidded eye. Humbert was absorbed in Lolita, and Lolita was absorbed in varieties of ordinary adolescent discontent as well as the extraordinary suffering of abuse. They traveled in mutual discomfort, each displaced with self and other, neither imagining a love beyond *eros* in one and compulsion in another. In this atmosphere of languid angst, Humbert was not actually going anywhere. The fact of travel, not any destination, was the end in itself. Keep going. Doesn't matter where. Keep Lolita isolated in car and cabin. Humbert had things to do all right, but he did not have places to go. Lovers, especially in that first flash of attraction and interest, are not yet connected to a journey. Journey comes when things might go somewhere, you might have a future; because of this girl you see your life differently. Humbert never got to that point. He was not willing to change anything. Journey is, after all, more internal than automotive.

Humbert's memoir made the road seem endless, and a day spent on a two-lane road would reinforce that impression. Humbert and Lolita had limits of endurance. Time to eat. Time to rest. The driver was adversely affected by the road as was the passenger, though Humbert was never bored. *Eros* is itself is never boring; and besides, driving on two-lane roads was work and required constant attention. Then came the time of decision. Which of the upcoming restaurants advertised along the roadside, and speed was slow enough so one could read the advertisements, seemed the best place to stop? No real way to tell, of course. Every stop was an adventure, and every decision had consequences. How about that small joint?

---

*Endless urban sprawl lay in the future. America, unlike the Europe that Nabokov remembered, is a land of space, and towns grow out rather than up. It's all a matter of efficiency and cost, two attitudes that Nabokov (and Humbert) held in contempt.

Chapter Three: Irregular Adventurers

It looked local. Maybe it was a hidden treasure of indigenous cuisine. Maybe not. And was it clean? Again, hard to say. Usually, the gaudier the sign, the more favorable the impression. Except for the chains, then few indeed. One standby, at least in the East, was Howard Johnson, then advertised as being on "all important roads." The food was undistinguished, the ice cream good, the rest rooms were better than those in gas stations, and at least you knew what you were going to get. But suppose you were between Howard Johnsons, or on an unimportant road? Then it was picking and choosing from local offerings. A soda at a gas station? The most temporary surcease of all, as the soda demanded a stop at a station a few miles further on. In towns, there were drug stores with soda fountains, some of which still had a grill for hamburgers. There were local restaurants, often time-consuming and requiring adult behavior, not always possible for Lolita. There were diners, proclaiming their wares as "Eats" or "Good Eats." The decision was never easy, and always a time of nervous concern for Humbert, who was endangered and offended by Lolita's moods.

Help did exist, in the form of paperback guidebooks, notably the one favored by Lolita, Duncan Hines' *Adventures in Good Eating*, and a competing handbook from the auto club.* Duncan Hines and his competitors tried to combine fact with support for the establishment, a difficult task, but were able to give some valuable general guidance. The traveling food tasters could not cover all places selling eats. There were plenty of eateries, even entire small towns, that fell below the notice of Duncan Hines. They were too small and obscure, too far off the important roads. Obscurity was a recommendation to Humbert, but Lolita preferred, as far as possible, to patronize places that Duncan preferred. Even when recommendations were available, Duncan Hines was not the *Guide Michelin*; Duncan and his troops concentrated on adequacy not excellence. Provincial America is not provincial France.

---

*It is fair to say that these guidebooks were a first step, a pre-digestive to the onrushing homogenization of the seething confusion of wide America's culture. The fact that not just Lolita, but Humbert too, loved using these guidebooks, meant that Humbert preferred getting pre-digested and homogenized information; he was aiming for what had been Accepted by the Ruling Culture, as opposed to being counter-culture and seeking out the undiscovered countries. No real traveler, he.

"Light of My Life"

Things were easier when it came to lodging. Auto courts and motels were quintessentially American, the exact opposite of the European inn and *les grands hotels*. In Europe, inns and hotels brought people together in a temporary community of conviviality and sharing. But American auto courts and motels had precisely the opposite effects on their guests. They isolated people from each other, into separate cabins or separate rooms in larger buildings. People parked in front of their rooms or cabin, thus retaining a more intimate relationship with their cars than with their neighbors. American motor courts imitated the anonymity of apartment life in a great city. People who are physically close do not know their neighbors, or even if they have neighbors. In the days before "continental breakfast" served in the lobby, and when restaurants were usually separate from motels, isolation was carried beyond lodging to meals. In Europe, one went to a hotel or to an inn to be part of a "set": in America, one went to a hotel to be alone, or with one's beloved. Humbert never commented on this aspect of the American road. No one would know this better than the son of an hotelier, who as a child had experienced the communal aspects of hotel living, and had enjoyed the bonbons given him by impecunious Russian princesses who could never pay their bills. Indeed, being part of "the group," being "one of us," was the way Humbert and Annabel met, brought together amidst the general bonhomie of coming together for a while in a *grand hotel*.

Yet isolation, not togetherness, was precisely the reason Humbert undertook the cross-country trips in the first place. Only in nameless motor courts, each isolated from the surrounding town, if even in a town, could Humbert enjoy fully the pleasures of *eros*. Moreover, isolation reinforced fantasy. Lolita could more easily be imaginatively subsumed into the Annabel idyll in the absence of company. Alone, it was just Lolita, pubescent body encasing an American soul, but for the moment, her body could be combined with his imagination into a "circle of paradise." Motels were the favorite spot for furtive assignation in postwar America, because they were comparatively inexpensive. Humbert showed inadequate respect for the American commercial establishments he daily frequented, and whose existence alone sustained and extended his sexual captivity of Lolita.*

---

*Ironically, Humbert self-consciously non–American, lived the fervent college dream of a

Chapter Three: Irregular Adventurers

Auto courts and motels were a sufficiently important part of American travel that the standard purveyors of travel information undertook to describe and catalog them. Duncan Hines and the auto club had guides, but, as with eateries, they could cover only part of what was out there. In 1947, roadside lodgings still resembled the auto courts that played so large a role in the Clark Gable and Claudette Colbert movie *It Happened One Night* (1934).* The lodgings were often wood frame cabins separated by sheds to protect the car. By 1947, auto courts had already had come to seem quaint and obsolete, the result of postwar motels built in the flush of victory-provided-prosperity. The new motels cost more, but the old courts still survived, and Humbert with Lolita in tow, often chose them. They were the best; all too often auto courts struck him as "frightening places," charging ten bucks "for twins," with screenless door, plenty of flies, noisy neighbors, and a "woman's hair ... on the pillow." Getting there is rarely half the fun.

But time was bringing changes to the outer world as well as to the travelers. Humbert observed that the old detached cabins were being welded together into a line of rooms fronted by an asphalt-paved parking lot. The lobby was shrinking to a cubicle devoted to reception rather than sitting. In these early motel days, many still retained local architectural motifs, such as faux mission in the great southwest all the way from Texas to "Los Angeles the Damned."†

The new motor hotels were a step or two up in comfort and cleanliness (usually), but that step was just beginning in these post-war years. The

---

sex-soaked road trip; in the case of Humbert the Clever, extended indefinitely. See the movie *Animal House*. Humbert also embodied the conventional and dingy dream of American businessmen, who take their secretaries and salesgirls out to motels at the edge of town, where they can enjoy (?) a squalid moment of forbidden sex. In Baton Rouge, Louisiana, a Howard Johnson's for years had on its sign the motto "Have Your Next Affair with Us." Doubtless, a great many took their advice.

*The movie was made without a script, with the actors discussing appropriate gestures and dialogue as they went along. They were good at what they did. The film has perfect pitch. Humbert and Lolita tried the same thing. They achieved dissonance. Schubert on the one hand, Schoenberg on the other.

†A phrase used by H. L. Mencken in the pre-war period to describe the massively growing settlement of Los Angeles. He referred to the people rather than the earthquakes; at least it pleases us to think so, and we have included this profoundly Nabokovian sentiment, noting also that Nabokov avoided the pathetic fallacy.

efficiencies of standardization were (are) the American response to the inadequate and the idiosyncratic in every endeavor, and motels and eateries were no exception. Adventures in lodging and eating were progressively replaced by sameness and predictability. The chains would arrive over a couple of decades, from the Golden Arches to variously named inns, and they would offer a standard level of comfort and cooking from coast to coast. Humbert and Lolita were at the dawn of this inevitable transformation from the local to the national. And Humbert preferred it; he was, after all, engaged in "insatiable illicit love." Motels were then still largely individual entrepreneurial efforts, surrounded by "enormous Chateaubriandesque trees."* For Humbert to prefer the new (and clearly philistine) lodging arrangements is a departure from his usual sensibility of irony and disdain. The lapse was only momentary. Humbert was back in form a paragraph later, commenting on the "Sunset Motels, U-Beam Cottages, Hillcrest Courts, Pine View Courts, Green Acres, Mac's Courts."† Compare these hostels, where a pretentious name attempted to conceal an ordinary reality, to the luxurious hotel on the Riviera, where Humbert spent his childhood before the war or safely out of its way, "in a bright world of illustrated books, clean sand, orange trees, friendly dogs, sea vistas and smiling faces." Humbert recalled that around him "the splendid Hotel Mirana revolved as a kind of private universe, a whitewashed cosmos." Keeping the Mirana in mind as he and Lolita shuttled from stop to stop must have increased Humbert's misery exponentially.

For Humbert the child, the Hotel Mirana had been an enclosed garden of joy and beauty, not an elegant collection of temporary homes to rent, which was the experience of its wealthy guests. For young Humbert it was the only home he ever knew, and his only indication of any attach-

---

*Nabokov, *Lolita*, Pt. I, ch. 1, p. 145. Humbert has probably merged his impressions of the Lolita tours with memories of the Rita tour. Motels ordinary in the Rita years were still in the future, after the mesozoic motel time of Lolita. This may be thought of as another Humbertian prevarication, but we do not base this essay on the notion that Humbert lied about everything.

†Nabokov, *Lolita*, Pt. I, ch. 1, p. 146. U-Beam cottages does not seem like a repetitious name. Author Hardy's family traveled quite a bit in the period 1946–56, and I do not recall seeing a single iteration of that establishment. We can find only a single definition of U-Beam contemporary to *Lolita*, and that is a steel support structure. Still, it certainly meant something specific to Nabokov. But what?

Chapter Three: Irregular Adventurers

ment to place. Everywhere else, whether the Pine View Courts or Ramsdale or Paris, Humbert was passing through.

Although Lolita had always known a home, though occasionally a difficult one, she was now as homeless as her captor. Humbert provided her instead with the same simulacrum he made do with for most of his own life: rental lodgings. Of course, Lolita got a cheapened form of lodging. While Humbert had known the real thing at the Hotel Mirana, with pre-war elegance and, later, "ruined Russian princesses," Lolita was put up in the American provincial version of hotels with pools, and, in California, tennis courts. Her taste for luxurious accommodations was not usually indulged by her "indulgent papa," whose criteria for lodging included privacy, the ordinary, the unobtrusive, and the economical.

The nocturnal substitute for home was succeeded, daily, by a search for amusement tedious for both parties. Humbert just wanted to keep Lolita from revolting; Lolita wanted respite from Humbert's insatiable assaults. The normal entertainments enjoyed by a traveling family held desperate though transient significance for both Humbert and Lolita. Museums, even movies and swimming pools, were barely adequate to keep Humbert's companion "in passable humor from kiss to kiss." None of these entertainments offered comfort.

Humbert found that Lolita was not much interested in scenery either, though they saw it all, from plantation homes to Yellowstone National Park to Jekyll Island, Georgia to the Corn Palace in Mitchell, South Dakota. Occasionally, they'd run across a ghost of "home" ironically surfacing. In a collection of old postcards, Humbert proudly pointed out one of the Hotel Mirana, "its striped awnings, its flag flying above the retouched palm trees. Lo was unimpressed, muttering "So what?" as she eyed a tanned and wealthy young man.* How could the uprooted Lolita evince any sentimentality for her captor's childhood residence? Home meant little to Lolita within that context.

The idea of home holds a central place in literature, and especially in memoir. Familiarity breeds a sense of comfort. Everyone (except, appar-

---

*A ghost of the young Humbert appears here in the Mississippi resort. Recall the photo of that tanned and wealthy young man taken during the Annabel episode.

ently, Humbert) feels the warmth of the *heimlich*, the home-like, with its pervasive sense of a known world where things are ordered and persons are in control.* This sense of the *heimlich*, of right order, excludes bare *eros*, with its intense and focused beam falling on one person alone, to the exclusion of place and general attitudes. Marital love is the natural abode of the *heimlich*; no one wishes to eat dinner alone. In spite of communal snacks at the soda shop, neither Humbert nor Lolita had a home in each other. For both, home was for other people. Humbert accepted this, but Lolita mourned it. Lolita recognized home in a poignant moment with Avis Byrd and her father. Did she grasp that home meant the connection of person to community, or was it merely a vignette of ordinary family life? She did love to read wedding announcements published in local papers of the towns that she and Humbert went through. No matter that she knew none of the couples. Was this simply movie fantasy? Or a sense that family merged into community? Humbert's memoir mentions but does not explain. No surprise for a man who grew up in a hotel, who as an adult imitated his father in peripatetic liaison. But for Lolita, home was never where Humbert was.

Nabokov illustrated the *unheimlich* by indirection, in Humbert's description of the scenery around them, in the towns they passed through, in the homes and histories of others, fading into the distance. The travelers gazed at endless scenery, both natural and social, from vistas of mountain and forest to graceful homes in quaint little villages. Humbert saw antebellum homes and "frontier lore" as scenes in a frame, hopelessly distant from him. Scenes from human life did not originate as *unheimlich*, but they now represented dislocation. The antebellum structures, now become museums, were no longer homes for anyone. The alienation of the *unheimlich* is something the war refugee Nabokov could represent very well.

The framed American landscape appeared in the memoir contrapun-

---

*See the essay by Sigmund Freud, *The Uncanny* (1919), intro. Hugh Haughton, trans. David McLintock (New York: Penguin, 2003). The German title is *Das Unheimliche*, which refers both to uncanny and unhomelike, and manifests itself in obsessive-compulsive repetition. Though this behavior is usually on a small scale, such as washing hands compulsively, the scope may be extended to include Humbert's obsessive return to *les fruits verts*. As we are not psychologists, we have not emphasized the Freudian connections, but we wish to note that they may be made. By others.

Chapter Three: Irregular Adventurers

tally with Lolita's moods and sulks and whines and distance, all becoming more irritating to Humbert as they did not diminish. What could be more pathetic, or funnier, than *eros* faced with whine? What could hurt the ardent and erotic lover more than a relentlessly normal, hormonal, trivial teenager? Only loneliness.

Humbert wrote almost nothing in his memoir about loneliness, though he did describe himself as self-marginalized, and also often alone. These functioned both as cause and effect, reinforcing each other in an endless circle of detachment, both social and psychological from the world around him. This applies to everyone, of course. For Humbert, isolation was physical, and exile far from home. Not psychological, exile far from comfort. Even though he was never more alone than when he was with Lolita, Humbert did not convert mere lack of company or friends into a permanent interior condition of loneliness. he did not succumb to the depths of existential angst. Or at least, he never admitted it.

Humbert's failure to connect being alone with being lonely shows Nabokov's skill at its most subtle. Here, the message appears more in what he did not write than what he did write. Always careful with chronology and setting, Nabokov omitted entirely the then-dominant cultural setting of existentialism in its endless explorations of aloneness.* During the two decades after Hiroshima, existentialism was fashionable, and thus a current aspect of literature and philosophy.† No less an authority than Anna Wintour, the present editor of *Vogue*, has asserted that no one is immune from prevailing cultural currents; they surround us and inform our attitudes. And yet, "alone" is in Humbert's memoir. He vaguely senses a problem with that. But he doesn't define himself as isolated by his own human nature. He thinks the problem is a lack of connection with another person. Everybody's made that mistake before.

Being grander than the rest of us, Humbert believes that his condition

---

*It is possible that Nabokov left existentialism out for reasons of personal hostility to, and disbelief in, philosophy. But we think that omission through hostility is not the case here. With Nabokov, one must always look for indirection. Just because a topic (existential aloneness) is out does not mean that it has no effect on what is in. Like Hamlet, one looks behind the arras.

†Need we go beyond Camus, Sartre, and Beckett? Or Nietzsche, for that matter, in the previous generation?

"Light of My Life"

is more dire, and the solution more dramatic and passionate than anyone else's. Fortunately, he is possessed by a great erotic and aesthetic spirit. Reserved for him alone are the full delights of love. Love can be the cure, not just the problem. For an ardent soul like Humbert, the Aristophanic connection can be made; he will be borne by the powers of erotic love. And then, whatever's wrong will become right. He will be cured. To the memoirist's bewilderment, that does not happen within the pages of *Lolita*.

Humbert's refusal to directly consider his essential aloneness has two main consequences. One, regarding his role as memoirist, and the other regarding the readers. In the case of Humbert, failure to recognize existential loneliness, like the absence of guilt, reinforces his story that his search for a nymphet to exploit is right and appropriate. For the readers, it is a subtle reminder that Humbert is not so different from us, and we are not so far from him. Matters of degree and intensity alone separate us from the writer of a memoir of unusual love. While readers do not generally follow where Humbert leads, all watch with uneasy recognition.

Humbert himself summed up his uncomfortable position in a single terrible moment, repeated with oracular emphasis in the various auto courts and cabins.

> And sometimes trains would cry in the monstrously hot and humid night with heartrending and ominous plangency, mingling poem and hysteria in one desperate scream.*

De profundis, Humbert understood that, perhaps screaming silently along with the Doppler-shifted wail of the engine's voice, always at its most mournful away from home. It goes without saying that Lolita screamed silently as well. Loneliness, for beloved as well as lover, is the inevitable accompaniment of love excessive, defective, or misdirected.

Lovers often hear loneliness as "heartrending plangency," the endless loneliness, the call of possibility missed, drifting through a "monstrously hot and humid night." So do prisoners. They too believe that their misery will be relieved, if only, if only, if only.... There was a half-believed story

---

*Nabokov, *Lolita*, Pt. I, ch. 1, p. 146. We all remember such moments, when loneliness seems overwhelming and distance endless. For most, it is a moment. For Humbert, it was a lifetime.

Chapter Three: Irregular Adventurers

that circulated through Parchman prison in Mississippi. If the head-light from a passing night-time train fell upon a prisoner, that man would soon be released.* "Let that light shine on me" was the fervent prayer of many an inmate, and that same prayer, with different words but similar meaning, fit Humbert's anxious moments between sex and sleep. As for Lolita, Humbert blandly observes that she broke into soft "sobs in the night — every night, every night," the moment she thought he had fallen asleep. Lolita was as much a prisoner of circumstance as Humbert was of lust, for "she had absolutely nowhere else to go." In an asymmetrical relationship, the lover is always importunate, while the beloved is always trapped.

As they traveled, Humbert and Lolita almost blended in, and the peculiarities of their relationship were never quite apparent to the Americans they briefly saw. Humbert and Lolita lived in the Twilight Zone of travel, where one is at a place but never of it. They were like butterflies, stilled for a moment in the warm air rising from a field. Then they were gone, both insects and irregular adventurers.

American Popular Culture

Humbert's discontent with the America through which they traveled began with Lolita, and spilled over into everything he saw.† Their difficult relationship merged into depressing exterior details, from hot fudge sundaes to movies and radio. If the center of one's life is broken, everything appears to poor effect, as less than it ought to be. Exterior environment often reflects interior disappointment.

Yet, even without a petulant Lolita in tow, Humbert would not have admired America. Lolita's embrace of song and show, which she preferred to him, merely added another level to Humbert's contempt. He believed in the essential trashiness of American popular culture, into which Lolita

---

*From Leadbelly.
†Oddly enough, the more European the scenery, the less Humbert desired Lolita. When he finally discovered an American beach that resembled the Riviera, he was shocked to discover that he felt no more desire for her than he would "for a manatee." Still, it must be suggested that what the manatee lacked in physical allure it made up for in friendliness.

constantly immersed him. Humbert, of course, was not alone in his disdain for American culture. It was fashionable then, as it is now, for Europeans, including Nabokov, to look down their noses at all things American, particularly popular culture. European culture was so much older, more elegant, less philistine, less commercial, less oriented towards consumption.* And the bad taste: Europeans thought that everything American simply reeked of it. Nabokov reflected the continental view, which he impishly inserted into the Humbert persona. Snobbish Americans, that is to say, the pretentious on both coasts, bought into this disdain with glee and enthusiasm. No one hated standard America, from suburbs to hamburgers to movies, more than an artistic, literary, or academic liberal.†

Americans had internalized this sense of cultural inferiority long before Nabokov described it. No sooner had the Civil War ended than Yankees (Southerners were now broke) began to go abroad to "get culture." Mark Twain, a journalist as well as a novelist, was the first to comment on this phenomenon in *The Innocents Abroad* (1869), but he was followed by others, notably Henry James, and the painter James A. MacNeil Whistler, both to England, and Mary Cassatt, to Paris. The custom did not end with the Gilded Age.‡ After the Great War came Ernest Hemingway, F. Scott Fitzgerald, and even Aaron Copland. Prohibition assisted in the migration, by adding booze abroad to a pervasive sense of disappointment in a country that would ban it at home. By the time Nabokov came to America in 1940, the sense of American inferiority was well established on both sides of the pond, and it would have been astonishing had

---

*Part of this attitude may have been poverty. See Fredrik Bergstrom and Robert Gidehag, *EU Versus USA* (Stockholm: Timbro, 2004). Bergstrom and Gidehag note that if the countries of the EU were compared to states in the United States in gross domestic product, only Luxembourg would have been in the top ten. The EU itself would have been in the bottom five, below Oklahoma but above Arkansas. Great Britain, Portugal, and Spain rank below Mississippi, which is pretty far down. This comparison was made almost sixty years after the setting of *Lolita*, and fifty years after its writing. Nothing like poverty to produce envy expressed as contempt.

†The conventional wisdom holds that the McCarthy-era hearings were a cause for this alienation. Perhaps, in part. The Beat generation was certainly well on its way by 1953. For the Cornell version, see Charles Thompson's *Halfway Down the Stairs* (1957).

‡In those days, of course, Europe was the place to make a pilgrimage to, not a place to flee from. Hitler would change all that.

Chapter Three: Irregular Adventurers

Humbert, an European refugee, not participated in the by now standard contempt.*

Nothing separated Lolita from Annabel so much as Lolita's lack of European cultural polish. Lolita was an American teenager to the core. Still, if she had really been the new Annabel, returning Humbert's passion, he might well have made himself at home in the land of the free. When love succeeds, there is less to criticize. During the period with Annabel, though Humbert had cordially despised the Leighs, everything else on the Riviera had seemed to please him mightily. He did not show, or at least did not include, the standard youthful disdain for the established culture of his elders. Had Lolita only loved him....

When love failed, as it did consistently for Humbert after Annabel, even Paris, the city of light, became dull and dingy. And Humbert never displayed a nostalgic thought for Paris of the *entre-guerre*. Nor was there any magic in postwar America, even though it was the center of competitive tennis. Snobbishness and sniffage is in part an affectation always.

So much for Humbert. What about Lolita? Her captor was forced to acknowledge that she was full of opinions and attitudes. If Lolita did not love Humbert, it did not mean she loved nothing at all. She delighted in romantic radio ballads, in movies, and in helpful magazine articles which gave counsel on how to succeed at youthful romance ("Girls, tuck your shirt-tails into your jeans"). Indeed, she loved the idea of love, of being

---

*See, for example, Robert Frank, *The Americans* (Paris: Robert Delpine, 1958), a book of photographs from the Humbert-trip years, 1947–1953. Frank came to America in 1947, touring in reality in the same year that Humbert and Lolita were touring in fiction. Like Humbert, Frank endeavored to portray the philistine vileness of American consumerism, highlighting the hypocritical contradictions in American culture, along with its vast mediocrity. Frank was particularly hostile to *Life* magazine, where photojournalism portrayed happy stories and tended toward narrative completion. The French, of course, were delighted to publish this kind of stuff, and it made Frank famous (on both coasts).

Since "getting culture" abroad usually involved disparagement of what went on at home, a number of Americans other than Frank published books on how bad things were here. But criticism of America could be done without succumbing to the disease of European superiority. See H. L. Mencken, who opposed much in America without supporting much of anything abroad. The norm was still to internalize foreign scorn. We note this ongoing phenomenon to indicate that Humbert was not alone in his sniffage, although his scorn came from a genuine European background. He plugged into an ongoing part of the American psyche. Nabokov specialized in irony.

"Light of My Life"

in love (at least in theory), despite a distaste for the self-described moodily romantic Humbert.

Lolita fit the time perfectly, that postwar interval where romantic love, so important a part of wartime relationships, still continued on as the soul of American popular culture.* She had the essential American optimism that things are going to get better, that love is just around the corner. Lolita absorbed a vision of life that had hope, beauty, and fulfillment. No surprise that popular culture just entranced her.† Out there somewhere was the guy for her. Out there somewhere was the home she did not have. It was then (and remains) the adolescent American dream. "Dream a little dream of me" is a perennial American sensibility of hope.‡

Her belief in the unifying and uplifting power of romantic love enabled Lolita to avoid the suffocating erotic attachment that Humbert pressed relentlessly upon her. Romance was then culturally defined as the lover respecting his beloved, rather than relentlessly attempting to engulf her. Humbert did not treat Lolita like the guys in movies treated their girls.

---

*This is before Bill Haley, and "Rocking Around the Clock" and "Shake, Rattle and Roll Those Pots and Pans." That didn't come before the early fifties. Before that, it was still the longing of love, as one can see from the stuff that appeared on "Your Hit Parade." In movies, romance and the longing of love continued on without missing a beat, although the great stars faded and their replacements (Sandra Dee, Bobby Darrin, et al.) were not up to the old standards. Of course, they never are.

†After the Great War, the Russian classicist Mihkhail Rostovtzeff remarked that one did not yet know whether a democratic society could produce a genuine high culture. Nabokov, in a work of fiction, answered that comment in the negative. But that judgment was strictly personal. The American historian and Librarian of Congress Daniel Boorstin published *The Image* (1961) in which he described the degraded, though not yet depraved, state of American popular culture. In *The Image*, Boorstin described American culture as nothing but surface, and gaudy and junky surface at that. He included the first definition of "celebrity," a person who is well-known for being well-known. Boorstin reflected Nabokov's attitudes and Rostostoteff's query in terms of an entire culture.

Of course, this was only 1961. In 1998, Neil Gabler published a sequel of cultural criticism, *Life: The Movie* in which he argued that the entire culture had become celebrity-driven, with acting now taking place, not on stage, screen, or radio, but in real life, with the media merely the message. In 1953–55, when Nabokov was writing *Lolita*, things had not gone that far, and popular culture was still something watched or heard rather than acted out.

‡This perennially popular song was recorded first in 1931 by Ozzie Nelson. In the 40s, it was a vehicle for Frankie Laine, in the 50s for Doris Day, in the 60s, The Mamas and the Papas. NPR produced a special on the song, declaring it one of the most important pieces of American popular music. The gentle, wistful hopefulness appealed to Americans across Depression, war, prosperity.

Chapter Three: Irregular Adventurers

Beyond her interest in love, Lolita also simply wanted to have fun, like girls do. She leapt at every opportunity to interact with the world around her. She would talk to anybody, shop anywhere; she longed to join the society that Humbert so shrilly despised. As time was passing, she was maturing into a citizen of this world. Teen-agers wish to fit in, to be part of the culture, not remain tourists of the passing scene. Love songs for Lolita replaced competitive tennis for Annabel. Since Lolita's insistent interest in American popular culture, an emblem of her drive to find a persona, nothing Humbert said or did could deter her. Of course, teens are like that.

The acculturation of this nymphet meant that she would fit the Annabel fantasy even and ever less. The more Lolita was shaped as American, the less Humbert could join fantasy and sexuality into a rational direction for his seedy life. Lolita was grasping America's unique national culture by the only handle she could, given her age and her orphan status — the portion produced by the entertainment industry. But Lolita's attention, distracted by radio and movies, did not diminish Humbert's erotic attachment, though it did stimulate his easily aroused sense of disdain and snobbery. Humbert did the sensible thing and took out his erotic dissatisfaction upon the world around him rather than upon his unloving beloved.

Eros going nowhere made Humbert grumble about Lolita's unsophisticated preferences and attitudes, and hardened his opinion of American pop culture. Lolita exhibited a (for Humbert) wayward aesthetic exuberance primarily in three ways, through movies, through popular magazines, including those devoted to movies (*Photoplay*), and through pop music disseminated by radio. Movies for Lolita and Humbert were a formal though frequent ceremony of surveillance and "togetherness" that required prior planning and time set aside, while the magazines were Lolita's private and silent devotion to the fads and trends of the day. The car radio, which Lolita insisted she must control, poured out popular music endlessly. It bathed listeners in sentimental popular music, sung almost off-key in the nasal tones which then passed for smooth and comforting. In the late forties, nationally popular music ran more to the romance of "Some Enchanted Evening," from *South Pacific*, than to the turmoil described by

Elvis Presley in "All Shook Up," a hit from the next decade. Lolita loved the singers and their songs, and the romance they purveyed. What should have favored Humbert, she used as a substitute for him. Popular music certainly suggested that love meant more than sex — at least in 1947 it did.

Lolita saw in magazines and movies a broader world than presented in the romance of "Your Hit Parade." They functioned as oracles of truth and style, infallibly bringing the secrets of instant popularity and belonging. Despite the cynicism of youth, Lolita believed in the silver cinema dreams and the ads in magazines. Worldly about sex, she was naive about all else. The entertainment industry of America in the late forties created a veneer of sophistication, of "glam," a hint of the smart, to which the aspiring teen or nymphet could measure current condition and social longings. These sensibilities were not confined to Lolita. Magazines from *Seventeen* to *Redbook* and *McCall's* both filled and expanded the cultural niche of feminine desires.

Lolita's romantic imagination, reaching for social confidence, became a primal means for blotting out Humbert's erotic overtures. He may have "worked his wicked will" upon her, as the old phrase went, but Lolita, while constantly touched, remained untouched. Romance has uses that are not primarily erotic, and *eros* is rarely romantic. This was clear to Humbert. The popular emphasis on romance, he glumly understood, contradicted the erotic desires that he inflicted upon Lolita, and undermined the impression of generosity of spirit that he attempted to convey in his memoirs. For Humbert, the message and its medium, popular culture, was the visible enemy.

It was also the outward manifestation of Lolita's interior independence. Popular songs and romantic comedies showed them both by contrast that this trip was merely an extended kidnap. Although reluctant to state that bald fact for the record, Humbert did not deny it. He retained the idea that the end justified the means, and kidnap was made legitimate by love, love as he defined it, at least.

Popular culture, in the structure of *Lolita*, represents the incompatibility between the irregular adventurers. That division Humbert could neither bridge nor finesse. As it grew, Lolita became more and more her own person. As she matured inexorably beyond the nymphet, her identification with her surrounding culture would only accentuate the abyss

Chapter Three: Irregular Adventurers

that divided her from Humbert. Humbert acknowledges this reality as he describes the moment of their return from the first road trip to house and school. Lolita, immediately upon entering the house, plopped herself down on the sofa and reached for her stash of popular magazines. Culturally, "home" was no different from travel.

Lolita's instinctive reach and grasp embraced the products of the entertainment industry whatever the location, as the need for self-definition is independent of place. Isolation with Humbert meant becoming an anti–Humbert. As Lolita began to integrate, however imperfectly, into a school society, Humbert moved from the center of her life to a pitied periphery. Before she left Humbert, all at once and cold turkey, as it were, she had long since left him psychologically and culturally. Slowly and imperceptibly, she slipped beyond his grasp.

Ironically, Lolita's road toward individual identity embraced the social conventions she did not live. She absorbed the attitudes of settled-and-living-at-home seventh-grade girls, while being as unlike them as one could be and still participate in mainstream American culture. Of course, it could hardly be otherwise. The road trips with Humbert were far removed from the ordinary rhythms of American teen existence. Still, a girl can dream.

In his memoir, Humbert derided America as a nation of philistines, from their incessant boosterism, to their gaudy ties, their crass passion for pelf, their popular "music" and movies and magazines, each thing separately philistine, all together a great philistine heap of trash and ersatz. But he didn't complain for the sake of complaining. If successful, his efforts would bring readers to his side. He called upon them to join a Humbertian clique of sophisticates, who were above it all, who appreciated a culture more sophisticated than "Eddy" and "Jo." Humbert derided the bogus substitutes for art, and he tried to carry the reader with him in a conspiracy of disdain and a fellowship of snobbery. He adopted the characteristic adolescent maneuver of trying to be one-up.

But, we suggest, Humbert went a sneer too far. It is not true that late 40's American popular culture, with its emphasis on love and romance and dream, lacked *philia*. Popular music may have been aesthetically pedestrian (and would get much, much worse), but the cultural intentions were not bad at all, defining the attitudes of the young in terms of love rather than death.* Moreover, the basic themes in postwar American media frequently centered around love as uplift, and was less static than Humbert recognized. Not only did the songs, movies, and mags of the day emphasize love as *romance* and *philia*, they usually believed in the good and the true, as two 1946 films, *The Best Years of Our Lives* and *It's a Wonderful Life*, innocently and successfully showed.†

The road, with its endless radio and movies, its motels, cafes, and tourist attractions, could be only a temporary solution to the problem of loving Lolita. Humbert was chasing a moving target. His adolescent beloved, like all adolescents, beloved or not, was always changing. Movement through space could not halt movement through time. Their trip could not last forever; anyhow, Humbert could only have been relieved to park the fractious adolescent among her own kind. In August 1948, Humbert settled in Beardsley, a town that housed a "comparatively sedate school for girls." Humbert himself would teach at the nearby college. Both would fit in well enough to escape hostile detection in the fluid society of a college town. Would this help? It would certainly relieve Humbert of the burden of entertaining a no-longer-nymphet whose interests and attitudes diverged ever farther from his own. Teens, for most adults, are in long stretches really tiresome. It can only have been worse for Humbert.

No matter where one lives, nor in what culture, instruction of the young is a universal human undertaking. Whether it's ballroom dancing or use of an atlatl, the young must be taught necessary and appropriate skills. It takes time. Teens learn slowly. It takes repetition. Teens don't pay attention very well. It takes organization. Teens will beat you down faster than anything, as Humbert was discovering. It takes law: rules with sanc-

---

*In *Madame Bovary*, Charles was a poor clod in nearly every respect, but his love was genuine and his intentions were always good. Humbert showed only half those virtues, and, lacking *philia* and good intentions, could well-read Humbert charm, entice, and win Lolita? No, he could not.

†Both movies are considered to belong in the top 100 films, by virtually every listing of that elite group that has ever been made. *The Best Years of Our Lives* had the additional distinction of employing an actual disabled veteran, Harold Russell, who won two Oscars, one for best supporting actor. Perhaps "Homer" is reflected in Dick's friend Bill. Perhaps not. To our knowledge, Nabokov never said.

Chapter Three: Irregular Adventurers

tions. Teens listen to power. Humbert could provide none of this on his own, but school could provide it all. School it would have to be.

The Beardsley school provided another element of American culture for Humbert to insult in his memoir. Humbert was contemptuous of the educational theories trotted out to impress credulous and philistine parents. Headmistress Pratt had the marketing patter down pat. Learn skills for success, which for young girls in 1948 generally meant marriage and family. Out with Shakespeare, in with social psychology As always, schools were serving parental and public demand. The school was interested in Expression, which included dating, dance, drama, and debate. These "four D's" were, of course, a burlesque, but not by much, as is the case with educational administration. Still, when Headmistress Pratt announced that "Words without experience are meaningless" she made some foggy sense.* The real goal of the school, honored in deeds as well as words, was to understand daily living, and the moral judgments that required.† Despite the Beardsley School's primitive presentation of its goals, they grew out of the same attitude about education that emerged from Aristotle's *Nicomachean Ethics*. Humbert scoffed, of course, but mainly to cover an uneasiness that the school was really interested in moral education. He did not, perhaps, wish to dip beneath the surface of the headmistress' words. They might apply to him. He might then have realized that the lines between school and camp and life had just about disappeared; his own endless extracurricular seminar in love was a particularly wicked illustration of the Pratt theory of education. Both emphasized "learning by doing" and ignored the traditional approach to education.

During her initial educational sales pitch, the accidentally apt Headmistress Pratt blundered into an historical allusion that bespoke fantasy to her and reality to Humbert. She asked, rhetorically, how could a modern

---

*Nabokov, *Lolita*, Pt. II, ch. 4, p. 178. In post–John Dewey America, educational aims, goals, and principles tend to appear in turgid circumlocution, an inheritance of Dewey's admiration for Marx. Nevertheless, just because educational expressions sound stupid, this does not mean that they are. Progressive education, no matter how it sounded, seeks to turn raw students into useful and moral citizens. In this case, the school administration worried that young Dolly, while looking prim enough, was swearing like a sailor. Routine blasphemy was not, in 1948, the road to social success, though that has probably changed.

†Aristotle: "For what we learn, we learn by doing."

girl like "Dorothy Hummerson care for Greece and the Orient with their harems and slaves?" Humbert himself had a one-slave harem, which he intended to keep, to which end he had been reassured to learn that despite terribly modern edu-babble, the school itself was still "as prim as a prawn."*
He doubted that Lolita would escape from Humbertian slavery within a school that was prim in fact. Beardsley would serve parental demand in this instance as well.

In fact, the clotted educational patter from Headmistress Pratt was one of the reasons that Humbert placed Lolita in the school. *En effet*, he didn't wish to give his "darling" a rigorous mental challenge. Sharpening her analytical skills might help her escape captivity. On the one hand, he complained about her ignorance and apathy; on the other, he needed to preserve it. Domestic slavery is always a difficult institution to manage.†

While Humbert mocked Headmistress Pratt's pitch, he liked her attitude. It appealed to Humbert the snob and to Humbert the captor. "We, who know and care, will lead and enlighten the unfortunate and probably unhappy masses who so obviously need our generous help." That attitude of condescension fit Humbert perfectly, who had a lifelong habit of looking disapprovingly down from a great height upon the place beneath. On this occasion, Humbert's disapproval in theory was matched by Lolita's disapproval from experience. A profoundly unhappy life at home added to typical adolescent rebellion made school particularly uncongenial for her, and she was soon cited for working below her potential and not finding an interest in her studies. Perhaps, indeed probably, Lolita's behavior deteriorated a bit at Beardsley since she was suddenly able to compare her life with that of other girls. The school's instinctive response was to call Humbert, not Lolita, to the principal's office. He was informed that Lolita's grades were "getting worse and worse." Pratt attributed this, in her fashionable way, to sex, though she had no idea exactly how. Fortunately for

---

*Nabokov, *Lolita*, Pt. II, ch. 4, p. 178. We have no idea as to the relative primness of a prawn. "Prim as a petticoat" has a certain resonance.

†*Lolita*, written between 1952 and 1955, appeared too early for modern feminism. Feminist criticism is, therefore, something of a cultural anachronism, unless, of course, one believes the laws of academic feminism have the same weight as the law of gravity. We have, therefore, omitted feminist critiques.

Chapter Three: Irregular Adventurers

Humbert. She fell back on psychobabble: Lolita was "still shuttling ... between the anal and genital zones of development." Pratt expanded on her analysis: "All I mean is that the biologic and psychologic drives — do you smoke — are not fused in Dolly, do not fall so to speak into a — into a rounded pattern."

Well. Pratt coupled the right instincts with the wrong words. She bumblingly sketched it as a failure of essential personal roundness (an ovoid psyche, or some protuberances, perhaps even disturbing rhomboidal tendencies) which could represent a developmental disorder. Pratt could not say more. The diagnosis may have been crazy but the malady was not, no surprise, since the nymphet was bearing, under constant sexual abuse, the loss of her mother, and of her home. It's what they call "acting out" these days. The Headmistress was not entirely a dim bulb. She had a prescription as well as a diagnosis. Lolita should take part in a play at Beardsley school, and thus participate in the "natural recreations of a normal child." The play would be by a modern playwright, relevant to a modern girl in modern America.

Lolita took a part in the play, enjoyed acting, began to make some friends: a tribute to her resilience, and, even, to Pratt's acumen. Perhaps Pratt was a better popular psychologist than Humbert, and knew more about Lolita than Humbert did. Had a few weeks in school yielded for her a better grasp on Lolita's personality than a year on the road had for him? Isolation dissolved into student community, something that Humbert could not prevent.* There were parties, dances, and then the play. Lo was becoming a full-blown adolescent.

And thus, as every parent could predict, Humbert was falling further into the periphery. Despite his constant effort, time and community were carrying Lolita beyond his reach. His lust remained intact, but nothing else did. Humbert's desire for stasis was contradicted daily by the energetic

---

*We argue, though only from anecdotal evidence, that junior high and high school are often the "worst years of our lives." This is probably not the fault of the school, but rather reflects the growing pains of puberty, social awkwardness, uncertain future, lack of useful work, and not being on the football team or the cheerleader squad. Nevertheless, school is not without its benefits, principally offering adolescents an alternative to the smothering, restricted world of childhood and home. At school, one has an opportunity to act and interact, however badly.

American culture around him, reinforced by Lolita's relentless development and growing connections to community. Lolita's relationship to the world around them provided an insight on modern America superior to Humbert's ancestral aristocratic European judgment. To the standards of class and aesthetics, Humbert added a personal contempt for the American interest in money and business.* A practical, business-doing people were Philistines, one and all.

Completely immune to Humbert's efforts to shape her personality, Lolita provisionally made a home within herself, first on the road and then at Beardsley. She never lost connection with the wider world. No Stockholm syndrome for Lolita. Her focused efforts to craft her own persona had defeated Humbert's voracious appetite to remake her into something who would always be his. Lo fought back, not just in what she rejected but also what she embraced. Humbert knew what the cultural divide meant: "Between a Hamburger and a Humberger, she would — invariably, with icy precision — plump for the former.†

Lolita's Langorous Glow

Love imparts value to the caress, more than the other way around. Age or stage aside, Humbert's central problem remained. Lolita did not love him, so his caresses, no doubt skilled, awoke in Lolita no ardor, but were felt by her as an irritant. Humbert was not unaware of this, but he suppressed an awareness of how ridiculous his situation had become. Over the years together, he was constantly oppressed and irritated by Lolita's

---

*The continuing tension, indeed, mutual exclusivity between *eros* and bourgeois materialism crops up in teenagers' blithe assertions that they don't need money to be happy. Flaubert's Madame Bovary stands as a permanent refutation of that airy youthful misconception. Emma, a woman of passion, found she could only be passionate in the presence of money. Money bought time, things, excitement, distance, and disguise, the raw physicality of sex in someone else's bed. What is groping in daylight becomes seduction and surrender through gauze and by candlelight. The upper levels of prostitution are built on this fact.

†Nabokov, *Lolita*, Pt. II, ch. 3, p. 166. And good grief, who wouldn't? Sexual abuse or nourishment — is the choice all that difficult? Only a moral blockhead like Humbert would blame Lolita's choice on brainwashing by crass "popular" culture. This excerpt brilliantly illustrates Humbert's enormous sin, swaddled here in his snobbery.

Chapter Three: Irregular Adventurers

"fits of disorganized boredom, intense and vehement griping," as much the result of her age as his own fervid abuse of her. Such anxiety is not uncommon of female early adolescents, in a period now called "the tweens," when they are entering the full social and hormonal horrors of the teen years. In this tempestuous time, vast mood swings alternate between "this will make me popular and cool" and "that will ruin my whole life forever." Mothers have long noticed that those years of full and glorious nymphetness, eleven and twelve, and perhaps thirteen, are the worst time of all, with girls at once sullen, depressed, weepy, uncertain, insecure, disorganized, passive, and more, always more.

Humbert noticed it too, despite his infatuation and erotic passion, and he took personally Lolita's "blue sulks" and her desperate passions accompanied by inconstancy, with everything deeply felt for a short time. In the nymphet years, the banal, the mutable, and the moment assume genuine importance, with neither judgment nor perspective to divide what matters from what does not. Humbert probably never understood that Lolita was displaying not the fickleness of the mature romantic lover but merely the constant kvetch of the young, along with sulks, temper, and endless demands for stuff, and an utter disregard for anyone's needs or convenience beyond her own. Everything aforementioned proclaimed the nymphet years, common to all passing through them, whether they were nymphets or not. It would have been true of Annabel had the brief idyll extended into life. That it did not left Humbert woefully unprepared to deal with a nymphet in the real, not magical and enclosed world.

This was bad enough for an adult, especially a European adult trained in decorum, but he saw worse: "presumption." Since she was an American, Humbert was convinced, Lolita lacked modesty, of any sort. She was "nervy," that is to say, she spoke her tiny little mind filled with conventional claptrap. She had been debauched, not just physically, which was bad enough, but morally and intellectually as well, by the American addiction to campfires, coeducation, and sexual license. Lolita was utterly absorbed into the adolescent world, which would come to be called "youth culture" in another decade. Humbert judged her as dangerously blasé about what mattered, especially sex, which she viewed as a part of life not dissimilar to cutting one's nails. Youthful cynicism had banished from their relationship all sense of wonder, of glory, of awe, and of hope, not surprisingly. But with all of those detriments and disabilities, she retained for him her "fey charm" as a nymphet. No doubt our memoirist wishes us to recognize how his powerful erotic nature masterfully overcame obstacles and challenges.

Lolita combined youthful cynicism with a deep sense of romance, which she located in popular music with its dreams of blissful love in a perfect world. This, ironically, was not so different from Humbert's own purple fantasies. He too was a romantic; he too looked for the perfect love. But the two similar dreams never connected. Instead, they ran in parallel, with Humbert looking for romance with Lolita (in bed, mostly), and Lolita looking for love on the radio, at the gas stations, and, generally, in every place and person except Humbert. Lolita's symbolic expression of romance came in the popular songs, which dribbled from the radio, note by saccharine lyric. In this, she was no different from every thirteen-year-old girl who wants to get out of the house and sees love as the way to do it. Hence, the popularity of popular music amongst adolescents (of all ages).

Popular music might have lacked aesthetic charm, but it did not lack social resonance. The songs of love implied a sublime experience. For Lolita, that did not come from sex, and she had yet to form, and would not form with Humbert, that net of affection and understanding that gave a context to sex beyond the stark and the furtive. Humbert hoped in vain for that sense of union, with its foundation in *philia*, which he could neither understand nor acquire. He blamed their failure to thrive on Lolita's bad attitude: "There is nothing more cruel than an adored child."

Humbert was forced to acknowledge that the "adored child" was changing, gradually but inexorably, and always for the worse. For Humbert, the change signified a moral failure. He could not, or would not, recognize, that Lolita was growing older. He diagnosed her more aversive (to him) behavior as proof that she was becoming "depraved." Her moral character stooped so far from romance as to demand money for sex. She dragged Humbert with her, as he searched her hiding places and stole the

Chapter Three: Irregular Adventurers

money back. "A fine romance" Fred Astaire had sung a decade earlier, but what was flirtatious there was ironic here.*

Humbert also observed that Lolita's "constant amorous exercise" caused her to cast a special aura, a particular "vibe" (to use slang anterior to this century but not yet begotten when Humbert and Lolita toured the country the second time). It never occurred to him to recognize that Lolita was growing into a teenage girl, beginning to radiate sexuality as a fact of life rather than a fact of moral intention. During the time at Beardsley, Humbert was alarmed to find that Lolita displaying the poise and self-possession of a woman. There was no doubt that the boys who came to the party produced a profound unease in Humbert's psyche. Later, Humbert would project his fear onto the young men who glanced at Lolita on the road. On Lolita's side, a "special langorous glow"; from the boys, "fits of concupiscence"; from Humbert, bewildered discomfort veering toward actual rage.

Lolita's glow, real enough in itself, was intensified by Humbert's guilt and unease. Had his "constant amorous intentions" produced this unholy aura of sexuality in his downy darling? Did his ardor, in true Marxist fashion, carry within itself the seeds of its own destruction? And if so, what in the world could he do about it? He could not stop abusing her. And she could not stop glowing. God, what a mess.

It all seemed odd, both to us and to him. Humbert thought that her sexual accomplishments, including the glow, ought to be turned towards him, the author of her experience and her constant lover. Instead, she charged him money and winked at boys, just the opposite of what it ought to be. We, readers and all, are aware that victims of abuse most often cower rather than glow and strut. They become ever-vigilant, looking always over their shoulders with suspicious glances. If it happened once, it can happen again. *Falsus in unum, falsus in omnium*, say the lawyers, and as with everything in law, it applies to life as a whole.†

---

*The movie was *Swing Time*, starring, of course, Fred and Ginger, with music by Irving Berlin. Who else? Like all Fred and Ginger movies, it concentrated on love. Katharine Hepburn remarked that Fred gave Ginger class, and Ginger gave Fred sex. This combination is a good one to have, both on screen and off.

†This is the prime and central indication of Humbert as an unreliable narrator. We cannot say whether he's trying to fool himself, or us; or if he has succeeded at either. We can merely

"Light of My Life"

Normally, Humbert watched Lolita with a glowering irritation in her moments of what he imagined to be sensual communication with boys. These moments seemed to increase, both in number and intensity, as the trips wore on. On one occasion, he suspected there was more than insolent stares met by soft smiles. He and Lolita were staying at the Chestnut Court, which boasted "nice cabins, damp green grounds, apple trees, an old swing — and a tremendous sunset which the tired child ignored." Among the other travelers was a good-looking young man. Nothing in that, but the guy "for some reason" grinned at Humbert as he passed by. Humbert had been away in town for an hour and a half; he found Lolita sitting on the bed "with a diabolical glow that had no relation" to him. Had the worst happened? There seemed to be evidence, from her filthy sandals, which betrayed "her sinful feet," to her "muddy, moony eyes" to the "singular warmth emanating from her." She had been out. Had she met that boy, the one with the grin?

Humbert went out on the porch to see the young man in the process of leaving. Alarmed, Lolita followed. He pushed her back into the cabin at once and stripped her clothes off. Pursuing "the shadow of her infidelity," he found nothing. The trail was so slight that it vanished from reality into imagination. The Platonic shadow and Aristotelian reality of infidelity remained naked in the cabin, while the boy drove down the road in a station wagon crammed with wife, children, and portable refrigerator. But had this been a hit-and-run encounter? Even that takes time, time that neither party must account for. Humbert had been safely away, but the pregnant wife was sitting on the swing. No matter. If Lolita's romantic swoon was merely the result of unfulfilled desire under the apple trees, the infidelity was still true enough. We recall Humbert and Annabel, so long ago, "unable to mate," but united in lust. Never mind what had really happened in the tourist court, Lolita was now what Humbert had been then. Humbert was excluded, his presence denied, and his erotic obsession dismissed as if it did not exist. In Humbert's "first circle of paradise" he dwelt entirely alone.

[*continued*] say that the phenomenon Humbert describes, while certainly real enough, has been applied to the wrong character.

Chapter Three: Irregular Adventurers

Here, Humbert is entirely honest, recording the paranoia and desperation of a lover not yet completely jilted, but who still knows that his beloved is slipping away, and no charm, no technique, no expense, no "certain manipulations" can arrest the drift apart. Certainly, Lolita was growing away because she was growing up. Age lay at the center of her slow escape. Humbert's memoir gave no reasons for Lolita's growing distance, beyond the malignant influence of (to him) sex-soaked and love-absorbed American pop culture. But the important causes remained at the edge of Humbert's recall. These were time itself, and Lolita's transition from green to ripe fruit.

Lolita's "special langorous glow" struck Humbert on the second trip with sufficient force that he remembered it as an element of virtually every encounter between Dolly and nameless young men. She was older now. The glow had begun to come from within. By now, she was a young woman, enticing to young men.* Humbert reacted to her glow with fear; it hinted at horrible possibilities. What he alone had enjoyed with Lolita might now be enjoyed by others. Lolita might, if everything fell into place, then, well.... The "goons" and "morons" showed interest. Humbert noticed. He tried to discourage their interest with (presumably) protective and paternal glares. And that usually worked, though that did not assuage his paranoia. While Lolita glowed, radiating the photons and pheromones of possibility, Humbert glowered with pride of possession and fear of loss.

Lolita's obvious attractions brought to the surface, from a rancid pool of worry, feelings of insecurity, jealousy, anger, exasperation and more insecurity. Suppose she strayed again, suppose she talked. Suppose she left, or was taken. Humbert knew that the glow was never meant for him. Only if Lolita loved him would her general glow reflect contentment.

---

*After World War II, there was a strong conservative cultural reaction to the dislocations of war. In no area did this more clearly occur than in relationships between respectable (that is, middle class) young people. The casual mores of wartime were swept aside. Society wished to reassert the values of domesticity, fidelity, and incidental sex was relegated to the social margins. This is in stark contrast to what occurred after the Great War, which was the increasing license of the Roaring Twenties. In the late forties and fifties, women were supposed to be both enchantingly attractive and available only for marriage. Men, of course, haven't changed; since then, probably since ever. It was the women who treated sex seriously. Of course, this was before the Pill.

"Light of My Life"

Humbert Tells His Tale

Before he told his tale of Lolita, Humbert had offered, by way of previewing coming attractions, an explanation of the entire nymphet phenomenon. Early in the first part of his memoir, Humbert had broken off the narrative in favor of explanation. We have examined this explanation before, in connection with Annabel, and we now refer to it again. Humbert's report of the magical allure of a nymphet, for those sufficiently sensitive to recognize it, is intended to justify Humbert's life and loves. Humbert was overwhelmed with erotic and aesthetic passion, which had claimed him as a devotee and led him from Annabel to Lolita to death. More, it is intended to induce the reader's admiration. He's so sensitive. His soul is so fine. His love is so immense. How can this person not be a source of wonder and respect?

Humbert needed his readers to sympathize with, if not understand, his situation. He had carefully placed himself in a specific sexual category, that of older men who were erotically attracted to young girls just entering puberty. While not a large group, it was not unknown, either. There were older, sophisticated lovers besides Humbert who were erotically enchanted by "green fruit." There must be reasons for such universal and overpowering erotic passion that could shape an entire life. The reader of the memoir would wish to know all about this. Humbert, who was at his most condescending when he seemed most reasonable, gave the reader two characteristics, as he saw them, of erotic fascination with young girls. The first was the age of the lover, and complementing this was the difficult-to-discern grace of the nymphet. The two must come together; nymphetic grace was useless without the sensitive antennae of the always-searching older lover.

Humbert carefully defined the nature of the nymphet in vague terms, making imprecision a part of his definition. That was the general category of things. In Lolita's case, Humbert was precise, frequently critical, often dismissive, and clearly of two minds. Lolita may have enchanted him with her nymphetic grace, but he did not like her as a person. That fact becomes clear only later. At the beginning, Humbert takes pains to present himself as an aesthete, who passionately admires a certain kind of girl-child. Most

Chapter Three: Irregular Adventurers

"girl children" are not nymphets, but a few are. It is not merely a matter of good looks, but includes

> certain mysterious characteristics, the fey grace, the elusive, shifty, soul-shattering, insidious charm that separates the nymphet from ... coevals of hers....

He was not very precise. His description consists less of visible characteristics than of internal impressions. So, how does one know a nymphet when she glides shiftily into one's presence? Most people, of course, do not. Only the most sensitive could be "in the know." Humbert never explained how one was able to do this. Humbert himself, of course, was a member of this tiny group of *cognoscenti*. He is able to recognize subtle signs, such as "a slightly feline outline of a cheekbone, the slenderness of a downy limb." A feline cheekbone, whatever that is, is not much to go on. You just have to know. Humbert knew.

A hint here and there was the best he could do to "to fix once for all the perilous magic of nymphets." Humbert knew, but did not say until later, that nymphet magic is not permanent. It fades as time passes. Nor was the magic of the nymphet absolute. One person's nymphet was another person's brat. All that Humbert could say with certainty was that the nymphet departed radically from the norm. He could only describe it as a *daimon*, an aberrant spirit. How often does one find a nymphet? Once in a lifetime is a lot, and a lot to ask. Even for Humbert, who recognized nymphets and searched for them relentlessly, that elusive sprite appeared only twice.

It didn't occur to Humbert to wonder at the inner life of nymphets, at their inability to reciprocate their older lover's intense erotic passion. But his own experience bears that out. For nymphets, the lover's skill in the arts of love was not enough; and for Humbert it was close to nothing. Lolita would remain stubbornly resistant. What Humbert called cruelty was simply adolescent indifference, which could be both personal and cultural and in Lolita was certainly both.* Lolita herself would put up with

---

*Humbert's approach to love resembles that of the medieval courtly lover, as in "I burn, and my cruel love ignores me." Lionel Trilling early recognized (and praised) the clichés of courtly love in *Lolita*. In terms of Nabokov's text, though, love in practice diverged from

some Humbertian annoyance, mutter, "Oh, no," when Humbert turned toward her in bed, shrug it off, and return to her own thoughts, which, though she was physically near Humbert, were not about him. The erotic lover is always alone, with no sustained interest in others.*

Although Humbert boasted that he possessed ample sex appeal for mature women, his memoir implies that this attraction did not cross the line to those still becoming women. Sex appeal tends to be culturally specific, being at least as much a matter of cohort fashion as personal dream. Ripe sirens who had sighed over Charles Boyer or Cary Grant were culturally different from the bobby-soxed teens and almost-ready-to-be-teens who felt themselves swept away by Frank Sinatra and his numerous epigoni. As time passed, Humbert's brooding good looks were passing out of style. His European charm and savoir-faire were dated and quaint. His violent need for Lolita also made him ridiculous, even a bit creepy. Alas, poor Humbert, he lacked the romantic tools even to woo Lolita, never mind to win her. For Lolita to love Humbert, the emotional surge would have to come from her, independent of his need or efforts, and that might only happen in the fullness of time, meaning years. That span of time was impossible for either Humbert or Lolita even to imagine.

But nymphets in time become adolescents. In describing this inevitability in Lolita's case, Humbert's rather vague description of a nymphet gives way to the ample compilation of specifics and anecdotes that collectively conjures up Lolita. The two descriptions seemed hardly to belong to the same person. Is it merely time that brings such changes? One would think. But Humbert, when it came to Lolita understood her less and less in terms of feline grace and more and more in terms of moral and sexual corruption. The nymphet ideal was pretty to think of, and Humbert was at some pains

---

[*continued*] the lofty sentiments of courtly love. Humbert slept with Lolita every chance he could, and there were plenty of chances. It's simply a case of an appropriate disaster resulting from an inappropriate erotic fascination. This doesn't happen all the time, and when it does happen, it goes pretty much as Nabokov describes it.

*The Western cultural prototype is no longer found in Ovid, but now resides in Dante. See Canto V of the *Inferno*, in which the pilgrim meets Paolo and Francesca. Actually, the pilgrim meets Francesca only. She tells her tale, filled with self-justification, while Paolo, who is endlessly attached to her, only moans. Her self-absorption is truly modern, worthy of the devil who wears Prada. Francesca refers to Paolo only occasionally, and never by name. He is always "that one."

Chapter Three: Irregular Adventurers

to lay it out for the reader, but the particular nymphet reality he experienced was both more worldly and more sordid. And Humbert was at pains to lay that out as well. After all, part of exalting the self is to diminish the other.

Humbert never did expound on how *any* nymphet, ideal or real, might experience the erotic relationship. He showed an astounding lack of sympathy for his main nymphet, Lolita, and her unhappiness in their constant sexual encounters. After all, he pontificated, her "crude" sensibilities and those of her debased American cohort were a deplorable social reality. Humbert ostentatiously sighed to his readers about Lolita's inevitable moral decline from those corrupting summer days at camp when she was twelve. He made his case that the fault belonged to Lolita in particular and America in general.

If he himself were at fault, too, then the fault was only in his high expectations. Humbert was just too decent. His European sensibilities simply could not encompass the American way of life, adolescent style. He regretfully admitted that his hopeful but mistaken moral sense "by-passed the issue by clinging to conventional notions of what twelve-year-old girls should be." Lolita herself falling even lower than some of her campmates did was no surprise, given the lack of societal controls over behavior. Adolescents were allowed, even encouraged, to develop their own independent styles.

Turning Lolita from a person into an example, he complained fatuously that the links between adolescence and the adult world had been in America utterly dissolved. America now sustained two cultures, adult responsibility and furtive adolescent adventure. Certainly this was Humbertian hypocrisy of a high and elegant order. In his complaints about Lolita, Humbert had forgotten his own efforts at debauching Annabel, and her enthusiastic participation in this (to adults) nefarious enterprise. Ah, well, it's easy to forget that what is good for oneself may be regarded as undesirable in another. It is also easy for Humbert to forget that he didn't want Lolita to become an adult, but wished that he himself could participate in adolescence, including the sex, including the furtiveness, including the realization that this was universally condemned by adults. Nevertheless, in spite of his own predilections, Humbert did not believe

"Light of My Life"

in the notion of "anything goes."* He saw American adolescence as a way of living as well as a time of life, and disapproved of both.

Lolita was, in point of sexual fact, no longer innocent in body, though her mind was another matter. She had been, from Humbert's point of view, debauched, and from Lolita's, initiated. With some coaxing she confessed/described. She had first been shown "various manipulations" for autoerotic or perhaps Sapphic sex by a schoolmate, who belonged to the local gentry. At camp, through a friend practicing with the thirteen-year-old son of a camp director, Lolita initially refused, but driven by a companionable curiosity, she gave it a whirl, and then more than one whirl. Soon, Humbert related, it was first one girl and then another. This is the everlasting male fantasy: not just the two girls, but the capacity to have intercourse seriatim. Although Lolita enjoyed, or perhaps tolerated, Charlie's mechanical attentions, she had only contempt for his "mind and manners." She regarded sexual play as therapeutic, "fine for the complexion." She summed up that summer of sex and swimming as "sort of fun," a tepid endorsement at the most. Lolita was twelve.

An indication of how young she was appeared as Lolita recounted the summer's activities. Addressing a crude detective-movie come-on to Humbert, she talked as if she were a moll. She was still too new to the game to know that cracking wise had consequences. But Humbert knew, and took advantage of a twelve-year-old pretending to be an adult. Perhaps he even believed it, because he wanted to. Humbert later would recall Lolita's bravado as a moment, for him, of bittersweet joy. She admitted having been "revoltingly unfaithful" and concluded with an evaluation of herself and Humbert, a "bad, bad girl," a "juvenile delickwent, but frank and fetching." Hollywood talk. At that time, it was popular for young people

---

*From the song of the same title by Cole Porter, a 1934 vehicle for Ethel Merman in the musical *Anything Goes*. The song described an America in which moral strictures previously observed were not discarded, in a time when "God knows, anything goes." The phrase "anything goes" passed into the language and was still alive after the war, used as an explanation for licentiousness specifically and social solipsisms in general. The year 1947 was not too late to hear the phrase, that is to say, in 1947, anything had not gone on long enough to make the phrase obsolete.

Ethel Merman had a brassy, expressive voice, and gave every song, even the most tender, an undercurrent of wisecrack and irony. Lolita's tone, in her initial conversation with Humbert after camp, echoed the Merman style.

Chapter Three: Irregular Adventurers

to imitate the silver screen's version of sophisticated patter.* During her patter, she pointed out that Humbert had run a red light while she was describing the summer's activities. Driving and sex, he concluded from her disjointed chatter, were related: both equally casual and part of a standard routine.† Only the very young or the very professional could think that. But Humbert could suppose that he had more charm than Charlie, so he would be more successful in engaging Lolita's emotions through sex. This would not happen. He would last longer than Charlie, but he would never become more important.

Humbert recalled Lolita's tone as well as her words from that first afternoon in the car. He interpreted her meaning that she was blasé about sex. It was just another thing to do, different from going to the soda shop in that it was private rather than communal, and different also in that sex, unlike the soda shop, did not imply communication. It is significant, though, that in chronicling all the succeeding years together, Humbert would recount no other instance of Lolita using those words or that tone. And he would have remembered.

Lolita's initial insouciance concerning sex was a function of her years. In spite of the fact that young girls imagine they know everything, the law wisely does not consider juveniles to possess the full powers of judgment. Perhaps the twelve-year-old Lolita came close. And perhaps not, as Humbert knew. Lolita no doubt expected that sex with Humbert would be an occasional event rather than a condition. Further, she was unaware of sex's immense power, both positive and negative. Sex goes beyond refining the complexion. It moves relationships into another category; it changes everything between a couple. In the best movie tradition, it can bind a couple

---

*Patter was a standard term in the 1940s, used both as a derogatory comment on useless verbiage, and as a description of film stichomythia, particularly between men and women. But not always. We recall 1942's *The Maltese Falcon*, written and directed by John Huston and starring Humphrey Bogart. When Bogart confronted Elisha Cook, Jr., 130-pound kid pretending to be a thug, Bogart commented: "The cheaper the hood, the gaudier the patter." If Bogart said it, it had to project the right image. This patter was particularly piquant when used by a girl. It was, of course, the bedrock characteristic of women in screwball comedies. See the *Thin Man* comedies.

†We omit comment on Freudian implications of driving a motor car, as they were then sometimes called. Everyone has talked about this. The relationships between various forms of thrust have become cliché.

"Light of My Life"

together, even through a life of time, children, and events; but movies to the contrary, it sometimes destroys couples. In *Lolita*, sex seemed to destroy more than to bind.

The twelve-year-old Lolita could not comprehend Humbert's passion, terrifying in its intensity and primal urgency. Besides, she, not unreasonably, did not equate sex with love. *Eros* was culturally separated from love for Lolita's generation, which thought in term of romance and marriage, followed by hearth and home. Lolita's ideas of love were developed out of the G-rated music and movies she saw, rather than from Humbert's words and deeds. Humbert lived in another world altogether. He defined himself as "enchanted," dwelling in an "elected paradise—a paradise whose skies were the color of hell flames—but still a paradise." How could Lolita accept or even tolerate that kind of passion? She clung to the security offered by the mundane and the immediate, not only because she was a teenager, but also because she needed order. The "color of hell flames" was not to Lolita's taste.

Humbert was forced to adjust, if not his desires, then at least his schedule. The young Lolita longed for some simple order in the day, and Humbert had to plan an itinerary to accommodate that. Routine works against *eros*. Nevertheless, Humbert was forced to create a routine for Lolita who, as a twelve-year-old, was easily bored. He had to devise a destination; they were on their way to see something special and particular. He had to make time for movies and lunches, since Lolita had an insatiable sweet tooth. Aimlessness was impossible for her. Every day must have a purpose. Humbert found it irritating, but necessary. *Eros* and anti-*eros* jostled uneasily through every together in the old blue car.

Even ordinary adolescents need structure, places to go and things to do, people to be with; the entire industry of schools is built on that single fact. The two problems intersected neatly. Humbert's erotic passion collided with Lolita's adolescent distraction and moodiness and leisure.

In Europe, adolescent girls from propertied families found their time tightly organized between school and family, and moodiness was not an approved or even tolerated activity. Had he known twelve and thirteen-year-old girls in Europe, Humbert would have found their behavior characterized by formal politeness and social structure. European girls had the

Chapter Three: Irregular Adventurers

same hormonal disorientation of their American sisters, but that stuff was tightly disciplined in the Old World. Humbert, used to the formality of bourgeois society in France, was unprepared for, and commented extensively upon, the freedom of activity and expression that existed in America after the war. Hence, disparaging comments about Lolita were aimed as much at America and its youth culture as at Lolita herself. Her problem was less her moods than her middlebrow, popular, aesthetic, commercial tastes.

Lolita was a post–Hiroshima American adolescent, part of the first full generation of such beings, which was a distinct psycho-social component of American life.* Public display of the emotional tsunamis of adolescent insecurity and fear routinely washing over the still disorganized psyches of teenagers were once seriously discouraged. But war loosens every tie. Adolescence as a distinct social category had appeared in America on a noticeable scale during the Roaring Twenties amongst the "Flaming Youth."† For those young in 1947, like Lolita but not Humbert, adolescence had become a specific time. Kids were now considered capable of independent doing and being, but were not fully responsible for the results of things done or personas adopted. Lolita at Beardsley was no exception, abuse to the contrary notwithstanding, and for Lolita, as for so many, school activities were both necessary to fill time and unable to fill it fully. Lolita, as described by Humbert, seemed to fit the adolescent paradigm perfectly. This may be thought of as defective observation on Humbert's part. No individual fits a general category perfectly, but it was in Humbert's

---

*See a thoroughly entertaining, cheerful, and essentially decent movie from 1945, *Junior Miss*, starring Peggy Ann Garner and Allyn Joslyn. The Junior Miss phenomenon, which included magazines and fashions, was rampant in the years between 1945–1948. As with all fashion, it was fleeting, though the magazine *Seventeen* still carries the torch. See also, *The Bachelor and the Bobby Soxer* (1948), a vehicle for Shirley Temple's post–Shirley Temple years. It may be thought of as near the terminus of the Junior Miss era, which consisted of entirely well-meant mishaps by a young lady in her effort to grow up into a responsible wife and member of society. No such movie could be made today, of course.

†The earliest use of the moniker "Flaming Youth" comes from a 1923 movie of the same name, which asks the immortal question, "How far can a girl go?" But the cultural prominence of the term "Flaming Youth" was enormously increased by a song in the 1927 Broadway musical *Good News*, which was a hit and ran for 551 performances. See also the 1929 version by Duke Ellington.

interest to define her by general American "youth-culture" characteristics rather than to acknowledge that his own behavior was part of the problem.*

Beyond angst and the absence of responsibility, American adolescence was also a time normally devoted to fun, fun, fun. Lolita, poor thing, did not have much fun until she got out of the car. Then she could go to the soda shop and the movies, though Humbert always lurked in the background. Things got better at school. Humbert was further away, other kids were closer, and, more importantly, she was older and savvier than the brittle kid who had been picked up at camp. Lolita began to settle in to a fuller adolescent existence which centered around school as much as the more distant emblems of movie and music. Lolita was resilient. In spite of Humbert, as she grew older, she had a bit more fun.

For a while, tennis was fun for her, and, happily, was insufficiently serious to be played seriously; that, of course, meant that the game ceased to have any point at all for Humbert. Lolita found that of all things, acting was the most fun: she was obsessed with acting. She plunged into the school play with an adult seriousness of purpose and an adolescent enthusiasm of discovery. It offered her the opportunity to become herself by playing others.

Age is a curious commodity. While the clock ticks equally for all, experience occurs differently to each. Painfully, Lolita would grow up. Humbert would merely get older.

Humbert and Repentance

Humbert's memoir tells a tale of doomed passion, bearing a striking resemblance to Jacques Offenbach's opera *Les Contes d'Hoffmann* (1881).

---

* Nabokov knew American adolescents only by disapproving observation, but he understood at least some of what he saw: leisure without responsibility, and a commercial enterprise tied to age. This is one of the few areas in which the omnipotent creator appears *in extenso* on the written page. In this respect, Humbert is not far distant from his creator. Though similar, Humbert is more limited. Nabokov was not in the habit of showing his whole hand, even at the end of the game, which in this case is the completed text.

Chapter Three: Irregular Adventurers

In both, the main character's grail is love, which overpowers him as it crumbles at his touch.* Because Hoffmann is a poet, at the opera's end his muse carries him off to the realm of art. At the end of his life, Humbert also appeals to the "refuge of art," in his case not sonnets but memoir. It's always better for life to imitate art. With art, one can at least save something.

Humbert's real goddess is more love than art; though the appeal beyond *Eros* to art adds a second theme, one of justifying *eros*. This was hard to do, given Humbert's monomania, and his need to write a memoir/statement that would evoke understanding from its judicial readers. Humbert (that is, Nabokov) did not take the easy way out and evoke a transcendental god. *Eros* just is, a part of life, which the fortunate (?) experience.† Lolita, therefore, is a novel without Providence of any sort except the nameless *deus ex machina* who appears briefly to obliterate Charlotte. Humbert does what secular men often do. At the point of desperation, he turns to religion. After Lolita has left him, he finds a confessor, though more for understanding than for absolution. *Ex post facto*, the memoir overlays his remembered feelings with religious terms, as if words had the power even at this point to provoke intercession. Of course, the words of religion do not automatically lead to the path of religion, even when, momentarily, Humbert's recollection of the act of love would assume religious formulae. He tells of moments "in paradise ... when ... I would ... mutely ask her blessing. ... (with my soul actually hanging around her naked body and ready to repent)."‡ Repent what? Did not Humbert really mean "repeat"?

The clichéd courtly love vocabulary has taken Humbert over, an odd

---

*Offenbach's opera appears to best effect in the sumptuous and lavish cinematic production by Powell and Pressburger, *The Tales of Hoffmann*, 1952. In this version, the opera is sung, of course, but it is also danced. With the exception of the tenor, we hear the opera while seeing the dancers. The opera was set in the 1820s, the height of the Romantic fever in Europe. Nowhere was the toleration for Romantic silliness stronger than in Paris. Of course, it formed a piquant cultural contrast to the eternal French attachment to money.

†On the (?), see Ovid, *Metamorphoses, The Art of Love, and The Heroiades*. See also the poems of Catullus. That kind of suffering and longing was certainly appropriate for the creation of at least a demigod or goddess.

‡Nabokov, *Lolita*, Pt. II, ch. 32, 285. We recall a contrary scene in *Anna Karenin* when Vronsky, after seducing Anna, falls upon her with kisses, and does *not* repent his love.

note, since he was essentially a secular character throughout his memoir. But toward the end, he tried confession and penance, and perhaps the vocabulary of medieval love remains in the midden of memory, as an artifact from that effort.

When it's all over, Humbert presents himself as having being alternately in Hell, or in a circle of Paradise. He repeatedly calls himself a sinner, a foul sinner; whatever might be meant by that, it is clear that Humbert does not mean felon. Humbert recounts a tale of love enjoyed and never repented. That is the pattern of the memoir. There is no moral or religious turn at the end of *Lolita*, no religious journey towards salvation such as found in *Crime and Punishment*. In *Lolita*, one person merely loves another, usually with unfortunate results, and that is the way life is. It's not a judgment of God. Unbridled *eros* is demanding, as Hoffmann and Humbert found, and the attitude of a postulant rather than a penitent is inadequate to exorcise passion.*

In *Lolita*, the absence of a religious sensibility is filled by a psychological one. In spite of his well-known aversion to Sigmund Freud, "the Viennese medicine man," Nabokov lets Humbert engage in a prolonged interior dialogue of memory. Other characters in Humbert's interior monologue are supporting players at best, and their sensibilities and attitudes matter only in relation to Humbert, an example of the techniques and practices of the "talking cure." Banished overtly, psychotherapy reappears as the very medium of the message.† The idea of the medium as message goes back to Marshall MacLuhan, who argued that, in effect, form trumped content, if any. In this case, the form of confession is supposed to distract the reader, but not the knowledgeable re-reader, from noticing that the content of the confession is entirely ersatz. As for the law, confessions are admissible, but of use only in terms of the felonies charged. It's no crime to love passionately, especially in courtly love or country music. A simple psychological confession, part of the "talking cure," has the distinct merit (or demerit, if one prefers) of being essentially trivial.

---

*Nabokov, *Lolita*, Pt. II, ch. 31, pp. 282–283. Significantly, Humbert only briefly describes this scene, and presents it far out of chronological order, at the very end of the book.

†At the end of the book you can just hear Humbert sighing, "Well, I'm glad I got THAT off my chest! I feel much better already."

Chapter Three: Irregular Adventurers

Psychology as a discipline ignores the moral and/or religious concept of life as a journey, as a pilgrimage toward moral growth and illumination. Psychology provides a comforting sense that everything is comprehensible, can be explained, will have resonance with the audience, and does not demand the hard strictures of free will and personal responsibility. Your desires drive you; you do not control them. Humbert was clear about that.

But Nabokov knew better. Comfort for the reader is not the same as insight for the author. Even in modern literature, as Nabokov clearly grasped, journey cannot be divorced from a spiritual/psychological gloss.* Do the characters on the road grow in understanding and sympathy? Often. Does movement edge toward momentum, or is it all Brownian motion, akin to running in place? Frequently. The Humbertiad actually includes both; while Dolly moves from adolescent sulks to marriage and family, Humbert stays as he was. The Humbert we liked with Annabel is the Humbert we deplored with Lolita. But it's the same Humbert. Context counts. He grew in understanding no more than did Emma Bovary, or Pavel Ivanovich Chichikov in the first volume of *Dead Souls*. Lolita's Augustinian journey towards self-knowledge slips quietly past, mostly offstage, leaving behind Humbert's inertia. When Humbert encounters a married Lo, he realizes in a rush of emotion that he was meeting her for the first time.

Humbert can be compared to Raskolnikov, whose wandering changed into pilgrimage and aimlessness into direction. Though Nabokov did not care for Dostoevsky's *Crime and Punishment*,† Dolly's *bildung* resembles nothing so much as Raskolnikov's journey, both physical and spiritual, within that great Augustinian novel. Dolly's marriage plays the same role in *Lolita* as does the second epilogue in *Crime and Punishment*, where the characters first understand love properly directed. But the novels end dif-

---

*Language has changed, not merely from Augustine's time from our own, but from Dostoevsky's time to our own. A basic indicator of this is the growth of an entire vocabulary of psychology, which has come to replace things that were once described in spiritual or religious terms. We are using the religious terminology that Humbert used. This is another example of Nabokov's subtlety: in a secular book, he has Humbert describe an emotional crisis in religious rather than psychological terms.

†Nabokov's dislike of Dostoevsky has not averted readers' eyes from the numerous parallels between the two writers' works.

ferently; Raskolnikov's recognition of his love for Sophia brought a reaction that Humbert would never know from Lolita. Sophia

> jumped up and looked at him and shivered. But at the same time, at that moment she understood everything. A boundless joy illuminated her eyes. She understood. For her, there was no longer any doubt. He loved her infinitely.*

Raskolnikov was transformed, from spiritual blindness to illumination, while Humbert's erotic obsession only made him more cunning and vigilant.

There was no angelic voice for Humbert as Augustine described in Book VIII of the *Confessions*, when he turned to the true path that made sense of life.† Humbert in the years after Annabel lived the flat life of incident without event, of movement without direction. After Annabel, through Monique, Valeria, Charlotte, Lolita, and Rita, there was only

> ... the bought smile
> Of harlots, loveless, joyless, unendeared
> ...
> Or seranate, which the starved lover sings.‡

The catastrophic results of unbridled passion, implicit in *Lolita*, are explicit in Hoffmann. Lucky Hoffman. He lived in a romantic age when passion itself was a positive value. Never mind the hideous and felonious results, which the opera strews along the road of Hoffmann's fierce infatuations. *Eros* was worth everything you paid, from disillusionment to death. Even though Hoffmann's heart was broken, more than once, it was always worth it, and the society around him agreed. Poor Humbert. He lived in a secular and prosaic age where *eros* run amok garnered social disapproval, and occasionally the attentions of the police. Postwar America was about as far as one could get from Paris in the grip of Romantic fever. Even if Nabokov disdained context, context still matters.

---

*Fyodor Dostoevsky, *Crime and Punishment*, second epilogue, quoted in Stanton and Hardy, "Introduction," p. xviii.
   †Augustine, *Confessions*, Bk. VIII. Another reversal of *Crime and Punishment*, where the murder happens early, an act of opening, not closure.
   ‡John Milton, *Paradise Lost*, Bk. IV, ll. 765–766, 769.

Chapter Three: Irregular Adventurers

Justified by Eros

Recapitulation forms the primary technique of plot development in Humbert's memoir. *Lolita* is a love story, usually gone to seed, followed by another. They differ according to the temperature of the passion. Some loves are tepid, others comprise erotic monuments in which passion is all that matters. Of course, the transcendent value given to *eros* properly belongs only to Humbert; it is, after all, his memoir. Humbert valued passion in himself, not others. He believed that passion justified him: with Annabel, for a moment with Monique, for what he swears will be a lifetime with Lolita. Without passion, Humbert sees himself as barely existing, an attitude similar to that exemplified by Emma Bovary and Anna Karenin. Of course, one recalls that things worked out badly for those two ladies.* For Humbert, it is always my passion; I am my passion and the memories of my passion.

Within the memoir, the many other characters never understand the depths of Humbert's passion nor does Humbert suppose they can possibly attain that temperature of love. The Farlows were tepid and companionable, Lolita's spouse Dick was "incidental," and Rita was "sweet and dumb." For Humbert, they barely existed. In spite of Humbert's patronizing attitude, he did admit that Charlotte loved him deeply. In terms of erotic passion, she was his true spouse, who loved him as he loved Lolita. Like Humbert, Charlotte blazed like a grease fire in an iron skillet. The plot demanded not merely her disappearance but her death. There's only room for one grand passion in this book.

In his memoir, Humbert circles back to Annabel, in order to understand his existence with Lolita. For Humbert, the past is more than prologue. It is the template for new loves. Monique could be made to fit the template for an hour, Valeria and Charlotte momentarily, but not for any sustained period. Humbert imagined that Valeria and Charlotte might

---

*It may or may not be of value to recall that in his university courses, which were informed by his general critical stance, Nabokov liked and valued *Madame Bovary* and *Anna Karenin* above all other novels. He regarded Anna as one of the greatest and most tragic heroines in western fiction. Possibly, Nabokov had Humbert, who was well-read but not wise, see himself in terms of Anna.

inspire passion, but for the most part, they were no more to his taste than was the accommodating nutritionist Dr. Anita Johnson, who shared her favors with everyone on the Arctic expedition. The recapitulation in *Lolita* is a constant search to find someone close enough to Annabel so that Humbert's interior template of *eros* seems to fit. Lolita would fit that template better, and longer.

For Humbert, everything happened again, but always with decreasing success. Nabokov had Humbert exemplify two of the dominant cultural trends of the twentieth century: the drift of the universe toward entropy, and Humbert's essentially Freudian explanation for his behavior. Therefore, the movement of the plot is not toward conclusion but toward repetition. The Greek view of life as tragic and circular is also an unacknowledged but still genuine frame for *Lolita*. "Play it again, Sam" may be regarded as a motto for this novel. Of course everything happens again, but with diminishing intensity. And, then, entirely by happenstance, Humbert felt his luck change: he ran into Lolita. In a novel which combines Freud with entropy, contingency must occur as a real, though not entirely comprehended, actor.

Of course, we are all memorialists of our own stories, and Humbert overtly attempts to invest his story with purpose and direction, the better to convince others that this gloss is accurate. This tendency works well in stories, less well in real life. Readers are eager for purpose and direction. They willingly suspend disbelief, try to go along, tentatively accepting morals and meanings even from unreliable narrators. Their efforts to swallow Humbert's story are complicated by Nabokov's red herrings, contradictory bits of information he allows the narrator to include, events which contradict Humbert's misty-eyed self portrait as martyr to love. Nabokov separates himself from Humbert by building into the narrative Humbert's continuing undercutting of his own story.

Recapitulation in *Lolita* occurs on a second level as well, not merely within the novel, but also within the readers' experiences. Nabokov may have disdained "real life" in novels, but he created a realistic Humbert, whom we recognize both from what he did and how he wrote. Humbert's tendency to shade the truth in self-serving ways is common to everyone. Humbert's recognition of the importance of love is common to everyone.

Chapter Three: Irregular Adventurers

And everyone experiences events that seem to have occurred before. "It's *déjà vu*, all over again," said Yogi Berra, in a clear statement that life as well as *Lolita* involves juxtaposition, recapitulation, and contingency as well as progress. Humbert emerged from the chrysalis of the Annabelic idyll as an essentially finished and functioning being. Not extraordinary at all. Every day the reader sees people who function well, even though they have not gotten beyond a trauma in the past. Yogi was more concise than Humbert, and he recognized reality just as clearly.

Stasis is not the only reaction to trauma, recapitulation is not the only way to make sense of the past. There is also movement. Lolita changed immensely from nymphet to mother-to-be. With Dick, she is a totally different person from the brat who took the first trip with Humbert. Behind Humbert's incessant demand for the center stage, Lolita's life appears incidentally as a progression toward maturity. Humbert scarcely notices it, but it happens. In *Lolita*, all of the action is not in the center ring. Indeed, most is not.

Nabokov took repetition and progress, and opposed these two modes of existence in a work of art. He didn't show how one reality leads to another, though that kind of relationship often shapes plots. *Lolita* is an inclusive, rather than exclusive, novel. It embraces both the Hegelian notion of progress, thesis-antithesis-synthesis, as well as the Manichean dialectic of constant, repetitive opposition, of the good and the dark side. And it does not exclude the despised "Viennese medicine-man" nor the essentially nihilistic idea of entropy. It's all in there. For Nabokov, life was complicated, while for Humbert, life was simple. For Nabokov, the complexity of life could *only* be satisfactorily depicted in art. Consequently, the distance between stasis and movement is presented by Nabokov as both a contrast and a process. *Lolita* drifts in that space between description and narration, proceeding in a circular way from episode to episode, from woman to woman, in a juxtaposition between women who move and Humbert who stays.

Chapter Four

EXEUNT OMNES

In Book IX of *Paradise Lost*, John Milton began to sing of the

> ... tragic, foul distrust, and breach
> Disloyal on the part of man....*

These tragic notes in Milton concerned the Fall, with Sin and Death to follow. In *Lolita*, a profoundly secular novel, the Fall is ignored, while Sin is psychologized and thus finessed.† Humbert whines endlessly about how badly things went, how difficult life had been, how love had seemed so hard to find, and once found, impossible to manage.‡ He writes in the pathetic psychological patter of self-justification. But despite Humbert's lingo, his memoir insouciantly confesses the sins of lust, violence, constant lying, betrayal, and murder. Sin is self-confessed, self-framed, and con-

---

*John Milton, *Paradise Lost*, Bk. IX, 6–7.
 †Critics generally place *Lolita* into the category of a psychological novel, although Humbert's memoir was more about sin than it was about attitude. See Leon Edel, *The Modern Psychological Novel*. We mention Edel because his theories were important and persuasive during the *Lolita* period, from about 1950 to the early sixties; and Nabokov in his instructions on how to read *Lolita* had Edel, and others, in mind. Nabokov himself disliked psychology and despised being categorized. His most prominent attitude toward contemporary critics and contemporary critical analysis was disdain. Nabokov did disdain well, communicating a genuine sense of contempt and distaste. Not surprising. He had the aristocrat's assurance and the exile's uncertainty. He also had the literary genius to allow an exile (Humbert) to hang himself with his own words, which Humbert himself misunderstood.
 Nabokov certainly wrote about a bad guy doing a bad thing: several bad things, in fact. But he did not place sin in a doctrinal or even religious framework. Nabokov never wrote about religion, and, at least at Cornell, he did not teach about it. Sin, plenty of that; doctrine, not at all.
 ‡If one strips away the décor of Humbert's road trips with Lolita, what is left is kidnapping, captivity, exploitation, and, protestations of love to the contrary notwithstanding, an overwhelming concern for Humbert.

Chapter Four: Exeunt Omnes

stantly justified, even as Humbert hopes to slip off the hook by terming it social heterodoxy.*

Death cannot be finessed. It is scattered broadcast through *Lolita*. Humbert's father, mother, and aunt, Annabel, Valeria, Charlotte, and Jean Farlow all perished within the confines of the "novel proper" (excluding Foreword and Afterword). So did Quilty. Lolita's death in childbirth, along with the death of her child, was hidden in plain view in the Foreword.† Humbert himself died in custody, after having completed his autobiographical statement, with the details of death, coronary thrombosis, and the date, November 16, 1952, duly given in the Foreword. With the passage of Humbert into the underworld, no one of consequence survives. All things sown have been reaped.

In *Lolita*, the enormous death toll included many victims who did not, in the ordinary meaning of the term, "deserve" to die. Many, apparently, were bumped off to make Humbert's plot flow more smoothly downhill, to his own death. Deserved both because he had nothing left to do, in narrative terms, and because whatever he might have done would have been too appalling to describe. The wages of *eros*, not sin, appear to be death. In *Lolita*, the reign of death fell upon the good and bad alike.‡

---

*In today's secular world, the term "sin" has been softened substantially and even turned into an adjective. For instances, taxes on cigarettes and booze are now called "sin" taxes, and certain rich varieties of chocolate cake are "sinfully" good. The word survives, but, as is common in a therapeutic society, the sense of judgment has been removed. Nabokov was not a practicing Christian, and did not belong to a specific church. But he had a clear grasp of right and wrong. As his memoir, *Speak, Memory*, shows, Nabokov had a role model (to use the modern term) in his father.

†The death notice is presented in the formal mode, under Lolita's married name of Mrs. Richard F. Schiller. The reader must be a Nabokovian re-reader to connect death early in the frame with marriage late in the story itself. Nabokov, who wanted *Lolita* read carefully and twice (at least) was as cunning and conspiratorial as Humbert.

‡Nabokov was enormously interested in the aesthetically pleasing, and he inserted this attitude into Humbert. In his lectures as well as in *Lolita*, Nabokov did not describe the beautiful; but he did describe, in a great many ways, the ugly. The ugly emerged in social attitudes and habits, ("Philistine"), in physical conformation (fat and waddling Valeria), and in moral attitudes (the pedophile chess-companion Gaston). Humbert, of course, is the ugliest character of all, and Nabokov endlessly describes him. Indeed, through *Lolita*, Nabokov reveals himself through the scrim of fiction as the antithesis of Ruskin. Nabokov is the literary aficionado of the ugly, the contemptible, the vile. Perhaps, we certainly cannot say for sure, Nabokov picked up more than he supposed from the artistic community of *entre-guerre* Berlin. See Georg Groscz.

"Light of My Life"

While writing *Lolita*, Nabokov was teaching *Anna Karenin* at Cornell, where the wages of *eros* was death. But only selectively. Anna succumbed while Vronsky survived. Nabokov was a more judgmental author than Tolstoy, and he wielded a more substantial scythe. Like Shakespeare with the cast of *Hamlet* or *King Lear,* Nabokov clears the board. Unlike Shakespeare with *Hamlet,* nothing remains that could continue the plot of *Lolita*; indeed, to borrow from Augustine, the novel is not able *not* to end. Humbert the unreliable narrator has described a reliable reality. Medium and message converge.

Many of the deaths in *Lolita* are essentially decorative plot elements, incidental to Humbert and the malodorous effects of his grand passion. That erotic passion was the core of Humbert's sense of reality, and he did not disguise this from either his intended readers (the prison officials) or those who might pick up the posthumously published edition. Humbert wrote (for both) a treatise on love, a defense of love, and an explanation of love, insofar as he understood it. He did not conceal the disasters of love; indeed, he reveled in them. He hid his malice as best he could, as any sensible felon would. Nevertheless, it peeped through, especially in his description of Valeria and his contempt for "the Haze woman." But in all of its manifestations, love was for Humbert an eternal condition. He was always, regardless of circumstance, either driven by passion, or looking to be driven by passion.

By the end of his life, experience had convinced Humbert that he could keep the erotic inspiration alive only with the assistance of art's "durable pigments." Hence, Humbert's desire to write the memoir was not less strong than the authorities' desire to establish motive.* But art, though it can appear to arrest time, though only for a time, cannot trans-

---

*The legal ramifications of Humbert's memoir remain part of the frame of the novel. The confession, which the authorities needed to convict Humbert, is of value only when motive is clear, comprehensible, and reasonable. We recall the movie *Strangers on a Train*, 1951. When Humbert agreed to write a confession explaining everything, the authorities were delighted to accommodate him. Humbert wrote, and wrote, and wrote. It probably disconcerted the warden; it would disconcert most wardens. But so what? Humbert was writing, and in the end produced a memoir of substantial length which did reasonably explain the murder of Quilty, within the context of love for Lolita, and at the same time justified Humbert to himself. Justification combined with incrimination. A masterpiece.

Chapter Four: Exeunt Omnes

form the fury of *eros* into a force that gives life. In the end, unfortunately, Lolita's "immortality" rested upon Humbert's intense regard for his flimsy skill as an artist, a testament to Nabokov's superb artistic skills.

Nabokov's Intervention: The God Visits His Creation

Vladimir Nabokov was careful about structure, which he considered an integral part of literary style, the author's signature of genius or incapacity.* In *Lolita*, precision in structure meant first of all a frame, a memoir by an author whose pseudonym, Humbert Humbert, has remained intact through the editing process. The frame of memoir, particularly with an unknown author, provided distance between Nabokov and suspicion on the part of reviewers and readers that he wrote from experience of some sort. But that frame, stout in literary terms, might seem less substantial in psychological terms. So Nabokov, for whom indirection was almost an alternate religion, added a second frame in the form of a "Foreword," written by an editor, a John Ray, Jr., Ph.D.† Humbert's manuscript had been entrusted to Dr. Ray by his attorney, acting upon instructions in Humbert's will. Dr. Ray obeyed Humbert's "dead hand" and prepared the memoir for publication. Both the lawyer and the editor had been professionally punctilious. Ray left Lolita's name intact from "real life," continued Humbert's pseudonym, and introduced appropriate disguises for the other figures in the "memoir." After all, he explains patronizingly, one must help those "old-fashioned readers who wish to follow the destinies of the 'real' people beyond the 'true' story."

The "real" people and "true" story of the "Humbert" manuscript pass into a legal and academic framework. These professions function in society

---

*On Nabokov's attitudes towards style, see his two collections of academic, *Lectures on Literature* and *Lectures on Russian Literature*, both ed. by Fredson Bowers.

†There have, no doubt, been a great many John Rays, but Nabokov may well have had a particular John Ray in mind. We mean the seventeenth-century English botanist, whose main work, a catalogue of the plants of England, appeared in 1670. Nabokov knew a great deal of botany, and the name of an important and insufficiently well-known botanist would strike him as an appropriate joke. John Ray provided the first definition of species in his *Historia Plantarum*.

to analyze and categorize, to contain and interpret and legitimize powerful forces in the culture. Nabokov, child of a lawyer, and an academic himself, understood the power of these professions in shaping society's views. In this case, the official validates the biographical. The information concerning editing, and concerning Humbert's retained pseudonym, (and what would be the point of a pseudonym for a pseudonym) are found in the Foreword. The Foreword acts, in these instances, as an afterword also, an economy of structure, an example of literary multi-tasking, and a clever piece of indirection.

In his own task of editorial tidiness, Ray included a sentence or a clause about the fate of many. The women in particular were accounted for. Rita married "the proprietor of a hotel in Florida," (a similarity to Humbert's mother, which must mean something) but Lolita did not enjoy (or endure) such a fate. The announcement of her death was terse and unadorned. *Sic transit* Lolita. Not a single first-time reader running across a mention of "Mrs. Richard F. Schiller" dead and buried in the Foreword will have any idea of whom that was. Only through re-reading, a Nabokovian requirement for an intelligent grasp of the novel, would the reader understand that brief remark.

The remainder of Ray's Foreword veered away from information into commentary by the Professor, which served to increase the realism of the second frame, thus further cooling the socially hot topic of pedophilia. Ray's commentary tended, unsurprisingly, towards the professorial, which Nabokov knew well and practiced often and equally often thought of as pompous in style and self-serving in message. Never mind, professors are what they are (and author Nabokov was one too).* The frames were not without their uses, both in plot and in interpretation.

Nabokov wished to steer the critics to an appropriate (and favorable)

---

*Nabokov is engaging with his own rivals: Published 1955 (in the air and in the works for years before) was Edel's *The Modern Psychological Novel*, which examined Modernist works (Joyce, most prominently, Nabokov's "aspirational peer" and artistic rival) and their stream-of-consciousness style: Edel insisted on examining the author's personality and how it made its way into the text. He asks the question "whether an artist drawing on the contents of his own mind (which is the only mind he can use in its creation) is really able to detach himself from his characters: that is whether their subjectivity is not, in reality, his subjectivity. In other words: is not a subjective novel but a disguised form of autobiography?" (p. 24).

Chapter Four: Exeunt Omnes

understanding of *Lolita*. He was not above caricaturing his rivals, whom he held in contempt and beneath contempt. Nabokov specialized in a magisterial style which excelled in gradations of disdain. Indeed, if you failed to read *Lolita* correctly according to the Nabokovian interpretive framework, neither Nabokov then nor his shade now would recognize your existence.

Nabokov's own critical tendencies lay within the (then) New Criticism, which asserted that the text alone, excluding biography, society, history, and ideology, is worthy of study. The text alone will, so to say, explain and illuminate itself.* Nabokov took this doctrine seriously, practicing it in his most extended critical effort, his college teaching. His portrait of Dr. Ray, therefore, displays his disdain for critics who might possibly "misread" *Lolita*. The "Foreword" was not addressed to his rivals or judges; that would have been too direct for the subtle Nabokov. Anyone could see through that. So he indicted Ray through Ray's own (Nabokov-given) words about biography and society and the moral lessons that might be drawn from *Lolita*. Ray ignored the Nabokovian standard of judging genius by the style and structure of the text. Still, Ray's academic postures were not without sense or merit. He is certainly not the only critic who asserts that social context adds depth and nuance to interpretation. This is an ancient and honorable interpretive stance. Both Plato (*Ion*) and Aristotle (*Politics*) worried that a poet's words would have an adverse effect upon hearers and readers. There is a world beyond the text, and if Ray only stumbled into it, at least he knew it was there.

Nabokov distorted Ray, however, into a scarecrow to drive critics away from undesirable critical readings of *Lolita*. The scheme worked magnificently. After all, no self-regarding critic (and all are self-regarding) wanted to follow Ray's lead. Nabokov's searing snobbery made sure of that. Therefore, a good bit of the commentary on *Lolita* in the succeeding

---

*The New Criticism was the refugee's signal form of criticism, and the lazy man's — it didn't require a library of reference books, or historical knowledge, or biographical backgrounds, or even a solid base of literary/cultural knowledge. You could do it out of a suitcase — perfect for Nabokov, who had other things to do besides teach his students, and perfect for Nabokov's students, educated in the increasingly rootless American educational system. New Criticism was perfect for a culture without culture.

decades has tended in the direction Nabokov intended, analyzing the book as self-contained unit, a closed system immune to the larger questions of context, purpose, and historical and ethical orientation.

All right: we stick with the text, playing Nabokov's game by his own rules, and consider the frame of the Foreword. John Ray, Jr., warns that the value of a work of art is not to be determined by the moral virtue of its protagonist "H.H." He was, according to Ray, horrible, abject, a moral leper, and plenty of other stuff as well. Nevertheless, there was a "desperate honesty" in his memoirs, even though he was, to say the least, "abnormal." Ray indicts harshly, though the same or worse could be said of many politicians. And worse does follow: "He is not a gentleman."

Nabokov, as was his wont, mixed into the same goulash attitudes he supported with those that he did not. Nabokov was not less judgmental than Ray, but certainly more manipulative, and he used Ray not just as a scarecrow but sometimes as a mouthpiece, and sometimes just as a goad to make the reader feel unbalanced. Ray's Foreword contains a tricky jumble. Nabokov clearly did not agree with Ray's assessment of Humbert as "abject," or "ponderously capricious," nor "desperately honest." But Nabokov would agree that Humbert Humbert was "not a gentleman." And with Ray's assessment, that Humbert was "horrible." Humbert's "moral leprosy" was not so much the pedophilia that captivated Ray as it was the habit of betrayal, of sacrificing everything and everyone to *eros*. Of course, Nabokov understood that this mixture of the approved and the disdained would guide commentary and inoculate the text against "ponderously capricious" critics. Furthermore, since this is a Foreword, the reader is thrown off balance from the start: unsure of what to agree with, what to ignore, and of the relationship of the author to the character. It serves the triple purpose of creating an alert reader, an uneasy reader, and a re-reader.

The Foreword, from a position before the beginning, tells what happened after the end. This circular technique, seen in Chaucer or Boccacio or Kierkegaard, deserves respect. Nabokov, moreover, went the extra mile, providing *Lolita* with a separate epilogue/afterword/critical explanation. Nabokov makes it appear that suggestions from readers and critics and publishers demanded it. So here, in Nabokov's comments "On a Book Entitled *Lolita*," we have a third frame, now Nabokov on Ray, added to

Chapter Four: Exeunt Omnes

Ray on Humbert, discussing Humbert's memoir. Nabokov could not resist a chance for irony, of misdirection, of changing voices and perspectives, of cameo peeps out from behind the curtain, even after the curtain had fallen on the show.

Nabokov also gestures through the afterword directly at the reader. He evokes a parade of lawyers and publishers, encouraging the reader to think again, and in contemporary terms, at the book just read. Was it a dirty book headed for censorship and lawsuit? Publisher Z is reported to have exclaimed that "...if he printed *Lolita,* he and I would go to jail."* Perhaps. There was a modest possibility of this in 1956, very modest indeed; so that Nabokov's explanation here was not *entirely* a work of supererogation.† He asserted the obvious, that the novel was not a dirty book. With indignation real or invented, Nabokov further pronounced that, in a free country, writers should not be held to account because the public cannot distinguish between the "sensuous and the sensual."

Fine, no argument there. Artistic freedom should mean something, even in the days of Senator McCarthy. Professor Nabokov announced that *Lolita* was not, as a reader may have suggested, "Young America debauching old Europe," nor the other way around. Further, he denied that *Lolita* was anti–American, a philistine accusation reminiscent of the charge (and trial) made in 1856 against *Madame Bovary.* Nabokov claimed that it was only natural that he had set the book in an American background of auto courts and restaurants and towns: after all, he was an American writer, like any other. Insulting America, which Nabokov certainly did in *Lolita,* was an established genre, and highbrow critics tended to approve of it. Dirty books, however, drew the ire of almost everyone else.

In the late fifties, popular critics often equated anti–American with "dirty," that is, they identified books that seemed to have a sexual theme. Americans committed plenty of sex in those days, but they weren't supposed to talk about it. In mixed company, they did not. *Lolita* seemed to

---

*Nabokov, *Lolita,* "On a Book Entitled *Lolita,*" pp. 313–314.
†We don't think Nabokov's second Afterword would keep the cops out of the printer's shop, or the judges out of the case. It just looks a little desperate, the gesture of someone who can't stop directing his readers how to read his book. Too much the professor. Whatever happened to "Go little book" *Envoi*-style comment?

some superficial readers to be perilously close to the category of books that were regarded as anti–American because they stimulated an immoderate interest in sex. It's hard to imagine *Lolita* stimulating an unhealthy interest in sex in anybody. However one read it, *Lolita* could not be regarded as a dirty book; in America, that's a pretty clear category, usually sold in "adult" bookstores.*

Finally, Nabokov warned that *Lolita* should not be read as an allegory, with some half-hidden but insistently implied *clef* which provides a higher meaning that explains everything.† He detested symbols and allegory, which he regarded with the same loathing as he did the "voodoo" of psychology. In their place, Nabokov insisted on guiding the reader's activities. His professorial direction was implicit in the novel, explicit and forceful in Prologue and Afterword, to say nothing of the comments he sprinkled among interviewers. But this directorial activity forces into the light Professor Nabokov's *bete-noir* question: "What is the guy trying to say?" Nabokov, as reader of other writers' books, did not waste much time listening to author's disclaimers and explanations. A reader must ask what the book is about, the despised question that Nabokov, both in *Lolita* and in his university classes, dismissed as a search for generalizations and patterns in the novel. And so it is. But is that a bad thing? Theme matters. We recall that Winston Churchill once declined a pudding because it lacked theme. Novels that lack theme have a similarly flaccid construction, and this applies to commentary as well. So, again, what is this guy up to with Ray's Foreword and his own Afterword?

We suggest that the main thing "this" guy (Nabokov) is "trying to say" is how to read *Lolita*. To understand *Lolita*, Nabokov argues, the reader must avoid thinking in terms of mutual cultural debauch, of pornography, of anti–American bias, of any hint of symbolism or allegory, of gen-

---

*This does not refer to romance novels. Housewives liked to read (and still do) books about romance sweeping characters off their feet in a delirium of bliss, which depicts *eros* rather than describing technical details of varieties of intercourse, which in those days was the subject of courses in abnormal psychology. Now, of course, this stuff can be found at every checkout counter in suburban supermarkets. Demythologizing has a way of turning the remarkable into the mundane.

†On allegory and symbol generally, the place to start is Augustine, *On Christian Doctrine*, Bk. 2, and Thomas Aquinas, *Summa Theologiae*, Prima Pars, q. 1.

Chapter Four: Exeunt Omnes

eralization at all, and see the novel as a story, independent of context, which is only stage decor, and concentrate exclusively on the writer's style, his wit, and the structure of the novel. In a perfectly Nabokovian world, the foreword would tell the critic what *not* to think, and the afterword would tell the critic, always a poor hack, how to think. Part of what "this guy" is "trying to say" is to influence the jury, not merely to get a favorable review but also to get a good (that is, correct) review. Well, why not.

Love Is as Love Does

Men are concerned with situations, while women are interested in relationships. When Humbert looked back over the five years with and without Lolita, he reexamined situations past to understand things now. He needed to make sense of things, to understand his life. But this could not be his only purpose in writing the memoir. Prison officials were looking over his shoulder. He had to explain the past in such as way as to engage their sympathies, if that is possible.

Beyond the official readers is the general public. Since the memoir was to go, and did go, to Humbert's lawyer for posthumous editing and publication, Humbert wished to appear sympathetic, even admirable; at the very worst, a man who loved too fiercely for his own good. Poor Humbert. He was really the victim, was he not? The love which exalted him also ruined him. A sad, sad thing. People should certainly sympathize with that. After all, many men have been in a situation where love betrayed them.

These two goals did not always mesh well. So Humbert wisely took the tack of explaining his story in a series of situations, of vignettes, of tiny glimpses rather than concentrating on how everybody felt about everything. He presented these episodes and descriptions chronologically, giving the impression of a coherent narrative. In "reviewing [my] case" Humbert recalled incidents which marked development or deterioration from one situation to another. Humbert looked for historical justification.* It worked

---

*This paragraph describes one of Eliot's purposes in *Four Quartets:* in order to find a meaning for our life, we try to make sense of the chaos of everyday experience, to find a pattern in

"Light of My Life"

well. The horrors of abuse were buried under layers of the mundane; chronology reassured everyone that what happened flowed inevitably from what happened. The kidnapping and molesting of a young girl became simply another incident in a trip across America and through puberty.

We suggest that Humbert understood very well the monstrous nature of his obsession and knew that Lolita, as the beloved, was the victim. The raw ruthlessness of *eros* had a firm grip upon him. He satisfied it as well as he might manage, hurting Lolita constantly, and spreading around a fair amount of collateral damage. As is always the case with *eros*, the hell with the damage. The lover knows he hurts others, but does not feel their pain. He feels his own, overwhelmingly, and that is the story he tells.

But he omits the monstrous nature of erotic passion. It is simply too shocking for either purpose of Humbert's memoir. He elides over its destructiveness, presenting an elegy rather than a tragedy. It is an elegy for love given, not returned, then gone, yet always at the center of the great lover's life. He had lived for love. And now he has nothing. Humbert wrote as if *eros* were a privilege instead of an affliction. And is not this the dual nature of love, according to the situation? But, as always, love is as love does.

Lovers Meet Again

Reunion of lost lovers is a constant theme in love stories (and on the internet). In *Orpheus and Eurydice,* Orpheus, returning for his lost love, found the predictable tragic conclusion: you can't go home again. In Humbert's memoir, Lolita reappears, reinforcing Humbert's unspoken contention that he is telling a love story. These reunions can go several ways. The lovers can say: "Those were the days"; or, "Thank God I've moved

---

[*continued*] the past.... Eliot concludes that that's almost impossible to do. Instead of trying to make sense of our life by searching for a pattern in the past, we need to accept our fallible human nature here in the present, especially our confusion and our sin. Humility is the Christian virtue we need to be a proper mode to receive inspiration and help. Of course Heracleitus was Eliot's favorite philosopher, and two quotations from Heracleitus precede the *Four Quartets* as epigraphs.

Chapter Four: Exeunt Omnes

on"; or "We must get back together again"; or "Fate has reunited us." Humbert implied that all but the second were true.

At the end of this love story, Humbert has met his "long-lost love" again. Dolly, Mrs. Richard Schiller, is now new-filled with life and purpose, though ruined as a nymphetic object of aesthetic and erotic desire. Although she had clearly changed, Humbert reacted as he had five years before in Charlotte's back yard. He realized that he loved her, still and always. And beyond the passion he felt for her, Humbert still had needs that cried out for fulfillment. With Humbert, it's always close to bedtime.

Now as before, he wanted her, to have, to hold, to possess, to engulf, to keep forever. At the time, he blurted it out, and asked her to run away with him. Of course she refused. As he spoke with her, Humbert saw again in his mind's eye the little Haze girl, "'pinging' pebbles at an empty can." What had become of her? He did not ask what had become of all nymphets. And in this case, this one special case, had Humbert done it? She had reassured him. Quilty had broken her heart; he had only broken her life. Humbert retreated to the safe ground of money. She needed some, and Humbert gave her more than she had asked for. He left, after hearing she would never return to him.

Looking back on it later, Humbert reported himself "weeping again, drunk on the impossible past." More importantly, he reported a moment of vision, seeing Lolita, perhaps for the first time, as a discrete part of his life. And what did that part mean? He was not able to say, exactly, though, in his most manipulative mode, he hopes the reader will see him as a changed Humbert.

As always, Humbert had thought of himself first. What he had understood, of course, was not primarily Lolita, although he would describe her in some (mostly unflattering) detail. Humbert realized that his own emotions had not changed. This could only mean one of two things. He had outgrown pedophilia. Not likely, the psychologists tell us. Once the lover becomes enthralled with "green fruit," nothing ever changes. Or, alternatively, Humbert had been faking it all along, the old masher. He was capable of loving mature women as well as nymphets. It can't be both ways. Either the reader takes a discussion of nymphets seriously, or the reaction on re-meeting Lolita seriously. They stand in unspoken contradiction. Is this contradiction due to the nature of erotic love, which can be explained only so far? Is it due to the needs of memoir? Humbert never says. Nabokov has slipped the contradiction in, without mentioning its existence.

Meeting again with Lolita is not, we suggest, less compelling in either narrative or emotional terms than the episode with Annabel, or Humbert's first sight of his "downy darling." Both of these nymphet-visions seem indelibly impressed on Humbert's psyche and memory. That sense of occasion recurs when Humbert sees Mrs. Richard Schiller for the first time. The reaction is slightly different. Here, weeping at the impossible past, or at least at something, replaced anger and frustration as Annabel was hustled off to Corfu or astonishment at first seeing Lolita. But the intensity of Humbert's reaction to all three situations is similar. That intensity confirms the contradiction at the core of Humbert's narrative. Love for Lolita the woman or passion for Lolita the nymphet: there is no way to discern which is the dominant attitude. *Lolita* does not conclude, in psychological terms. It leaves only a question.

We suggest that Nabokov intended the contradiction, opening up alternative interpretations of Humbert's memoir. In his fiction, generally, Nabokov did not foreclose possibilities; instead, he added to them, multiplying ambiguity. Nabokov also understood the conventions of love stories, and particularly the meaning of reunion. In *Lolita*, he consciously spurred his readers' conventional expectations about the lovers' reunion. In a meeting of an hour or two, we see Lolita unmoved, and the contradiction in Humbert's life exposed. He leaves to murder Quilty. All of it without comment of any sort. The narrative conceals rather than reveals. In this, it functions a lot like Scripture.

The Popish Cure

In describing his years with Lolita, Humbert presented his travels with her as an era, not just a series of episodes. He smugly insisted he had achieved clarity. But clarity does not necessarily impart wisdom, either for writer or reader. Humbert, by implication, agreed with his contemporary T. S. Eliot's (and Augustine's) view of "clarity" as an enlightenment, though

Chapter Four: Exeunt Omnes

still incomplete, gained through retrospection. In the second of the *Four Quartets*, Eliot accepted

> There is, it seems to us,
> At best, only a limited value
> In the knowledge derived from experience.
> The knowledge imposes a pattern, and falsifies,
> For the pattern is new in every moment
> And every moment is a new and shocking
> Valuation of all we have been. We are only undeceived
> Of that which, deceiving, could no longer harm.
> .... Do not let me hear
> Of the wisdom of old men, but rather of their folly....*

Eliot acknowledged the fact of seeing through a glass darkly, of our inability to make more than transient sense of the past. We are never *fully* undeceived. Somehow, Humbert seems to have missed that.

Humbert's efforts at making order of the situation had begun a "couple of years before" with a conventional but frequently successful tentative. He had sought a Roman Catholic confessor. He dismissively put it down to "a moment of metaphysical curiosity," and pursued it with substantial reservation. Still, he kept at it for more than a year, a testament probably to his misery rather than his faith.

The "popish cure" Humbert pursued, in spite of the efforts of "an intelligent French-speaking confessor," failed utterly. It did so for reasons that had nothing to do with the *cure*, or the cure. Humbert was not looking for grace, which he did not understand, but wished to make sense of his life in general and, more specifically, to make sense of what Lolita had undergone, and, perhaps suffered rather than enjoyed. Confession would for Humbert become the road to comprehension, and perhaps also peace, but this should entail no unseemly effort on his part.

In the *cure's* theology, the sacrament of confession requires the sinner to do more than confide his sin. It consists of three actions, performed in the following order. First, the sinner feels and shows true contrition, not

---

*T.S. Eliot, "East Coker." Eliot doubts the pattern we discern in past experience, because of our fallible human nature, that tends to obscure our own failures, and isn't able to generalize anyway. Nabokov would not disagree.

only a genuine sorrow for sin committed but an equally genuine resolve to lead a new life with that sin omitted. Only after contrition, which alcoholics call "hitting bottom," is one ready for confession.* Here, in the second part of the sacrament, one speaks the sin aloud. Speaking the sin means accepting responsibility for it. It is my fault, it is only my fault, it is my great fault, and I have got to start the process of fixing it. Only then can the third part of the sacrament of reconciliation begin. Satisfaction, which alcoholics call making amends, involves penance. The symbolic penance may be a few tours around the rosary, the personal form of community service. The genuine and extended penance involves life apart from the sin that inspired contrition and confession in the first place.†

Humbert could not choose to live without his sin, which was also his soul, and the light of his life. In the memoir's opening line, Humbert had actually misstated his case. Lolita was not his sin. His lust was. And when she left him, his lust remained. Certainly the *cure* knew that. The *cure* also knew that grace received equaled the effort expended, and that Humbert was unlikely to make any effort at all to recover or repent. Humbert would never repent, though he would again attempt to assuage his guilt after his last meeting with Lolita, years after his sessions with the *cure*. Even then, the new life he intended to lead was far from exemplary, consisting of rationalization, self-justification, and murder.

Humbert asked from the confessor, whose skills he commended, what the sacrament could not give. Humbert wanted only a modest dollop of comfort, a hint of closure, and a proof of God's forgiveness, to be found by deduction backward from effect (pain) to cause (sin). Like Dr. Faustus,

---

*The twelve-step program for recovery from addiction, begun in the 1930s by Bill Wilson, is an extended, continuing, and public form of the sacrament of reconciliation. The tradition of the twelve-step program began with the *Handbook* of Epictetus, who began his work on practical ethics with the simple yet profound statement, "Some things are up to us, and some things are not up to us." The Serenity Prayer comes from this, of course, along with the addict's ongoing effort to understand his life as a whole, to see his life in social, personal, and divine context, and to recognize the steps that he can and must take.

†Reparations, making the other person whole insofar as possible, was not really at issue here. Dolly could not be de-assaulted, de-abused, or de-kidnapped. Apology alone would have to suffice. No reader will be surprised to discover that Humbert did not apologize, to Lolita or to anybody else. "Well, one does what one can," which is the conclusion of H.L. Mencken's essay on Theodore Roosevelt.

Chapter Four: Exeunt Omnes

Humbert resisted the process of Augustinian turning. Faustus did not turn, but Humbert did not even grasp that he ought to repent, or to regret, or to turn, nor did he grasp that this alone would close the gaps in his life — there is a struggling implied but not described. In his memoir, Humbert slides over it all, as if it had not happened. Existentially, it had not.

Humbert had found that his difficulty lay in being unable to get over "the simple human fact that ... nothing could make my Lolita forget the foul lust I had inflicted upon her. This memory involved Lolita, not Humbert, but Humbert was the putative penitent. He had attempted to confess what he had not done, focusing instead on Lolita's pain rather than his role in causing it. That Lolita could not forget was the *gravamen* of his distress.* And what was it that Lolita could not forget? Why, it was nothing less than Humbert's extraordinary "foot of engorged brawn."† But Lolita's memories themselves were not Humbert's sin. They were merely a manifestation of his discomfort, from which Humbert had wished for release, though without the cost of changing anything that had caused Lolita pain. Just the fact of her memory, that was what tormented him. In such a situation, alcohol would produce more immediate relief than would the sacrament. For more extended relief, a memoir would better soothe the misery.

In sacramental terms, it was Humbert's "foul lust" that alone mattered. The secular Humbert could accept forgiveness *only* from Lolita. That opportunity was yet to come. Even then, when Lolita accepted the genuine (for Humbert) but spiritually suspect penance of money, she did not forget and may not have forgiven. Humbert did not even offer the satisfaction of an apology. He wanted a change in another, not in himself.

---

*The question of pain was current in literature at the time: T. S. Eliot extensively considers the past, and how we can define ourselves through our past. He concludes that we are not constituted out of just the sum of our happy moments, but also of our pain. Any real attempt to make meaning must include the problem of pain.

†No woman could ever forget Humbert's virility, which acted as these things always must, as a paean of praise to a woman's desirability. It is not uncommon for women to judge that the work involved in sex exceeds the flattery implied by sex; nevertheless, the flattery of being wanted is pretty powerful stuff. The idea that Humbert could, by confession, obliterate Lolita's memories, either of desirability or exploitation, is so preposterous that only acute psychic need can explain its existence in the memoir.

"Light of My Life"

The final meeting with Lolita would reinforce the attitudes he had brought to his earlier efforts at "confession" in Quebec. Humbert never sought forgiveness, nor moral illumination, nor reconciliation, and certainly he was not interested in a new life, but he did call for Lethe, primarily for Lolita. Humbert wanted sin to be washed clean of consequence. The prayer for a reversal of the natural law would be regarded by the *cure* as improper worship of the true God, as far from a cry for grace and reconciliation as it is possible to be. So Humbert's effort at confession failed. How could it not?

While Humbert did not confess a sin, he did posit a question of the logic of pastoral theology. He had been confused about the nature of his undertaking. He had deprived Lolita of her childhood, and of the opportunity to grow up in a more or less normal way, in a more or less normal environment. Did that matter? Did it have consequences beyond his own discomfort and her deprivation? Humbert was unable to answer those questions, as so many had been in the wake of the Holocaust. What did it all mean?* Humbert, an aesthete, fell back on his usual answer: only art could redeem, only art could justify. Perhaps Humbert's sexual play with Lolita had been particularly artful. At any rate, he would go on to produce his memoir, and then die.

Failure at confession did not imply a final failure of Humbert's introspection and search for understanding. He would continue that search primarily by combing his memory. If illumination could not come from above it could come from within. The memoir took shape slowly, but also inexorably. It percolated beneath the story, perhaps unconsciously, but always present. While Humbert is doing things, from traveling with Rita, to seeing Lolita married, to murdering Quilty, memoir as a source of explanation, like magma under the surface, slowly rumbled and grew until it would emerge as the last resort for understanding life. This took years. No surprise. We all know how the mills of the gods grind.

Humbert's romantic imagination would recall (create?) events in his

---

*The movie *Alfie* asked the question "What does it all mean?" in a tuneful way. But the charm of melody did not diminish the intractability of the question. And in fact, no answer can be given. The answer you find, and we all find one, is the answer we have brought with us. "The Christ you seek you will not find, unless you bring him with you."

Chapter Four: Exeunt Omnes

trips with Lolita clearly enough, including his feelings and her response. He treasured the memory, grandly giving it a Dantean ring reminiscent of the *Commedia*, Humbert regarded it as "our first circle of paradise." Alas, it was not all *Paradiso*. Humbert admitted that he knew he was not Lolita's boyfriend, nor even, as he fondly imagined, an international glamour-puss, nor a friend, but just "two eyes and a foot of engorged brawn."* No point in not giving yourself as much credit as you can.

Humbert's imitation of Dante's descriptive technique revealed the basic truth of his relationship with Lolita. In the *Inferno*, Dante allowed his characters to descend to synecdoche in their relationships with others, indicating how they used people as objects. Synecdoche is literally a hellish style. Humberto, like Francesca di Rimini, remembered the beloved as a feeling, not as a person. And he was also sure that Lolita remembered him as parts (one of which was dubiously and ostentatiously measured out as "a foot of engorged brawn"). Humbert transposed the circles from the *Inferno* to Paradise, unsurprisingly.

Not everything had looked like Paradise, even to Humbert. As he looked back on things, he allowed himself to acknowledge "smothered memories, now unfolding themselves into limbless monsters of pain." The monsters may have begun in Lolita's physical discomfort, but Humbert appropriated them as his own pain. From Humbert in love to Humbert suffering because he had inflicted lust upon another, it is always Humbert's narrative, even when told through reference to another. Empathy was not something Humbert was good at. He might recognize another's pain, but he did not feel it.

Humbert's memoir reveals Lolita's pain as real and sustained, and his "smothered memories" reported her despair and embarrassment as continuing conditions. Looking back, he admits Lolita bore signs of pain. Once he glimpsed her unawares, wearing an expression of abject helplessness that even he recognized as the mark of captivity, injustice, and the absence of options. That expression revealed, her response to another of Humbert's broken promises. It might have been to take her to a movie or a similar

---

*Measurement is a male preoccupation and Humbert's reportage is a self-administered pat on the back. Humbert's numerous other pats are discreetly *askene*.

outing, promises carelessly made and cruelly broken (the reader recognizes, as Nabokov knew he would, that it is Humbert, not Lolita, who is cruel). Lolita's helplessness came from hopelessness, from being trapped and used, from "love" in the form of *eros*, so often expressed as capture, lust, isolation, and jealousy. Humbert recognized at the time that Lolita was drifting toward despair, not reaching it but veering off into the direction of injustice acutely felt. Nevertheless, Humbert did nothing.

Humbert recognized an exceptionally painful moment, for Lolita, not himself, that came unexpectedly, in an ordinary moment at home. One of Lolita's more dumpy friends, Avis Byrd, was visiting. Her father came to get her. Avis promptly "perched plumply" on her father's knee. Lolita reserved for social occasions an "absolutely enchanting" smile, which projected "a dreamy sweet radiance" to strangers.

Humbert mistrusted the sincerity of that the smile, because it appeared to be directed at things rather than people, and seemed to vanish at the moment everyone looked away. Then the dimple "became a frozen little shadow." That shadow emerged when large and lumpy Avis embraced her father and he put an arm around her. An ordinary embrace within an ordinary family, paternal rather than erotic, brought Lolita to an unbearable sadness. Humbert attributed the grimace and the pain behind it not to exploitation but to family. Avis had everything, from dogs to siblings to parents. All of it, combined into a real home, while she, Lolita, "had nothing."

Humbert explained Lolita's sadness as stemming from what was missing rather than what was done. Growing older, she realized more and more clearly that "the most miserable of family lives was better than the parody of incest." That, he admitted, was all he could offer his orphaned captive. In Humbert's version of events, that's just the price that has to be paid. By others. *Eros* is a demanding mistress.

Humbert's sense of contrition never outweighed his sense of loss, both before and after Lolita left him. Humbert eluded easily enough the formulae of psychological healing, but he did not, on that account, participate in (or endure, perhaps) the sacrifice and benefit of religious healing. Reflection only begins the journey toward contrition. Repentance and reconciliation are relationships, not situations.

Chapter Four: Exeunt Omnes

Foul Quilty's Murder (and It's About Time, Since It Gets Humbert Off the Street and Brings the Memoir to an End)

Though Humbert was unable to experience contrition, he was perfectly capable of murder. Existentially, Quilty's death continues the confession episode: satisfaction for injured Lolita, but performed by another. The murder is Humbert's third attempt to understand his life. The "talk therapy" in the confessional having failed to give meaning, the lovers' reunion having failed to bring closure, Humbert now tries understanding through deed. In this effort, which succeeded in terms of Quilty and failed in terms of Humbert, he moved further away from confronting the spiritual consequences of his erotic passion.

Killing people is not an act of contrition for sin, nor a contribution towards self-understanding. Yet Nabokov had Humbert kill. Nabokov knew what he was doing. Having Humbert make this colossal action at the end of the novel seals all the preceding Humbertian errors of judgment into a single comprehensive whole. Self-indulgent Humbert repeatedly drifts into serious error. Of course, his excuse. "Love made me do it" is a common enough justification for "many a foolish blunder," including those which land you in prison. Humbert's creator is implacable in his devotion to the obvious consequences of moral missteps.

The death of Quilty appears in Humbert's memoir as a day of surreal but lucid madness alternating with childish self-justification and the crazed calm of homicidal intent, all enacted in the sunlight of the everyday world. Its complement may be seen in Joyce's theatrical chapter on Nighttown in *Ulysses*, where surreal madness, disjointed self-justification, and antic allusions co-existed within a dark dream-vision. While Joyce extended the text with dead ends, profusion of chatter, allusions to anything, tangents of tangents and anguish without stint or limit, Nabokov constructed a tight chapter relentlessly focused on the single topic of the murder of Quilty. Nabokov agreed with Marcel Proust, who said, "I prefer concentration, even at length."*

---

*An uncited quote used by Lydia Davis in her introduction to her translation of Marcel Proust, *Swann's Way* (New York: Penguin, 2003), p. xvii.

"Light of My Life"

 Concentration and surreal contrast describe the salient characteristics of the death of Quilty chapter. Quilty's blood-red and purple death did not end Humbert's wandering or memories. The inconsequential Quilty, whose primary narrative function as *deus ex machina* to separate Lolita from Humbert had long since been fulfilled, also gave Humbert another chance to face the moral realities of his Lolita years. And Humbert did face them, in his usual manner of frank and open evasion and a cloud of moral unknowing. Humbert, as always, found fault with others. "Because" Quilty had done this and that, mostly taking "advantage of my essential innocence," Humbert was justified, entirely justified, in substituting for his redemption the murder of the abominable and incidental Quilty. For Humbert, confession was a sub-division of explanation and evasion of responsibility. Humbert as a wounded vessel of "inner essential innocence"? Does not the entire memoir refute that plaint? And Humbert's much-repeated "because" merely casts blame without establishing cause.

 Humbert remembers the murder of Quilty through a haze. A comically crazed Humbert finds a hung-over and not completely *au courant* Quilty, who sees him as "some familiar and innocuous hallucination." Quilty must undergo the same process of examination, confession, and understanding that he, Humbert, had failed to complete in the *cure's* cure. The deed itself would not just be murder. It would be enlightenment, an outsourcing to Quilty of Humbert's efforts to see the meaning of sin. If Quilty could understand, then Humbert would understand, a breathtaking *non sequitur* that only the "lucidly insane" could possibly entertain. Humbert begins an intense and concentrated interrogation of Quilty. "Composition of place, come to my aid!"* After all, it had worked for Ignatius Loyola and for Stephen Dedalus. Why not now?

 Humbert asked a slightly dazed Quilty, point-blank, if he remembered Dolores Haze. Recollection took time, passed with conversation, and motivation, supplied by Humbert's pistol. Quilty's light came partially on. If Dolly the girl was lost, Dolly the incident returned. Quilty denied kidnapping, and substituted rescue. He announced that he'd saved the poor girl from a "beastly pervert." Tactless, under the circumstances. Dolly

---

*Ulysses, Episode Nine, "Scylla and Charybdis."

Chapter Four: Exeunt Omnes

had escaped on her own, without any help. Humbert overlooked the accuracy of Quilty's remembrance. Quilty must know why he was being executed, which was not less important to Humbert than the actual demise.

To aid Quilty's understanding, Humbert, pretentious always, had prepared a poetic confession, which Quilty had to recite aloud. It was a pitiful parody of the sacrament as well as a silly imitation of Eliot's "The Hollow Men." The poem was stage-setting, but for Humbert a necessary part of the décor of death. It did communicate, however, the sense of sin common to the sacrament and to Eliot:

> Because you took advantage of a sinner
> because you took advantage
> because you took
> because you took advantage of my disadvantage

That's how it started, with the fault of another. Humbert was good at that. The guilt of one must imply the innocence of the other; no wonder Humbert had had problems with his confessor. Eventually, the poem ended. And then Humbert shot him, several times, in several places, in several locations.

Juxtaposition of the fatal to the ordinary made the scene work: as Humbert descended to the ground floor he found a party going on. Humbert looked in at the party and announced to all: "I have just killed Clare Quilty." That was exactly the right tone to take. Humbert was good at casual social interactions, catching the spirit of the moment, making an apt comment. Indeed, it was a Humbert moment: a furtive killing late at night in a dark alley was certainly not the Humbert style, but shooting somebody during a party certainly was. Humbert's announcement made the dead (actually, not quite dead enough) Quilty a part of the party scene, a slightly offbeat festive touch which only the best parties can provide. Of course, at the same time and in the same words, Humbert was continuing his confession, or rather expanding it, to include a new *delit* which he hoped would bring better results than his earlier, more formal effort.

The partygoers caught the Humbertian public spirit immediately. "Good for you," replied a "florid fellow," followed by an addition: "Somebody ought to have done it long ago," from the "fat man." The party went on, music, conversation, sexual attraction, all of which make a party a success. And then there came a "sudden noise on the stairs": Quilty had implausibly survived multiple gunshot wounds, staggering out onto the landing and collapsing there, bubbling and bleeding.

Quilty's unseemly interruption seems to have had no effect. It was in bad taste but no one minded. The party continued. Humbert, having provided all the entertainment he could, stepped out the front door and drove away. And the band played on.

The murder of Quilty, which made no difference to the party, seems to have made no difference to Humbert either. His confession had been understood as a party joke, bringing approval rather than condemnation. For Humbert, alas, the deed had brought no more understanding than the effort at sacrament. Humbert's life was still a turmoil of unknowing. He drove away, not particularly to escape but more in quandary over what to do next. What would come next, and last, was memoir.

Looking beyond murder and confession, the Humbert who emerged from the Quilty house was a man who had come to the end of the line.* From his "confession" to his "poem," Humbert had advanced to himself plausible explanations from what he had done and was about to do. Looking back over it all, the murder of Quilty did not appear to be an appropriate satisfaction for abusing Lolita. As he drove away, Humbert began composing his memoir where he distributed blame broadcast. The memoir would allow Humbert a final way attain an understanding of his experiences. What had it all been about?

Humbert's reflective mood in the aftermath of bidding leave to Lolita and Quilty was simultaneously a first draft of his confessional memoir and a conclusion to the things he needed to do. Lolita was gone. He had forgotten Rita. He had murdered Quilty. He had tied up every loose end. Goodbye to all that.

Humbert takes pains to include a final elegiac moment in the concluding pages of his confession. He presents this coda of purity and joy as conclusion, as the last messy episode in a narrative of a still incomprehen-

---

*The most celebrated of the situational ethicists was Harvey Cox, *The Secular City* (1965), which, we suggest, combined the intense modern concern for intention (malice or accident with the ancient Greek Sophism of Protagoras and Gorgias in its modern form of existentialism. The core of situational ethics appears to be a social context combined with an ambiguity of moral result.

Chapter Four: Exeunt Omnes

sible life. It is as if he is proffering a little flower to the reader. *Here you are; I'm not so bad. I really couldn't help it. But I have changed.* However, the change is suspect since the incident is a flashback. What takes place after Humbert has murdered Quilty is the memory of children singing, not the sound of children singing. The little flower offered the reader is a moment of recollection, dredged up and served out.

It's a saccharine moment, to be sure: the murderer, run to ground, yet revealing (or pretending to reveal) an essential decency. Humbert is waiting on the hillside for the police to arrest him. Inspired by the wonders of nature (another sure-fire trope), he recalls the moment when his evil nature gave way to the powers of goodness. And all (of course — you guessed it) inspired by childish innocence.

What could be more Humbertian than a Damascus moment inspired by children? What could be more Humbertian than a Damascus moment that fades, leaving his behavior and intentions unchanged? What could be more Humbertian than a Damascus moment inserted out of chronological order? No wonder he calls it "a last mirage."

That moment is recycled from years before; it's a memory dating from after Lolita's escape. The scene was quite picturesque. Humbert recalls having stopped on the road above a small mining town, hearing happy children's voices in the distance. He had not been able to distinguish individual word or voice in the music. But the sound had inspired him with "poignant" emotion. (A bad sign. Readers of *Lolita* know by this point that every time Humbert has been overcome by his emotions, he's behaved badly.) Still, we give him the benefit of the doubt as he explains the source of his emotion: he had been heartbroken at Lolita's "absence from that concord."

What is he saying here, in the Hallmark-card scene of happy children and lovely mountains? That Lolita was not down the hill playing with the children? Piffle. Lolita then was a child no more. She had run off with another man, evincing a greater interest in passion and relationships than with toy wagons and hoops. The time when she could have been playing is long past. Reading carefully, we do not hear Humbert mention his own responsibility for Lolita's absence from children's play groups, then or ever.

"Light of My Life"

Humbert addresses the flashback directly to the reader. "Reader!" The "hopelessly poignant thing" isn't the fact that he's lost Lolita, but "the absence of her voice from that concord." Humbert regrets an impossibility — that Lolita could be a child now, playing with those children. It is the loss of childhood itself. His abuse was irrelevant Humbert is not alone in that universal regret. Gerard Manley Hopkins caught the truth of the fallen world diminished by death:

> It is the blight man was born for
> It is Margaret you mourn for.*

Time is "the hopelessly poignant thing."

Regret, however, is not contrition. When the careful reader considers that after Humbert had this Damascus moment, he spent two years doggedly hunting her down, intending to recapture her, and finally made a desperate attempt to do so, despite the fact that she was married, pregnant, and "ruined," that final moment in his narrative is revealed as suspect as the rest. Nothing has changed.

Even if we were to understand Humbert's realization as oblique regret over his own part in Lolita's lack of childhood, we question the depth of his regret. "One swallow does not make a summer," as Aristotle reminds us; one (more) Damascus moment does not make a reformed or enlightened pedophile. It might just make him seem more harmless. We recall, throughout the memoir, Humbert's infatuation with children's voices, and it was their innocence that he valued. Childish innocence, however, could hardly survive contact with Humbert, who lived a life professionally, as it were, engaged in destroying the thing he valued most, nymphetic innocence.

Purity and joy do not last, but irony does. The closing pages of Humbert's "confession" cannily conclude with children's song rising in the clear cool air. It represents the final self-justification and moral equivocation in a memoir which explained nothing, confessed everything, avoided responsibility, and wallowed in the shallow sentiment of the "hopelessly poignant." And so it goes.

---

*"Spring and Fall" (written before 1889, published 1918).

Chapter Four: Exeunt Omnes

Humbert as Everyman

In his university lectures Nabokov opposed the notion that works of literature should be understood and interpreted historically, as illustrative of a particular time and place. He denied that literature existed as an historical artifact. One could not, he sententiously informed his students, learn about French provincial bourgeois life from reading *Madame Bovary*.* Nor, he implied by not discussing it, could one learn about pre-war urban life in Dublin from reading *Ulysses*.† Nabokov supported, though he never admitted it, the Greek myth of the Muses, who gave talent to writers in ways and for reasons that remained always mysterious. If the Muses were hidden, literary talent was not and works of genius were easily distinguishable from grade B literature, which comes in bottles, and grade C, which comes in pails.‡ It is the grade B and C (and D and E) stuff that can function (perhaps can only function) as an historical artifact. Class B and C literature, which lacked the full approbation of the Muses, was hardly worth discussion, except in terms of its historical and social setting. In his courses, Nabokov ignored it.

Lolita, which Nabokov correctly thought was an important (and good) book by a major international author, could not be read as illustrative of mid-century America. Of course, it was set in post-war America, but every book has to be set somewhere. But *Lolita* was not about place, but about person. Its emphasis on character leads inevitably to the suspicion that Humbert was, on most of his self-recorded days, only a little, little worse than the rest of us (the readers) on our bad days. We all search endlessly for *eros*, and sometimes, to our sorrow, we find it. When we find it, we usually find disaster, for ourselves even more than for others. We betray our best intentions and our preferred self-image. We root mercilessly in the lives of others, to their great sorrow and permanent damage. We make

---

*Nabokov, *Lectures on Literature*.

†Nabokov, *Lectures on Literature*. This refers, of course, to the extent one can read Joyce's *Ulysses*, a notoriously difficult book, a truly brilliant book, a terrible book, but one that must be read and reread, alas. But what Nabokov thought was too narrow; *Ulysses* was an act of memory as well as creation.

‡Nabokov, *Lectures on Literature*.

"Light of My Life"

excuses. We pretend all will be well. Love, after all, conquers (and justifies) everything. We echo Humbert.

Of course, *eros* rarely consumes anyone to the extent that it utterly absorbed Humbert. Like Narcissus, *Lolita* is a parable. *Lolita* rests, *au fond*, upon the reality of Original Sin, which is the universal human failure of the will to do, or be able to do, the good we know and know we ought to do. Called *hamartia* by Aristotle in the *Poetics,* human failings are the inevitable and universal imperfection of people.* Humbert was a snob and predator, given to effortless self-mitigation. For all, it is the same, or we could not recognize the patterns.† Though judgment should be made in consciousness of the human condition, it should not be withheld because of the human condition.

Humbert was, upon reflection, an exaggeration, not someone unrecognizable. His passion was more focused, his actions were gaudier and more damaging, his self-justifications were more elaborate, his deception more disingenuous than was the common run of experience or imagination. Whatever the arrow of *hamartia*, the mark was missed by an unusual distance. Unusual, but not unknown, not unheard of, not unimaginable, not impossible.

Life as a Work of Art, and Love

Beyond *eros, Lolita* examines time through the device of memory, which is subject to the faults of the human condition. Memory is our own, and we distort it how we will. Memory has a way of drifting always towards correction, towards making sense of the past. Memory highlights this and ignores that, bringing patterns out of happenstance, and giving purpose to contingency. Not a bad thing, really. It's hard to go through life when everything, including ourselves, is a mystery. So our internal memoir runs

---

*Aristotle, *Poetics*. *Hamartia* did (and does) not mean "tragic flaw," which is thus confined to tragedy. The emphasis ought to be placed on the mark missed, a universal thing, rather than the arrow shot, a discrete event.

†"From wrong to wrong the exasperated spirit/Proceeds": T. S. Eliot, "Little Gidding," II, ll. 91–92.

Chapter Four: Exeunt Omnes

along the lines of Humbert's formal autobiographical exposition. Every story (as did Humbert's) acquires a theme; a moral theme, if at all possible, or at least an exculpatory one. Humbert had more to justify than most, but no one is immune to the need to excuse. So we remember, in part, to understand by excusing, by cutting some slack. And if we can't forgive ourselves, or others, we try as best we can to reduce what is painful in our past to what is vestigial in our present.

Humbert increasingly towards the end of his memoir, wrote his life as a "work of art."* The very last words of *Lolita* evoke "the refuge of art. Through the memoir, which marked the end of his life, Humbert had combined life and memory, and confused both with art. Art would make the sordid life immortal through its power, its beauty and its passion.

In this, Humbert imitated (in his own estimate, re-created) the ideal of Renaissance Italian aristocrats, particularly rulers. These princes lived their lives on the public stage, and understood themselves as artistic emblems of excellence. Excellence was expressed through power, style, or even artistic representation by others. Love mattered. Only through love of art and of life as art could a Renaissance aristocrat gain immortality, given only to those whose life is lived greatly. Humbert, toward the end, and perhaps even earlier, aspired to the same goal of *fama*, of deserving the favor of Fortuna, because he lived an elegant and artistic life, with graceful touches, charming postures, and elegant taste. *Manque* as a scholar he may have been, but the memory filtered into memoir shows Humbert's true *métier* was as a sophisticated lover (of green fruit). Of course, Humbert neglected to grasp that to be possessed by *eros* disabled one's ability to exercise artistic moderation, judgment, and discretion. Well, Humbert did what he could.

Life as a work of art had entered the Renaissance International style via Baldassare Castiglione, *Il Cortigiano (1508–1528)*, conversations before it was essays, a blockbuster before it was even published, translated into every known language. It became the ideal of the gentleman, and that ideal remained essentially constant until the second war. The importance

---

*See Jakob Burckhardt, *Civilization of the Renaissance in Italy, 1859–60*. The initial section of vol. 1 was entitled "Life as a Work of Art," and carried Burckhardt's main thesis.

of this notion of a gentleman, as a life being a work of art, can be seen in Nabokov's unselfconscious comment, attributed to John Ray, Jr. in the Foreword: "He was not a gentleman." It can hardly be surprising that Humbert, born into the bourgeois class most conscious of gentlemanly behavior, would reflect the older (by 1955) style of understanding one's life.

Trying to turn a life dominated by *eros* into a life gracefully arranged as art was a difficult task. Humbert struggled manfully with it. But *eros* is by nature sloppy, boundless, overpowering, and art is always bounded and controlled. Humbert himself announced at every turn how love overpowered him. In life and other books, love has been pronounced "the word known to all men." Not in *Lolita*. In Humbert's memoir, love is known only to Humbert. All the rest of the characters slide along the edge of that enormous emotion, while Humbert, in a hero-journey of struggle, experiences love in all its power and violence. Or so Humbert says. We take his word on these matters with a grain of salt. But Humbert was certainly right about one thing. The black hole of *eros* was endless, and endlessly destructive.

Humbert also claimed to be writing a memoir of morality. He always tried to do the right thing. He chose marriage over philandering, he attempted to let Charlotte down easy, by pretending that his love for her daughter was part of a novel. He put up with Lolita's sulks and pouts, tantrums, rages, despairs, and distance. He attempted to make amends for Lolita's pain, through confession, though, it is true, that he never offered the necessary apology. Well, no one is perfect. Everyone has moral lapses. At least he searched for her when she was gone. And when he found her, he paid her the money that was owed. Nor did he drag her away from her husband. At least he killed the abominable Quilty. And finally, he surrendered peacefully to the police and confessed all *in extenso*. Humbert recognized that art had a moral dimension, and was not about chaos, but was about love, even prayer. This is certainly the formal structure, the proffered surface, of Humbert's memoir.

A moral book about an amoral life, or an immoral life, perhaps, requires the one thing that Humbert never did. It requires a genuine contrition and a genuine apology. It is no different with a book about the

Chapter Four: Exeunt Omnes

ecstasies and monstrosities of love. A lot of wrong has been done to a lot of people in the name of erotic love. Humbert only understood that kind of love. Other forms were beyond his ken and appreciation. Love for Humbert remained a Hercules shirt of flame which he wove for himself, of pain transformed into pain, of *eros* descending into itself. It was the same with time and memory, both wrenched into a simulacrum of artistic pose. Humbert did, however, write a sleek and plausible memoir, finessing the betrayals, the contradictions, the ambiguities that often make readers uncomfortable. But do not betrayals, contradictions and ambiguities form the soul of a story about erotic love?

BIBLIOGRAPHICAL REFLECTIONS

This work, with its attendant allusions and obscurities, is served better by a bibliographical reflection than by a bare list of books. This list tells only the books used, already clear from the footnotes, but does not indicate why or how we used them. So we append a small bibliographical comment, explaining (we hope) why this work has taken the form and direction it has.

In any work on love and time in the post-classical world, the starting point, whether the authors admit it or not, reflects the influence of Augustine. This is not because Augustine was lovable: he was not; but because he discussed at length and in depth several basic ideas on love, its opposite in sin and selfishness, and on human time that have become a continuing part of Western culture. At times, Augustine's ideas have enjoyed wide cultural approval, with Aquinas in the thirteenth century and Calvin in the sixteenth, and have also been held at grave cultural discount, with Rousseau in the Enlightenment and Marx later. But Augustine has always been at the core of western discussion about love and time.

We begin with the *Confessions*, which may be found in many convenient editions. See Father John K. Ryan, trans., intro., notes, *The Confessions of St. Augustine* (New York: Doubleday Image Books, 1960). Many of the major works are in Philip Schaff, ed., *A Select Library of the Nicene and Post-Nicene Fathers of the Christian Church*, 14 vols. (New York, 1886–1890), particularly Volume V, though *On Christian Doctrine* is in Volume II. The Schaff edition may be found online in the Christian Classics Ethereal Library at http://ccel.org/. The Latin may be found in the Loeb Classical Library, and, less conveniently, in the immense J. P. Migne, ed., *Patrologia Latina*, which can be found online through subscription.

Bibliographical Reflections

The *Confessions* contains the best-known and most accessible, in Augustine's case a relative term, version of the journey of love away from the self alone and toward God. The seeker/postulant begins in a condition of *aversio*, facing toward the ways of the world and away from God. Then comes, and it does not come for all, the salvific moment, when all understanding about the nature of the world change. This is the moment of turning, of *retorqueo*, when life now comes to be seen in terms of *conversio*, the facing toward God and away from the world. *Conversio* changes life from a wander or a meander or a trip into a journey, with love of God, *agape* at its center. The Augustinian journey of living forward and understanding backward, of learning about life in youth and grasping its meaning in age, was placed fully into the task of reunion with God, giving life a pattern and a direction greater than events or individuals.

The modern retelling of Augustine's journey through the *Confessions* is Fyodor Dostoyevsky, *Crime and Punishment (Transgression and Atonement)*, trans. Sidney Monas, intro. Leonard J. Stanton and James D. Hardy, Jr. (New York: Signet, 1999). Rodion Raskolnikov begins in *aversio*, self-deceived by the "new word." He kills, confesses, repents, and his *retorqueo* is a turn toward love and Sophia (both as woman and as wisdom) and arrives at *conversio*. We have mentioned this in the text, but the Augustinian journey, though rhetorically simple, is psychologically complex, and a bit of repetition in the Afterword is both appropriate and needed.

We have also mentioned that Humbert was not on an Augustinian journey, that he was one of those who lived but did not learn. He looks back with intense concentration but sees only a cognitively flat life. In this he resembles Agamemnon, who also failed to grasp that his actions and attitudes had meaning. See Aeschylus, "Agamemnon," first of the *Orestia* trilogy, trans. and intro. Richard Lattimore (Chicago: University of Chicago Press, 1953). Like Humbert, Agamemnon died in custody, charged with a capital crime. In both cases, blindness about love was a central factor in things ending badly.

A second Augustinian idea that undergirds *Lolita* was the theologically separate but psychologically connected *theologeo* of original sin and free but damaged will. Original sin, the idea that humanity is not able not to sin (*non posse non peccare*), describes human nature as naturally evil. G.

K. Chesterton described original sin as the only Christian doctrine that is empirically verifiable, since people have shown the same betrayals, disorders, and criminality *simul, semper, ubique, et ad omnibus*. Consciousness of sin does not, however, mean sin avoided. Humanity has free will, and people may choose what they wish, but the will is degraded and people cannot attain virtue. They can do better, but not well.

These theological positions essentially describe Humbert, who sins against Lolita (and Quilty, and Valeria, and Charlotte, and Rita, though he gave more to her than the others). Humbert knows he has sinned, and repents (sort of), and sins further, and so on. As do we all, Humbert seeks confession and absolution, but sins confessed and absolved are not undone. Humbert can accept nothing less since he is not embarked on an Augustinian journey. Since there is no human "fix" for original sin and damaged will, it is hardly surprising that Humbert's search for that fix fails.

For Augustine, there was a fix for original sin and damaged will, not a fix that undid these psychological realities, but an amelioration of their damage. That was grace, or, in another context, providence. The grace of God gave a purpose to life, a meaning to life beyond the worldly, allowed forgiveness for sins that were "grievous unto us" as their "burden was intolerable." Humbert, the secular memorialist of *Lolita*, found no such forgiveness in the non-providential world he described. Whether grace un-sought may be found is a question too far for *Lolita;* the text itself is haunted by its absence.

There are, of course, many treatises that help in understanding the Augustinian view of the world. We have chosen three, in part because they are on point and in part because they deal with Augustine in terms of literature and cultural history. See Alan Jacobs, *Original Sin: A Cultural History* (New York: HarperCollins, 2008), a beautifully written book that examines original sin within the cultural context of western literary thought. See also Gale H. Carrithers, Jr., and James D. Hardy, Jr., *Age of Iron English Renaissance Tropologies of Love and Power* (Baton Rouge: Louisiana State University Press, 1998) for an explanation of the tropes of religious life (Augustinian journey, salvific moment, ambassadorship of good will toward the community, human theatre of betrayal). See also

Bibliographical Reflections

Jeanne Shami, ed., *Renaissance Tropologies: The Cultural Imagination of Early Modern England* (Pittsburgh: Duquesne University Press, 2008) for an examination of the tropes as a method of discussing literature and culture.

In the opening line of the *Confessions*, Augustine wrote that "our heart is restless until it rests in Thee," and there are not many lines from the Confessions more quoted. Wherever one feels that rest lies, the restless heart is certainly universal. Disquiet, we suggest, is the nature of love, and the common experience of lovers. Certainly, *Lolita* reflects the unquiet heart syndrome, with the *bildung* of Lolita from "blue sulks" to marriage and Humbert's fixation on the erotic first circle of "paradise." Humbert reflected, unwittingly, of course, Augustine's comment on the human condition. It's not as easy to shake sin off as modern therapists presume. Nabokov knew that. Like Plato before him, Nabokov was primarily a moralist.

In a novel as secular as *Lolita,* Augustine can only be "deep background," providing a fuller understanding while remaining unnamed in dispatches. We have used in addition authors, ancient and modern, that Nabokov knew and, in some cases, taught. We have tried to keep these authorities on love to a minimum, since this essay deals with *Lolita*, and have tried to keep our comments to the situations Humbert describes. We have dealt at length with only the two classical authors, Plato and Ovid. Both thought about love in the world, from narcissism to *eros* and *phile*, and both placed a higher value on love in a community than in a bedroom. Social disorder was a greater problem than personal longing or despair or fulfillment. For Ovid, we used *Ovid The Metamorphoses,* ed., trans., intro. Horace Gregory (New York: Viking, 1958) and for Plato, *The Symposium*, ed. Alexander Nehamas and Paul Woodruff (Indianapolis: Hackett, 1989).

We have also left classical authors in the background, including Virgil, *The Aeneid,* trans. Robert Fitzgerald (New York: Random House, 1984). In books IV and VI and XII, Virgil described the Roman sense of public duty as the primal social obligation, with family also understood as public institution. At the apex of obligations was Roman destiny, thought to be of interest to the gods as well as men. As for *eros*, the passion of one person for another, this was dangerous, to be avoided if possible, since it often, usually actually, blinded the individual to duty. Humbert valued *eros* as much as Virgil feared it, but even for Humbert, a certain wistful tone about being *manqué* indicates a vague sense of unease in substituting *eros* for duty.

Personal and social obligation includes family, as Mercury reminded the then-less-than-pious Aeneas, who was involved with Dido. Beyond the *Aeneid* with its approval of Stoic Roman public virtue, we have used the Medea myth as described in drama and epic. See Ovid's *Metamorphoses,* Book VII, along with Euripedes' *Medea*, trans. Lattimore and Grene (Chicago: University of Chicago Press, 1971), and Apollonius of Rhodes, *The Voyage of Argo: The Argonautica*, edited by E.V. Rieu (London: Penguin, 1959). All three versions of the Medea myth dwelt upon the twin themes of *furor* and *pavor*, and the betrayal that flowed so easily from erotic fixation outside of communal restraint and blessing. We have read Virgil, Homer, and the Medea myth as base-line analyses of home and family and as an implied commentary on both in *Lolita*. In Humbert's experience, family meant problems, with marriage itself as the most serious problem of them all. No family in *Lolita* survives dissolution (Valeria) or untimely death (Charlotte, the Farlows, and the Schillers), and none produces children. Humbert thought that intense erotic connection was preferable to marriage and family.

Social and familial obligation can only exist successfully if the participants possess a moral/social code (*boni mores*) and attempt to live up to it. Here we come, as all critics inevitably must, to Aristotle, particularly the *Poetics* and the *Nicomachean Ethics*. The Master of Those Who Know can be conveniently found in the Loeb Classical Library, in twenty-seven volumes. See Aristotle, *Poetics* and *Nicomachean Ethics*. The Loeb translations are rarely felicitous, but they are precise, and with Aristotelian philosophy precision really matters. And should discussion arise, the Greek is on the facing page, which can be used to settle every argument.

We have paid particular attention in the *Poetics* to Aristotle's comment on *hamartia*, literally missing the mark in archery, and more broadly missing the mark in moral and social duty. *Hamartia* may be defined as the inevitable imperfection in things and people, thus encompassing both the local and general application of the term in dramatic commentary. For

Lolita, the Aristotelian concept of *hamartia* is entirely appropriate, since it expresses the broken will and self-acknowledgement of moral failure that constitutes the core of Original Sin, without the religious connotations and contexts that term embodies. Things in *Lolita* go badly and choices are made badly without any reference to Providence, just as in Aristotle's interpretation of Greek religious drama. But for causality, for reasons why everything in *Lolita* ends (and often begins) badly, if sin and providence are to be avoided, then *hamartia* or its modern form of Murphy's Law must suffice. A psychological explanation is common amongst readers and critics, ever since Freud and Edel saw psychological dysfunction as a cause of behavior in literary characters.

The *Nicomachean Ethics* contains both a guide for happiness, and a recommendation for moderation (*sophrosyne*), and social involvement, which Humbert avoided. Humbert chose isolation in society and excess in love, and Aristotle advised against these things. We suggest the *Nicomachean Ethics* as the general antidote to Humbertian (and Quiltyish) living, and, therefore, as the proper point of contrast to understand where, exactly and in a general way, things went wrong and stayed that way.

To jump directly from Aristotle, Ovid, and Virgil to modernity is too extreme for an essay dealing with love, loss, and time. So we have appropriated the insights of Dante Alighieri and John Milton, with William Shakespeare and John Donne appearing, as does Augustine, at vital places here and there in the essay. For Dante we have used Dante, *The Divine Comedy*, 3 vols., trans. Mark Musa (New York: Penguin, 1971); for Milton, John Milton, *Paradise Lost*, ed. Scott Elledge (New York: Norton, 1993); for Shakespeare, William Shakespeare, *The Norton Shakespeare: Based on the Oxford Edition*, gen. ed. Stephen Greenblatt (New York: Norton, 1997); and for Donne, John Donne, *Selected Poems*, edited by Ilona Bell (London: Penguin, 2007).

We have treated Dante's Augustinian journey from sin to salvation as being the opposite story from the one told in *Lolita*. Humbert's brush with the confessor aside, there is nothing of the transcendental in *Lolita* beyond borrowed vocabulary. What Dante the pilgrim experienced and did, Humbert did not do, and what the pilgrim surmounted Humbert fell prey to. Francesca is the Dantean Humbert, and she is in the *Inferno* (Canto V), not the first circle of paradise. Milton's paean to marriage is also un–Humbertian: Milton, who did not avoid marriage but managed never to be anything beyond legally married. Like Dante, Milton thought in terms of salvation, and Humbert, who had certainly heard of that, did not mention it in his memoir.

Shakespeare and Donne appear as general background referents on love, marriage, and duty in our essay. In most of his plays Shakespeare dealt with marriage: as a problem, as a benison, as an absence; and an implied reference to Shakespeare was always in our minds. The same with John Donne, who had an unerring eye for *eros* and its limitations. The room was not a universe; the busy sun kept rising, right on schedule. The world is always with us, and with it the obligations to kith and kin. Humbert's efforts to isolate Lo through travel, to make the room a universe by changing rooms, was doomed from the start, and made sense only as an instinctive response to o'ermastering passion. Even at best, it could be only a stall for time, not utterly irrational as time is always altering passion and nymphets. Nevertheless, keeping Donne and Shakespeare in mind means that the reader is thinking, while reading, of what we were thinking, while writing.

In the inevitable contrast between the ancients and the moderns, the thoughtful consensus, though it inclines decisively toward the ancients, does not exclude modern re-examination of perennial social, moral, and personal concerns. Things have changed greatly, though people have not, and the old ways, even if fundamentally the only ways, still deserve more recent reconsideration. Nabokov attended to this task in two venues, in the books he wrote and the books he taught. From the latter we have chosen four books, one that he did not think so highly of, and three that he loved. The one less praised was Fyodor Dostoyevsky, *Crime and Punishment*, and we have used the edition trans. Sidney Monas, intro. Leonard J. Stanton and James D. Hardy, Jr. (New York: Signet, 1999). The three Nabokov more admired are Lyov Tolstoy, *Anna Karenin*, and we have used the translation by Louise and Aylmer Maude, ed. Georg Gibian (New York: Norton, 1970), Gustave Flaubert, *Madame Bovary*, trans. and ed. Paul de Man (New York: Norton, 1965), and Nikolai Gogol, *Dead Souls*, trans. Bernard Guilbert Guerney (New York: Knopf, 1997).

Nabokov himself needed no translation for any of these books, and he often in class commented on their unnecessary and appalling mistranslations, adding correction to invective. But, while word mal-usage is an artistic matter, it is also a technical matter: in a commentary on love and time, we have felt it sufficient to mention the problem (for Nabokov) without plunging into the tangential remarks on the details of translation horror.

Crime and Punishment (and we have suggested that *Transgression and Atonement* would be a more accurate but less dramatic title) is an overtly Augustinian Christian tale of a journey toward light, redemption, and love. Raskolnikov was saved by love, through Sophia, and there is no doubt that his soul was what was saved. Nabokov was emphatic that nothing of this sort would be found or could be found in *Lolita*. *Bildung* for Dolly and *agon* for Humbert do not lead to salvation in a world without Providence. Regardless of transgressions, there is not much in the way of atonement. We have used *Crime and Punishment* as a point of triangulation, as an example, a primary example, of what *Lolita* is not.

Madame Bovary is closer to what *Lolita* is. Flaubert wrote about a lot of things, from class and caste to bourgeois life, from provincial France to the glitter of Paris, from gauzy romance to corrosive realism, but at the heart of it all is the heart. Emma Bovary's passion for erotic passion leads to debt, despair, and death. The direction of life for Emma anticipates that of Humbert, in both cases an effort to recreate and relive an early and primal romance, vicarious for Emma and physical for Humbert, but real for both. And for both, erotic obsession led to a life lived not so much forward as repetitiously.

Nabokov regarded Tolstoy as the greatest of the many Russian novelists (amongst them himself), and thought that *Anna Karenin* was a masterpiece. He taught it with reverence, emphasizing the varieties of families in what students thought was a long novel, perhaps because students did not like the harping on the evil effects of *eros*, their main activity. That theme appeared in the opening sentence: "All happy families resemble one another, but each unhappy family is unhappy in its own way." Nabokov contrasted two couples, Anna and Vronsky and Kitty and Lyovin. There could be no doubt about love; the passion felt by Vronsky and Lyovin was not inferior in intensity to Humbert's passion for Annabel or for Dolly. The issues lay in the areas of social propriety, as Anna was still married to Karenin and Vronsky was single, and Christian sacramental and spiritual completion, which the married Kitty and Lyovin possessed while Anna and Vronsky did not. The latter component of a happy marriage did not even occur to Humbert, though it did to Charlotte, and certainly could not be fulfilled with either Annabel or Dolly. In *Lolita*, marriage for Humbert must be outside love, love must be outside marriage, so the social and the erotic could never converge. *Eros* and *philia* were, in *Lolita*, always strangers.

The final modern novel that Nabokov taught which bears directly upon *Lolita* is Nikolai Gogol's *Dead Souls*, and perhaps Nabokov's shade might agree. Humbert's narrative is largely about life on the road, both with Lo and afterward, giving *Lolita* almost a picaresque character, and a striking similarity to *Dead Souls*, also a novel (volume one, that is) about travel that is not a journey. Chichikov in the first volume of *Dead Souls* traveled across the 1830s Russian provinces on an errand of fraud, buying dead serfs and mortgaging them as still living to the government. Humbert traveled across late 1940s America to retain control, avoid detection, and prolong the time for passion. Redemption was not the goal. Humbert was much the more distressing character. He was snobbish and condescending and alone, where Chichikov was amiable, polite, and involved in the provincial society around him. Chichikov was only defrauding the government, hardly a *delit* under any conditions and usually a virtue. Humbert engaged in child abuse and murder. And add whine and self-pity to that. Picaresque protagonists are not always a fit object for emulation.

In addition to the prose that Nabokov taught, we have given some attention to certain modern poetry, which Nabokov, also a poet, certainly knew. We emphasize T. S. Eliot's *Four Quartets* (New York: Harcourt, Brace & Co., 1971) because one cannot comment on love, loss, and time in the modern vein without recourse to it. Nabokov never refers to his contemporary Eliot in either text or *excedra*, though he allowed Humbert to imitate the *Waste Land* in the poem he wrote for Quilty. Well, so many poor poets have. Humbert did understand Eliot's insistence that time was more than a measure; it was also a cause. Humbert did recognize that

Bibliographical Reflections

Lolita would not be a nymphet much longer, certainly true, and she would outgrow the nymphetic glow, true again, and that he would love her forever anyway, a pious but probably false romantic hope. *Humbert* did not see time in terms of the Eliot journey, of returning to origins and knowing them for the first time. But that is exactly what Humbert hoped would happen. Nabokov, of course, knew better. The perspective denied to Humbert made him in that fundamental way, the non–Eliot. Here, more than Nabokov diverged widely from Humbert.

In terms of modern criticism, we have noted, where appropriate, some books and articles as helpful, though most were nowhere near as helpful as the epic, drama, poetry, and novels previously described. An exception is Alfred Appel, ed., *The Annotated Lolita* (New York: Random House, 1991). Appel took Nabokov's course (or courses) at Cornell, and stayed in touch with Nabokov afterward. Appel's annotations reflect a substantial knowledge of both Nabokov and his work, and they are enormously useful in understanding *Lolita*. Nabokov was lavish with often obscure allusions, enjoying little jokes at the non-re-reader's expense. Appel points these things out, enlightening the reader on numerous obscurities.

Finally, we suggest that Rebecca West, *The Meaning of Treason* (New York, 1947; Viking) is a useful book in understanding *Lolita*. Again, it is a matter of contrast. Rebecca West knew what poor Lolita knew, that home radiates outward from the hearth. Humbert understood home differently. For him it was passion. Humbert was at home only when engulfed by erotic desire for a nymphet, and treason was not the betrayal of people but of passion. When passion is home, betrayal is inevitable, for time works not to cement *eros* into obligation but to lead to the look, the word, the gesture that turns noon into night.

Bibliographical essays can run on and on forever, mentioning first this book and then that one and then a few more, similar to an endless evening of karaoke. For us, it is time to stop. The list is not complete but it is sufficient. The bibliography does not contain every source we mined to write on *Lolita*, but it does indicate the sensibilities we brought to this work. As with Nabokov in his afterword to *Lolita*, we hope this will be helpful.

Index

Actaeon 42
Adventures in Good Eating 113, 115
Aeneid 45n, 67n
Aeschylus 100
Agape 40, 43, 46, 63, 96
Aleichem, Sholem 45n
Alfie 169n
Also Sprach Zarathustra 92n, 119n
The Americans 123n
Anna Karenin 5, 7, 14, 47, 48, 49, 49n, 79, 147n, 151n, 156 [see note † page 47]
Annabel 8, 9, 14–32, 53, 54, 58, 59, 60, 65, 67, 70, 71, 74, 75, 79, 86, 89, 89n, 97, 101, 114, 117n, 123, 125, 136, 138, 141, 151, 152, 153, 155, 166
Apollonius of Rhodes: *Voyage of the Argo*, 40, 80n
Appel, Alfred J. 11n
Aquinas, Thomas: *Summa Theologiae* 36, 162n
Arachne 40
Aristophanes: *The Frogs* 100n; *Symposium* 25, 38, 93, 120
Aristotle: *Nichomachean Ethics* 13n, 28, 67n, 129, 129n, 136; *Poetics* 180
Art of Love, Heroides 147n
Asch, Sholom: *Three Cities* 45n
Astaire, Fred 135, 135n
Athena 40
Atlas, James 55
Augustine of Hippo: *Confessions*, 50, 63n, 91n, 150, 166, 169; *On Christian Doctrine*, 162n
Austen, Jane: *Mansfield Park* 7, 34, 48, 49n

The Bachelor and the Bobby Soxer 145n
Barry, John: *The Great Influenza: The Epic Story of the Deadliest Plague in History* 29n

Baton Rouge, Louisiana 115n
Beardsley, Aubrey 128, 129, 130, 132, 145
Beckett, Samuel: *Waiting for Godot* 9, 19n, 93, 119n
Belle Epoque 51
Benchley, Robert 19n
Benjamin, Walter: *Paris, Capital of the Nineteenth Century* 52n
Berlin 155n
Berra, Yogi 153
The Best Years of Our Lives 128, 128n
Bildungsroman 7
Blake, William: "The Clod and the Pebble" 88
Bleak House 7, 48, 49n, 79
Boccaccio, Giovanni 160
Bogart, Humphrey 143n
Boorstin, Daniel: *The Image* 124n
Boyer, Charles 73, 78, 140
Burckhardt, Jakob: *The Civilization of the Renaissance in Italy* 181n
Byrd, Avis 118, 172

Cambridge University 34
Camus, Albert 119n
"The Canonization" 25n
Cassatt, Mary 122
Castiglione, Baldassare: *Il Cortigiano* 181
Charlotte 37, 60n, 63, 64, 73, 74, 74n, 76–86, 89, 92, 94, 95, 100, 103, 105, 106, 150, 151, 155, 156, 165
Chaucer, Geoffrey 160
Chesterton, G. K. 67n
Chichikov, Pavel Ivanovich 27n
Chrétien de Troyes 43n
Christianity 42, 43, 44, 166, 172
Churchill, Winston: *The Second World War* 54; *The World Crisis* 61, 162

Index

The Civilization of the Renaissance in Italy 181*n*
"The Clod and the Pebble" 88
Cloisters 19*n*
Clytemnestra 35
Coca-Cola 110
Cocteau, Jean 19*n*
Colbert, Claudette 115
Colette: *Claudine* 51
Commedia 5, 13, 33, 34, 43, 140*n*, 171
Confessions 50, 63*n*, 91*n*, 150, 166, 169
Les Contes D'Hoffmann 146, 147, 147*n*, 148, 150
Cook, Elisha, Jr. 143*n*
Copland, Aaron 122
Corfu 166
1 Corinthians 37
Corn Palace, Mitchell, South Dakota 117
Cornell University 7, 154*n*, 156
Il Cortigiano 181
Courtly Love 43
Cowan, Christine ix
Cox, Harvey: *The Secular City* 176*n*
The Crack-Up 61*n*
Crime and Punishment 93, 109*n*, 148, 149, 149*n*, 150, 150*n*

Daimon 139
Dante Alighieri: *Commedia* 5, 13, 33, 34, 43, 140*n*, 171
Darrin, Bobby 124*n*
David Copperfield 53
Day, Doris 124*n*
Dead Souls 74*n*
Death and Transfiguration 92*n*
Dedalus, Stephen 76, 76*n*, 174
Dee, Sandra 124*n*
Deus ex machina 85, 174
Dick (Mr. Richard Schiller) 7, 88, 91, 92, 93, 151
Dickens, Charles: *Bleak House* 7, 48, 49*n*, 79; *David Copperfield* 53
Dido 5
Dr. Pepper 109
Donne, John; "The Canonization" 25*n*; "A Lecture Upon the Shadow" 25, 26
Dostoevsky, Fyodor: *Crime and Punishment* 93, 109n, 148, 149, 149n, 150, 150*n*
"Dream a Little Dream of Me" 124
"The Dry Salvages" 15, 15*n*

Duchamp, Marcel: "Nude Descending a Staircase" 76
Duenna 21

"East Coker" 166, 167, 167*n*, 169
Edel, Leon: *The Modern Psychological Novel* 154*n*, 158*n*
Edmundson, Mark 1*n*
Eisenhower, Dwight 108*n*
Either/Or 5, 30n
Eliot, T.S.: "The Dry Salvages" 15, 15*n*; "East Coker" 166, 167, 167*n*, 169; *Four Quartets* 164*n*; "The Hollow Men" 175; "Little Gidding" 44
Ellington, Duke 145*n*
Epictetus: *Handbook* 168*n*
Eros 7, 10, 11, 13–17, 21, 22, 23, 25, 26, 27, 31, 32, 33, 35, 36, 38, 40, 41, 43, 44–49, 51, 51*n*, 63, 66, 76, 77, 78, 87, 91, 92, 97, 98, 99, 101, 102, 107, 120, 125, 135, 138, 140, 144, 147, 148, 151, 152, 155, 156, 157, 162*n*, 163, 166, 169, 172, 183
Eros in the Belle Epoque 51*n*
Eudaimonia 13*n*
Euripides 5

Farlow, Jean 155
Faust 169
Fitzgerald, F. Scott: *The Crack-Up* 61*n*; *The Great Gatsby* 59*n*; *Tender Is the Night* 9, 19*n*, 51*n*, 59*n*, 60, 61, 69, 122
"Flaming Youth" 145*n*
Flaubert, Gustave: *Madame Bovary* 5, 7, 14, 47, 48, 49, 109, 128*n*, 151*n*, 161
Fortuna 181
Foster, Gaines ix
The Four Loves 2, 2*n*, 6*n*
Four Quartets 164*n*
Francesca di Rimini 171
Frank, Robert: *The Americans* 123*n*
Freud, Sigmund 24, 34, 100, 143*n*, 153; *The Uncanny* 118n
The Frogs 100*n*
Frost, Robert: "The Oven Bird" 101n

Gable, Clark 115
Gabler, Neil: *Life: The Movie* 124n
Garner, Peggy Ann 145*n*
General Motors 108
G.I. Bill 108
Gilded Age 122

Index

Gogol, Nikolai 27n, 49n; *Dead Souls* 74n
"Good News" 145 n
Gorgias 19n, 176n
Grant, Cary 140
The Grapes of Wrath 89, 89n, 108n
Graves, Robert: "Recalling War" 58
The Great Gatsby 59n
The Great Influenza: The Epic Story of the Deadliest Plague in History 29n
Great War 54, 57, 61, 112, 124n, 137n
Groundhog Day 107n
Guide Michelin 113
Gurdon, Meghan Cox 3n

Haley, Bill 124n
Halfway Down the Stairs 122n
Hamartia 36, 180
Hamlet 60, 156
Handbook 168n
Harding, Warren 49n
Helen of Troy 3n, 35, 49
Hemingway, Ernest 19n, 122; *The Sun Also Rises* 59n
Hepburn, Katharine 135n
Heraclitus 74n, 90n, 154n
Hercules 183
Hines, Duncan: *Adventures in Good Eating* 113, 115
Hiroshima 119, 145
Hitler, Adolf 122n
"The Hollow Men" 175
Hollywood 142
Holmes, Oliver Wendell, Jr.: *United Zinc and Chemical Company v. Britt* 31n
Homer 81n
Hopkins, Gerard Manley: "Spring and Fall" 178, 178n
Hortus inclusus 19
Howard Johnson 113, 115n
"Hugh Selwyn Mauberly" 57
Humbert 1–5, 7–11, 13–34, 36, 37, 41–46, 49, 50, 52n, 53, 54, 55, 58–61, 64, 64n, 65, 66, 67n, 68, 68n, 69, 69n, 70, 71, 71n, 72–90, 90n, 91–95, 95n, 96–101, 101n, 102, 102n, 103, 104, 104n, 105, 105n, 106, 106n, 107–112, 112n, 113, 113n, 114, 114n, 115, 115n, 116, 117, 117n, 118, 118n, 119, 120, 121, 121n, 123–128, 128n, 129–132, 132n, 133, 134, 135, 135n, 136–139, 139n, 140, 140n, 141–148, 148n, 149, 150, 151, 151n, 152, 153, 154, 154n, 155, 156, 156n, 157, 158, 160, 161, 163–169, 169n, 170, 171, 171n, 172–183
Hybris 40

Idyll 18, 26, 27, 31, 32, 53, 70, 86, 97, 101, 114
The Image 124n
The Innocents Abroad 122
Interstate Highway System 108n
Ionesco, Eugene 19n
"It Happened One Night" 115
Ithaca, New York 88
"It's a Wonderful Life" 128

James, Henry 106n, 122
Jason 25n, 41
Jekyll Island, Georgia 117
Johnson, Anita 152
Joyce, James: *A Portrait of the Artist as a Young Man* 76, 76n; *Ulysses* 7, 9, 11, 14, 49n, 57, 58, 109, 174n
"Junior Miss" 145n

Kafka, Franz: *Metamorphoses* 90n
Kerouac, Jack: *On the Road* 108n
Kierkegaard, Søren: *Either/Or* 5, 30n
King Lear 156

Ladies' Home Journal 62, 63, 64, 99
Laine, Frankie 124n
Lange, Dorothea 89, 89n
League of Nations 58
"A Lecture Upon the Shadow" 25, 26
Lectures on European Fiction 14, 34, 84n, 157n, 179n
Lectures on Russian Literature 13n, 179n
Leda 33
"Leda and the Swan" 34
Leed, Eric: *No Man's Land* 58n
Lewis, C.S.: *The Four Loves* 2, 2n, 6n
Life: The Movie 124n
"Little Gidding" 44
Lolita (Lo, Dolly, Mrs. Richard Schiller) 7, 15, 17, 20, 26, 28, 31, 35, 42, 43, 50, 59, 66, 67, 74–79, 84–96, 99–102, 102n, 103–106, 106n, 107, 111, 112, 113, 113n, 114, 115, 115n, 116–119, 121, 121n, 123–128, 129n, 130, 131, 132, 132n, 133–138, 140–146, 149–153, 155, 155n, 158, 164, 165, 166, 168n, 169, 169n, 170–174, 177, 178
Lolita (novel) 1–5, 5n, 7, 9, 11, 11n, 12–15,

Index

19n, 28, 32n, 33, 34, 38, 42, 44, 47, 48, 48n, 50, 51n, 54, 55, 58, 60, 61, 62, 64n, 67, 71n, 75n, 78n, 80n, 88, 88n, 89n, 95n, 96n, 99, 100, 103, 104n, 106n, 116n, 119, 120n, 122n, 124n, 129n, 130n, 132n, 139n, 144, 147n, 148, 148n, 151–154, 154n, 155, 155n, 156, 156n, 157, 159, 160, 161, 161n, 162, 166, 179, 181, 182

Los Angeles 115, 115n

Love 11, 12, 14–18, 21–27, 29, 31, 33, 35–40, 42, 43, 46, 47, 48, 55, 61, 66, 71n, 75–78, 81, 82, 83, 85, 86, 87, 87, 89, 91, 102, 104, 111, 120, 123, 125, 126, 134, 140, 147, 151, 163, 166, 172, 173, 180, 181, 182

Love in the Western World 3n

Loyola, Ignatius 174

Lycaeon 42

Lyrics of the Middle Ages: An Anthology 43n

MacLuhan, Marshall 148

Madame Bovary 5, 7, 14, 47, 48, 49, 109, 128n, 151n, 161

"The Maltese Falcon" 143n

The Mamas and the Papas 124

Mansfield Park 7, 34, 48, 49n

Marriage 7, 13, 14, 22n, 26, 43, 45–48, 52, 62, 63, 64, 68–72, 77, 78, 81, 82, 87, 90–92, 155n

Mass 71n

McCall's 126

McCarthy, Joseph 161n

McCaughey, Dorothy ix

The Meaning of Treason 13n

Medea 40, 41, 71n

Mencken, H.L. 95n, 115n 168n

Metamorphoses 13, 34, 39–43, 48, 66, 67, 81n, 90n, 102, 140n, 147n

Miller, Henry 9

Milton, John: *Paradise Lost* 13, 34, 43, 46, 46n, 47, 154, 154n

The Modern Psychological Novel 154n, 158n

Monique 31, 53, 65n, 86

Murphy, Gerald 19n

Murphy, Sara 19n

Myth 3, 34, 37, 39, 40, 41, 42, 98, 104n, 162n

Nabokov, Vera 7

Nabokov, Vladimir 1–5, 7, 9, 11–14, 17, 18, 19n, 21n, 23, 27n, 28n, 32–35, 37n, 42, 43, 45, 47–50, 58, 61, 62, 63n, 64n, 68n, 74n, 75n, 77, 78n, 79, 80n, 84n, 85, 85n, 86, 87, 88n, 89n, 90n, 92n, 93, 97n, 99, 100, 100n, 104n, 106n, 109, 109n, 112n, 115n, 116n, 118, 119, 119n, 120n, 122, 124n, 129n, 130n, 132n, 139n, 140n, 147, 147n, 148n, 149, 149n, 150, 151n, 152, 153, 154, 155n, 156, 157, 158, 158n, 159, 159n, 160, 161, 161n, 162, 163, 166, 172, 173, 179, 179n, 182; *Lectures on European Fiction*, 14, 34, 84n, 157n, 179n; *Lectures on Russian Literature* 13n, 179n; *Speak, Memory* 1, 1n, 45n, 155n

Narcissus 7, 14, 27, 39, 69n, 86

Nardo, Anna ix.

National Public Radio (NPR) 124n

Nehring, Christina: *A Vindication of Love* 3n

Nelson, Ozzie 124n

New Criticism 3, 4, 159, 159n

New York 59, 73, 80, 88, 96

Nichomachean Ethics 13n, 28, 67n, 129, 129n, 136

Nietzsche, Friedrich: *Also Sprach Zarathustra* 92n, 119n

No Man's Land 58n

"Nude Descending a Staircase" 76

Nymphets 12, 15, 19, 27–31, 42, 53, 68, 69, 75, 76, 78n, 81, 82, 103, 104, 125, 126, 128, 133, 134, 139, 165, 166

"Ode to Joy" 19n

Odette 14

Offenbach, Jacques: *Les Contes D'Hoffmann* 146, 147, 147n, 148, 150

Okinawa 108

On Christian Doctrine 162n

On the Road 108

One Thousand and One Movies You Must See Before You Die 98n

"The Oven Bird" 101n

Ovid: *Art of Love, Heroides* 147n; *Metamorphoses* 13, 34, 39–43, 48, 66, 67, 81n, 102, 140n, 147n

Paradise Lost 13, 34, 43, 46, 46n, 47, 154, 154n

Parchman Prison 121

Paris 9, 51, 52, 52n, 59, 64, 65n, 68, 69, 72, 122, 123, 150

Index

"Paris, Capital of the Nineteenth Century" 52*n*
Parker, Dorothy 19*n*
Paul: *1 Corinthians* 37
Pearl Harbor 107
Peckham, Irvin ix
Pennsylvania Turnpike 108*n*
"Peter Quince at the Clavier" 30
Philia 3*n*, 5, 49, 69, 96, 127
Philistine 82, 115*n*, 127, 129
Picasso, Pablo 19*n*
Pickford, Mary 51*n*
Pietàs 40
Plato: *Symposium* 34–39, 41, 42, 105, 136
Poe, Edgar Allan 16*n*
Poetics 180
Porter, Cole 19*n*, 142*n*
A Portrait of the Artist as a Young Man 76, 76*n*
Poulet, Georges: *Studies in Human Time* 27*n*
Pound, Ezra: "Hugh Selwyn Mauberly" 57
Pratt, Headmistress 129, 130, 131
The Prelude: Growth of a Poet's Mind 14, 15
Presley, Elvis 126
Prohibition 122
Prostitution 52
Protagoras 119*n*, 179*n*
Proust, Marcel: *Swann's Way* 14, 15*n*, 173

Quebec 169
Quilty 87, 91, 93, 102, 155, 156*n*, 165, 166, 173–176, 182

Rampton, David 18*n*
Raskolnikov 150
Ray, John, Jr. 4, 157, 157*n*, 158, 162
"Recalling War" 58
Redbook 126
Der Reigen 4*n*
Rita 94–97, 97*n*, 98, 99, 106*n*, 151, 158, 176
"Roaring Twenties" 137*n*
Rogers, Ginger 135*n*
Roosevelt, Theodore 168*n*
Rostovtzeff, Mikhail 124*n*
Rougement, Denis de: *Love in the Western World* 3*n*
Rousseau, Jean-Jacques 45*n*, 50

Ruskin, John 155*n*
Russell, Harold 128*n*

St. Petersburg 51, 109*n*
Samsa, Gregor 90
Sartre, Jean-Paul 19*n*, 119*n*
Schiff, Stacy 7*n*
Schiller, Friedrich: "Ode to Joy" 19*n*
Schneider, Stephen J.: *One Thousand and One Movies You Must See Before You Die* 98*n*
Schnitzler, Artur: *Der Reigen* 4*n*
Schoenberg, Arnold: *Death and Transfiguration* 92*n*
The Second World War 54
The Secular City 176*n*
Seventeen 126
Shakespeare, William: *Hamlet* 60, 156; *King Lear* 156
Shenandoah 98
Singer, Isaac Bashevis 45*n*
"Some Enchanted Evening" 125
Sophia 150
South Pacific 125
Speak, Memory 1, 1*n*, 45*n*, 155*n*
"Spring and Poem" 178, 178*n*
Steinbeck, John: *The Grapes of Wrath* 89, 89*n*, 108*n*
Stevens, Wallace: "Peter Quince at the Clavier" 30
Stewart, Jimmy 98
Strangers on a Train 156*n*
Studies in Human Time 27*n*
Sullivan, Louis 107*n*
Summa Theologiae 36, 162*n*
The Sun Also Rises 59*n*
Swann's Way 14, 15*n*, 173
"Swingtime" 135*n*
Symposium 25, 34–39, 41, 42, 93, 105, 120, 136

Temple, Shirley 145*n*
Tender Is the Night 9, 19*n*, 51*n*, 59*n*, 60, 61, 69, 122
Tennyson, Alfred 8
Texas 109, 115
Thompson, Charles: *Halfway Down the Stairs* 122*n*
Three Cities 45*n*
Thurber, James 73*n*
Tolstoy, Lyov: *Anna Karenin* 5, 7, 14, 47*n*, 48, 49, 49*n*, 79, 147*n*, 151*n*, 156

Index

Trilling, Lionel 17*n*, 43*n*, 71*n*, 87*n*, 139*n*
Truman, Harry 107
Twain, Mark: *The Innocents Abroad* 122

Ulysses 7, 9, 11, 14, 49*n*, 57, 58, 109, 174*n*
The Uncanny 118n
United Zinc and Chemical Company v. Britt 31*n*

Valeria 37, 59, 60*n*, 64, 69–73, 76, 79, 80, 83, 85, 86, 88*n*, 94, 95, 150, 151, 155, 155*n*, 156
A Vindication of Love 3n
Virgil: *Aeneid* 45*n*, 67*n*
Vogue 119*n*
Voyage of the Argo 40, 80*n*

Waiting for Godot 9, 19*n*, 93, 119*n*
Waldberg, Patrick: *Eros in the Belle Epoque* 51*n*

West, Rebecca: *The Meaning of Treason* 13*n*
Whistler, James A.M. 122
Wilhelm, James: *Lyrics of the Middle Ages: An Anthology* 43n
Wintour, Anna: *Vogue* 119*n*
Wordsworth, William: *The Prelude: Growth of a Poet's Mind* 14, 15
The World Crisis 61, 162
World War II 29*n*, 107, 108, 137*n*
World's Fair (1939) 108

Yeats, William Butler: "Leda and the Swan" 34
Yellowstone National Park 117
"Your Hit Parade" 124*n*, 126

Zeus 34

www.ingramcontent.com/pod-product-compliance
Lightning Source LLC
Chambersburg PA
CBHW032059300426
44116CB00007B/812